Water Rights in the United States

A Guide through the Maze

Charles R. Porter Jr.

Bernan Press

Lanham • Boulder • New York • London

Published by Bernan Press
An imprint of The Rowman & Littlefield Publishing Group, Inc.
4501 Forbes Boulevard, Suite 200, Lanham, Maryland 20706
www.rowman.com

86-90 Paul Street, London EC2A 4NE

British Library Cataloguing in Publication Information available

Library of Congress Cataloging-in-Publication Data

ISBN: 978-164143-413-3
E-ISBN: 978-164143-414-0

Contents

Acknowledgments

Over the course of this multiyear project, my wife, Connie, has been overwhelmingly supportive. Writing a book with fifty moving targets is a challenge that interrupted our lives from time to time. Thank you, Connie, for your support.

I also thank Will Myers in Austin. Will has dedicated over forty-five years of his life to protecting the seashores and bays in Texas, with special emphasis on saving seagrass. He is deeply concerned about water issues and provided me, almost every day, with nationwide articles about water; he served as an old-timey clipping service used to do for members of the Texas legislature. I sincerely thank Will for his support and dedication to preservation of our water resources and environment.

Three other people deserve much thanks: first, the late Tim Brown, the man I refer to as "the dean of Texas water law." He supported me, guided me, and taught me water law for decades as my mentor. I so appreciated his friendship and professional acumen.

Jason Hill, the finest young water law attorney I know, also supports my work as a lecturer and author of water law and policy. I so appreciate his continuing guidance through the maze of water law and policy.

Robin DeShayes, a California attorney and owner of Miltonian Capital, was very helpful in my research into California water laws and policies. I so appreciate her wise support and guidance.

Introduction

> *Water helped ancient man learn those first difficult lessons about the rights of others and responsibility to larger society. Even the most rudimentary irrigation system required organization, discipline, cooperation, and a measure of social cohesion. Mutual need begets mutual aid. Notions of sharing, of equity, of compromise, and of the common good first floated precariously on this liquid foundation to be later cemented in philosophical thought and codified law.*
>
> —Michael C. Meyer[1]

Water is the common denominator of life on earth—every living thing on our planet must have water to survive. Water is constantly in motion, moving through the one *hydrologic cycle*,[2] seeking a way to reach sea level at all times. Water freely moving about in nature is fugitive, quick to disappear, and is best described as fleeting.[3] We face a changing climate, a growing population of hundreds of millions that flushes human waste into our water systems many times per day, an aging water infrastructure system, some of which has changed little since the nineteenth century, and a travel system with imperviously covered streets, highways, driveways, and parking lots that catch and directly divert rain and flood water into the overall hydrologic cycle, carrying with it the filth, debris, and chemicals of our daily transport. In some cities, such as New York City, the underground pipes carry both human waste and storm water, creating, at times of heavy rainfall, raw waste flow into our

1. Michael C. Meyer, *Water in the Hispanic Southwest* (Tuscon: University of Arizona Press, 1984), ix.

2. The United States Geological Survey defines the *hydrologic cycle* as follows: "Earth's water is always in movement, and the natural water cycle, also known as the hydrologic cycle, describes the continuous movement of water on, above, and below the surface of the Earth. Water is always changing states between liquid, vapor, and ice, with these processes happening in the blink of an eye and over millions of years." http://water.usgs.gov/edu/watercycle.html (accessed many times but specifically on October 31, 2019).

3. Charles Porter, *Public Water Policies: The Ultimate Weapons of Social Control* (Lanham, MD: Bernan Press, 2018), 4.

surface streams. Estimates by the U.S. Environmental Protection Agency and the Government Accountability Office claim as much as $400 billion is needed to repair our nation's sewer infrastructure.[4] I think this is an optimistic estimate.

It is important to the overall understanding of the reader for me to share that this has been the most challenging book I have attempted. Why? Trying to analyze each of our fifty states' water rights policies in one book is like attempting to put together a puzzle of ten thousand sky-only pieces on a small coffee table. Each piece must be examined for its shape, not its image, as the images are all quite similar; each state has a separate water policy for surface water and groundwater. Several states have set up the jurisdictions of water regulatory agencies around political boundaries, not based upon the geological boundaries of the water they are attempting to regulate. "Water ignores political boundaries" should be a mantra our schoolchildren learn from the earliest possible age. Throw in the fact that state-by-state water policy changes continuously with rulings by the legislatures, the courts, and the regulatory agencies at the local, state, and federal levels, and you have the perfect conditions for a headache filled with frustration. The overlapping jurisdictions alone are not only complex but often vague and ambiguous.

As political leadership changes, water policy interpretations change as well. My last book, *Public Water Policies: The Ultimate Weapons of Social Control* (2018), attempted to explain to the public that throughout history, all around the world, governments have used water to control people. Water, used to accomplish political goals such as determining where people should live and how and punishing resistance to the agenda of the political leadership in control at any given time, is truly the most potent weapon to force one's political will on another.

Everyone on this planet shares a common pool of water as there is only one finite amount of water in one hydrologic cycle. We are now acutely aware of that fact as climate change and global warming are drastically impacting the natural distribution of water across the earth.

Take just one simple example: The Rio Grande River that makes up the border between Texas and Mexico is administered by a 1944 treaty. Both parties genuinely make a diligent effort to honor the agreement in a friendly relationship. However, one simple unofficial change in policy along the Concho River in Mexico will likely limit the potential water contribution Mexico will make in the future. Why? At La Junta de la Rios in the far West Texas town of Presidio, the Concho provides major inflow to the Rio Grande—or at least it has throughout history. Over the past few years there has been a large

4. Charles Duhigg, "As Sewers Fill, Waste Poisons Waterways," *New York Times*, November 22, 2009.

increase of diversion in Mexico from the Concho for irrigation, a wonderful use of the water to support life. Of course, this vital use of the water in Mexico decreases the potential downstream flow in the Rio Grande. Yet how can anyone blame the people of Mexico who live on the Concho—they have the right to try to enjoy a happy, healthy life. Isn't their more efficient use of the water just the same as when the United States lined the All-America canal to stop the seepage waste along the Colorado River at the border of Mexico at Mexi-Cali? The consequences for the irrigators in Mexico was a loss of sixty thousand acre-feet of seepage into their aquifer annually. The only difference between the Concho situation and the All-America canal situation is that the United States has provided the required annual 1.5 million acre-feet of water to Mexico. The United States simply wanted to better manage its water resource. Should the United States tell the irrigators in the Concho River basin in Mexico to stop diverting the water? Is this a fair thing for us to do? Should the treaty be revised?

Water policy must be based on science, not politics. There is no fair or even possible way to create a one-size-fits-all water policy for our nation or even for many of our states. In Texas, for example, the worse drought in Beaumont's history would be a year with only fifteen inches of rainfall, as its normal rainfall is sixty or more inches. Yet El Paso's best year for rainfall is twelve inches; a year with fifteen inches would be a blessing. A one-sized policy from the legislature in Austin won't work; it would be unfair and ridiculous.

I wrote a book titled *Sharing the Common Pool: Water Rights in the Everyday Lives of Texans*. The best and most interesting twist in a comment I was not meant to overhear was made by a Texas state senator just before I was to testify for a bill I wrote and presented to a committee of the legislature. The senator whispered to his transcriber while looking at me, "He's the author of *Water Rights for Dummies*." I've yet to decide if that was a compliment or insult, but it did indicate to me I had accomplished my goal—to introduce Texans to their water rights. It was never meant to be a law book; it was never meant to be a graduate school textbook. It was a survey of Texas water rights to make everyday main street Texans aware that water rights were critical to their daily lives, that water must be respected, and that water rights screamed out for clarity, transparency, and common sense. I am hoping the book you are now reading accomplishes a similar goal.

The book is an attempt to help the reader to carve a path through the maze of water rights and regulations. The appendices contain current links to each state's starting-point regulatory agency responsible for water policy. Please be aware that government agencies often change URL addresses with little or no notice, but as of the date of publication of this book, all the listed links are active. Essential to every reader, above all else, is to keep in mind that you simply *must* consult an attorney with expertise in water rights in your state in all matters pertaining to water rights issues.

You will find that I selected one or two sample states for each region purely by personal choice. In order to keep this book from reaching thousands of pages in length, I selected the sample states in each region for detailed in-depth water rights analysis while still briefly describing the remaining regional states in basic detail. I provide the contact information for the main regulatory agency (if one exists) in each of the fifty states.

Before entering into my water rights and regulation analysis, some basic concepts about water rights must be understood. These basic concepts are shared by all the states in a variety of uniquely local ways at times.

What do I mean by *analysis* in the context of this book? Most dictionaries define analysis as “the process of breaking a complex topic or substance into smaller parts in order to gain a better understanding of it.” In this book I am conducting a survey of U.S. water rights as the preliminary step to assist the reader, who could then conduct a detailed analysis or systematic examination and evaluation of a specific state’s water rights.

Analysis is a systematic examination and evaluation of data or information by breaking it into its component parts to uncover the interrelationships, including cause-effect/action-reaction relationships to problem-solve and help the everyday American decide how to develop fair, transparent, and acceptable public water policies. In each region I discuss in this book, I select several states that are either experiencing water crises at this time or whose water policies are typical of other states in the region. In our changing world, which now likely faces more droughts, floods, and potable water shortages, more than ever before our public water policies must be responsibly determined. Water is the cornerstone that determines where all government is located and financed and how all people are fed and clothed and gain the opportunity to live healthy lives.

Unfortunately, oftentimes across the United States, water policy is hindered by *analysis paralysis*. Analysis paralysis in water policy happens when policymakers overanalyze or overthink a decision because the subject matter is so complicated (or they perceive it as such) that the group together is unsure any pending or proposed solution will work. In Texas, water policy seems to move forward during or just after a major drought period; in nondrought legislative sessions the complex water issues tend to be not necessarily ignored but simply put off to a future session. The opportunity that is always missed is the chance to act in advance of the sure-to-come next drought period. Our droughts across the nation west of the Mississippi are worsening and are likely to worsen more. In Texas, our population growth is putting enormous pressure on our water resources even in nondrought periods. Acquisition of right-of-way for water pipelines usually takes years to process due to landowners' just compensation rights. In Texas, our state water plans since 2007 have warned of the impending doom in 2030 when our potable water supplies will not meet demand in any drought year. Planning for the absolute worst and hoping for the best is what each and every water policymaker should be doing right now—today.

Generally, most Americans do not have a working knowledge of the water rights in their state. Since water across the nation is simply available at numerous taps in our homes, until it is declared damaged (as in Flint, Michigan) or comes under short-term volume restrictions for watering yards, no one thinks past their monthly water bills. This book is another effort to reach people so they can gain an understanding of water rights in their everyday lives and the critical importance of fair water policies to their future security.

In the words of one of Texas's most qualified and responsible past Texas House of Representatives members, Mark Strama (who now serves as the head of Google Fiber in the western United States), "Given the extraordinary efficiency with which human industry and innovation have developed food supplies, it's clear that Thomas Malthus was wrong when he predicted that population growth and limited food resources would eventually arrive at a cataclysmic intersection. In Texas, at least, it's clear that the resource most likely to lead to Malthusian consequences for population growth is water, if we do not find ways to conserve, manage, and expand our water supply."[5]

I would expand Mark's perspective to include the entire United States (if not the world). His astute comment is one of the catalysts of my continuing efforts in water policy studies.

5. From a June 23, 2012, email to the author.

Chapter One

Fundamental Concepts of Water Rights in the United States

Water is the ultimate zero-sum game; the volume of water used by one right holder sourced from our common pool of water ultimately diminishes, to some degree or other, the volume of water available to other water right holders.

—Charles Porter[1]

Nothing is more basic to successful human congregate settlement than the management and sharing of scarce freshwater resources. As Nelson M. Blake, chairman of the history department of Syracuse University, said of water and cities in 1956, "Without it, cities simply could not exist."[2]

Water rights and policies in the United States evolved from ancient native cultures through Spanish and other European colonial influences. Generally, water rights and policies in the area of the United States west of the Mississippi River grew from laws and standards brought to the "New World" with the Spanish colonizers; the water rights and policies of the land east of the river arrived with the English and were based on English common law ideas. This concept naturally makes sense: the land west of the Mississippi tends to be arid and enjoys less natural rainfall; hence, the legal concepts of the colonizers from arid Spain learned over two thousand years in dry Iberia were and still are well suited to meet the challenges of living in varying degrees of aridity. The land east of the Mississippi tends to enjoy more natural rainfall and other forms of precipitation, making water policies more

1. Charles Porter, *Sharing the Common Pool: Water Rights in the Everyday Lives of Texans* (San Marcos, TX: River Books, 2014), 1.
2. Nelson M. Blake, *Water for the Cities* (Syracuse, NY: Syracuse University Press, 1956), 2.

appropriately based on those developed to suit the wetter English or British Isles environment.

Falls on the Upper Hudson River in New York

WHO OWNS WATER IN THE UNITED STATES?

A first most fundamental question arises: Who owns water in the United States, the public or the individual citizen? The answer is the eternally favorite answer: it depends. Ownership of groundwater varies somewhat from state to state, but surface water in rivers, streams, and watercourses across the states is owned by the individual state and held for the people.

The path to finding the answer to the puzzle of water ownership begins with a look into the three geological containers in which water resides: *surface water*, *diffused surface water*, and *groundwater*. (In some states, a fourth nongeological container is referred to as *developed water*, or water that has been extracted or diverted under some use, at which point its development changes its ownership.)

Surface Water Rights: Riparian or Appropriative?

Surface water is water that runs naturally in a river, creek, or stream, most accurately defined as a *watercourse*. Many states refer to surface water as flowing in a watercourse. The most understandable and well-argued definition of a watercourse arises from a 1925 Texas Supreme Court case, *Hoefs v. Short*,[3] in which the court approved the legal requirements for it. According to Wells A. Hutchins, author of *The Texas Law of Water Rights*, "There must be a channel, comprising well-defined bed and banks, a current of water, and a permanent source of supply. The flow of water need not be continuous, and the channel may be dry for long periods of time."[4]

Surface water is the first geological container to consider the study of water rights in the United States. Much different than the geological container we know as groundwater, surface water is owned by the individual states in each of the fifty states.

The list may be misleading to a degree as one can see that the state of Texas is not listed in the following list of states; yet we know that surface water is owned by the state of Texas, held in trust for the people, and regulated by the Texas Commission on Environmental Quality. Texas, by its historical court-defended policies, claims full jurisdiction over its waters within the agreed-upon compacts with surrounding states. Even those compacts, some in place for decades, can fall into conflict from time to time. Currently, Texas and New Mexico are in an extended court battle over shared water in the Rio Grande.

---

3. *Hoefs v. Short*, 114 Tex. 501 (Tex. 1925), 273 S.W. 785 (decided May 13, 1925).

4. Wells A. Hutchins, *The Texas Law of Water Rights* (Austin: Texas Legislature and Texas Board of Water Engineers, 1961), 25.

Aside from the waters of the United States issues, what are the fundamental conceptual ways in which surface water rights in the United States are determined? First, a comment from a commission of the state of New Jersey that is sadly applicable across the United States in each and every state: "Riparian rights have a long and somewhat checkered history in New Jersey. It is a subject that for too long has been difficult for most people to understand because of developing and shifting administrative policy, technical jargon, and unnecessarily complicated statutes. The result is that riparian land management is understood by very few that it most directly affects. In fact, there is an absence of general agreement concerning the meaning of essential terms."[5]

Water policy across the country, state by state, is difficult for folks, outside very qualified water law attorneys and some water policy regulators, to understand. Why?

1. Water policies shift continuously due to the weather and political whims and will.
2. Water policy is full of technical jargon, including words and phrases that are ill-defined even in the statutes.
3. Without doubt, in all the states, the water statutes are unnecessarily complicated.

The Texas Supreme Court judges I have known, to a person, have hated water cases as the precedents are at times antiquated, and changes in the statutes, in their opinion, should be made by the legislature, not the courts. Maybe the infinite permutations of water relationships that exist in nature cause the statutes and regulations to be a mess. Unfortunately, my expert observations inform me that the norm for legislatures is to react to water issues, not to proactively try to solve obvious inherent policy problems.

In surface water policy and laws, there are two basic surface water right concepts state by state: *riparian rights* and *appropriative rights*. Both basics are *usufructs*, or rights that allow use but not ownership of the water. Each does convey some level of property right to the riparian or appropriator, but the extent of the property right is continually in debate in some court somewhere in the United States.

---

5. Lewis P. Goldshore, *New Jersey Riparian Rights Handbook* (State of New Jersey County and Municipal Government Study Commission, 1979).

Riparian water rights are based upon ownership of land *appurtenant*[6] to or adjacent to a surface water river or stream. English common law concepts of water rights are *riparian* based or tied to the ownership of land appurtenant to surface watercourses. According to law professor Joseph Dellapenna,

> Since the 1950s, about half of the states east of Kansas City, along with Hawaii, have enacted administrative permit systems to replace tradition riparian rights. Rather than importing appropriative rights into the east, these states have developed a highly regulated system of water administration based on riparian principles that amounts to a transition to a public property system. The transition from extremely limited regulatory intervention to more or less comprehensive regulation often occurred incrementally rather than from a conscious design to transform the system of water rights. There thus is disagreement over when a true regulated riparian system emerged in a particular state and even today one could debate whether certain states have in fact crossed over from largely unregulated common law riparian rights to a regulated riparian system. Bearing this in mind, the following list indicates the states that have enacted regulated riparian systems and the approximate date of that step: Alabama (1993); Arkansas (1957); Connecticut (1982); Delaware (1959); Florida (1972); Georgia (1977); Hawaii (1987); Iowa (1957); Kentucky (1966); Maryland (1957); Massachusetts (1985); Minnesota (1973); Mississippi (1985); New Jersey (1965); North Carolina (1973); New York (1979); Virginia (1989); and Wisconsin (1957). In addition, several states have applied a regulated riparian system to groundwater without applying it to surface waters.[7]

Most water rights in the states in New England are riparian; this makes sense as English common law came from a country with little or no water resource problems. "New" England is appropriately named regarding water rights based on geographical conditions such as rainfall and moisture amounts. Riparian rights were best described in *Haas v. Choussard* in Texas in 1856. According to the conclusion of the Texas Supreme Court,

---

6. *Appurtenant*: According to *Black's Law Dictionary*, an appurtenance is something that belongs to something else; an adjunct; an appendage. The watercourse and the land could be said to be appended to each other. Another term used is *adjacent*, or the land is adjacent to the watercourse. *Black's Law Dictionary* defines *adjacent* as lying near or close to; sometimes contiguous; neighboring. Most riparian rights are appurtenant to the land and cannot be severed from the land in the United States. I prefer *appurtenant* to describe a riparian location and right. Some legal scholars prefer the phrase "abutting a water body" to describe the basic characteristic of riparian rights.

7. Joseph Dellapenna, "The Evolution of Riparianism in the United States," *Marquette Law Review* 95: 53–90; Joseph Dellepenna, ed., *The Appropriative Rights Model Water Code*. Report of the Committee on Laws and Institutions (Reston, VA: American Society of Civil Engineers, 2007); also from an out-of-print white paper written by Professor Dellapenna. See also A. Dan Turlock and Vicki C. Krueger, "Water Rights: A White Paper Report," National Association of Realtors, September 2015, https://realtorparty.realtor/wp-content/uploads/dlm_uploads/2020/07/State-Local-Issues-Water-Rights-2.pdf.

> Every proprietor of lands on the banks of a river has naturally the right to the use of the water which flows in the stream adjacent to his lands as it was wont to run, *currere solbat*, without diminution or alteration. No proprietor has a right to use the water to the prejudice of other proprietors above or below him, unless he has a prior right to divert it, or a title to some exclusive enjoyment. He has no property in the water itself, but a simple usufruct while it passes along. *Aqua currit et debet currere* is the language of the law (Water runs and ought to run as it used to run). Though he may use the water while it runs over his land, he cannot unreasonably detain it, or give it another direction, and he must return it to its ordinary channel, when it leaves his estate. Without the consent of the adjoining proprietors, he cannot divert or diminish the quantity of water which would otherwise descend to the proprietors below, or throw the water back upon the proprietors above, without a grant or an uninterrupted enjoyment of twenty years, which is evidence of it.[8]

Appropriative rights are based upon a grant or license to use the water from the appropriate state government. In many states, appropriative rights are allocated based upon *first-in-time, first-in-right*, or what is referred to as *prior appropriation*. Many states, such as Texas, have completed an adjudication process to determine the water right held or granted to whom, for what use, and to memorialize the date of the water right to determine priority rights. The earliest priority date is entitled to the surface water before those later priority dates, which are generally referred to as junior rights. The adjudication of surface water rights is a highly complex, time-consuming, and at times controversial process. Once this has been accomplished (Texas took almost thirty years to complete the adjudication process), much of the dispute over who has first access to surface water is much clearer, of course, but it certainly continues to be discussed years later.

Another fundamental concept of surface water rights is *reasonable use*.

Reasonable Use

The revised American idea of *reasonable use* represents an advanced concept over simple riparian rights in earlier English common law. An opinion rendered in 1827 by Circuit Justice Joseph Story in a Rhode Island case styled *Ebenezer Tyler and others vs. Abraham Wilkinson and others* and legal scholar James Kent's 1832 *Commentaries* together "mark the inception of reasonable use"[9] in American law. In 1963 professor of law T. E. Lauer wrote in the *Missouri Law Review*, "The origin of the American riparian doctrine of water use, whereby each owner of land upon the banks of a watercourse has

---

8. *Haas v. Choussard*, 17 Tex. 588 (1856), 589–590. See Also Timothy L. Brown and Jason T. Hill, "Surface and Groundwater in Texas," *The Water Report*, October 15, 2019.

9. Lauer, 61.

the right to make a reasonable use of the water, is customarily placed shortly after the year 1825. Traditionally, the creation of the riparian doctrine has been ascribed to two of the greatest early American jurists, Joseph Story and James Kent."[10]

In my review of the opinion in the case, Circuit Justice Story wrote these opinions, which became the recognized underpinning of the reasonable use concept in American law:

> Primâ facie every proprietor upon each bank of a river is entitled to the land, covered with water, in front of his bank, to the middle thread of the stream, or, as it is commonly expressed, usque ad filum aquæ. In virtue of this ownership he has a right to the use of the water flowing over it in its natural current, without diminution or obstruction. *But, strictly speaking, he has no property in the water itself; but a simple use of it, while it passes along* [emphasis added]. The consequence of this principle is, that no proprietor has a right to use the water to the prejudice of another. It is wholly immaterial, whether the party be a proprietor above or below, in the course of the river; the right being common to all the proprietors on the river, no one has a right to diminish the quantity which will, according to the natural current, flow to a proprietor below, or to throw it back upon a proprietor above. *This is the necessary result of the perfect equality of right among all the proprietors of that, which is common to all* [emphasis added]. The natural stream, existing by the bounty of Providence for the benefit of the land through which it flows, is an incident annexed, by operation of law, to the land itself. When I speak of this common right, I do not mean to be understood, as holding the doctrine, that there can be no diminution whatsoever, and no obstruction or impediment whatsoever, by a riparian proprietor, in the use of the water as it flows; for that would be to deny any valuable use of it. *There may be, and there must be allowed of that, which is common to all, a reasonable use. The true test of the principle and extent of the use is, whether it is to the injury of the other proprietors or not* [emphasis added].[11]

Note that Justice Story clearly declares the riparian has no ownership in the water but a usufruct right only. Note that he also considers water a "common" for all, each having a perfect equality of right. Further, Justice Story declares the test of a reasonable use to be whether one's use is to the extent that it injures another's use. Justice Story simply makes logical sense covered in fairness and justice. James Kent followed Justice Story's lead in 1832 in a part of his voluminous and amazing *Commentaries on American Law*, commonly known as Kent's *Commentaries*.

---

10. T. E. Lauer, "The Common Law Background of the Riparian Doctrine," *Missouri Law Review* 28 (winter 1963). Lauer also refers to the case as 24 Fed. Cas. 472 (No. 14,312) (C.C.D.R.I. 1827).

11. *Tyler et al. v. Wilkinson et al.*, Circuit Court, D. Rhode Island. June Term, 1827.

James Kent[12] wrote in his *Commentaries*, in the section titled "Of Real Property," "All that the law requires of the party, by or over whose land a stream passes, is, that he should use the water in a reasonable manner, and so as not to destroy, or render useless, or materially diminish, or affect the application of the water by the proprietors below on the stream."[13]

The reasonable use concept opined by Justice Story in 1827 was further supported by well-known and respected legal scholar Justice James Kent in 1832. Within a few years, the doctrine of reasonable use became often used in water laws across the United States.

Today, the reasonable use concept is alive and well in many states. There are movements from time to time in states such as Texas to incorporate the concept into groundwater law, but to date, neither the Texas Legislature nor the Texas courts have implemented the idea. A modern explanation of reasonable use is outlined by the National Agricultural Law Center: "The riparian landowner has the right to make 'reasonable use' of the watercourse. This means that the riparian landowner may make a reasonable use of the water as long as that use does not interfere with the reasonable use of another downstream riparian landowner. Reasonableness is determined by comparing the proposed use with the other uses of other riparian landowners. Any natural uses, such as water for drinking, watering livestock, or watering a garden, are considered reasonable under the law. Artificial uses, such as those for irrigation or industry, are considered reasonable uses under most states' laws."[14]

The American rule of reasonable use is a foundational legal concept in many states; in most it applies to both surface water and groundwater rights. Wells Hutchins wrote of the rule, "Under the American rule, however, the use of water by each landowner must bear some reasonable relationship to the use of the overlying land. Export of the water from the area for commercial purposes or waste of the water to the injury of others is not a reasonable use; otherwise, the specific criteria governing these relationships have not been well developed."[15]

Reasonable use is actually quite complicated and easily becomes a matter of hot debate between water users in modern times. Brian E. Gray of the

---

12. James Kent was a U.S. attorney, judge, and scholar who played a central role in adapting the common law of England into the common law of the United States. As a justice and later chief justice of the New York Supreme Court and a chancellor of the New York Court of Chancery (then the highest judicial officer in New York), Kent wrote many decisions that became foundations of nineteenth-century law. Kent's great legal treatise *Commentaries on American Law* (1826–1830) offered the first comprehensive analysis of U.S. law. From https://law.jrank.org/pages/7982/Kent-James.html.

13. 3 Kent Commentaries 354 (1st ed. 1828).

14. https://nationalaglawcenter.org/overview/water-law.

15. Wells Hutchins and Harry Steele, "Basic Water Rights Doctrines and Their Implications for River Basin Development," *Law and Contemporary Problems* 22, no. 2 (1957): 284.

University of California's Hastings College of Law wrote of the complexity of the term:

> This seemingly simple and innocuous sentence masks a world of meaning and complexity, however, because the requirement of reasonable use embraces at least four interrelated concepts. The determination of reasonable water use is utilitarian: the law seeks to encourage relatively efficient, economically and socially beneficial uses of the state's water resources. It is situational: the evaluation of individual reasonable use concerns not only the water right holder's own uses but also other competing demands (both consumptive and ecological) on the water resource. The reasonable use doctrine is also dynamic: the definition of reasonable use varies as the economy, technology, demographics, hydrologic conditions, environment, and societal needs evolve. And, because all uses of water must be consistent with this interdependent and variable definition of reasonable use, the law renders all water rights fragile. A water right that was reasonable when first recognized, and which may have been exercised reasonably for many years, may become unreasonable as hydrologic conditions change.[16]

Gray points out four interrelated characteristics of reasonable use that make the concept complex: it is

- utilitarian;
- situational;
- dynamic; and
- consistent.

A reasonable use in the past may not be a reasonable use in the future due to many events that humans cannot control. Above all else, the situational aspect of reasonable use is *subjective* and determined in the eyes of the stakeholder; the same specific use can be argued for or against easily and credibly. A few states broadly define reasonable use as irrigation, agriculture, municipal, domestic and livestock, and even some industrial purposes. Imagine you are an irrigator from a surface water source, and over time your use, which was considered "reasonable" for decades, suddenly becomes "unreasonable" to protect a species or the environment. It may very well be that once your use becomes unreasonable as determined by a court of law, you lose the relief of just compensation to your water right because unreasonable uses are not compensable rights. Are we heading toward those type of decisions in our heavily drought-laden West? Will a court decide an irrigator's crop, such as

16. Brian E. Gray, "The Reasonable Use Doctrine in California Water Law and Policy," in *Sustainable Water: Challenges and Solutions from California*, ed. Allison Lassiter (Berkeley: University of California Press, 2015).

almonds, is an unreasonable use of the water right because either the use of the water damages the environment or a municipality needs the water for health and safety? If the prolonged drought in the West continues a few more years, surely questions will be asked about someone's reasonable use of their water right.

Another foundational doctrine in water rights is the idea of *beneficial use.*

Beneficial Use

In Texas, according to Texas Water Code 11.002 (4), "Beneficial use" means "use of the amount of water which is economically necessary for a purpose authorized by this chapter, when reasonable intelligence and reasonable diligence are used in applying the water to that purpose and shall include conserved water."

What exactly are *reasonable intelligence* and *reasonable diligence* when applied to water law? Surely both of these ideas are highly subjective and sources of strong argumentation. In 1972, with updates in 1996, California defined many beneficial uses of water—so many in fact that the list is five pages in length! Some states provide comprehensive lists of beneficial uses; others do not. What constitutes a beneficial use of water can be very controversial. The prime example of the beneficial use controversy centers on the use of water to frack oil and gas exploratory wells. Is using the water for fracking a beneficial use?

As mentioned in the introduction, water policies tend to be overlooked during wet periods before and during legislative sessions around the country, even in dry climates like Texas. Other areas east of the Interstate 35 corridor have, until recent times, had weak regulatory policies, especially in groundwater, due to the simple fact that these areas enjoy more adequate moisture and precipitation. Villanova professor of law Joseph Dellapenna opined correctly in 2006 that "the relative lack of administrative regulation of water use in Pennsylvania perhaps reflects the Commonwealth's relatively wet climate."[17] His comment is especially true in the US Northeast, but with climate change and global warming, the attitude to increasing regulation of groundwater and other water resources, even in the "wet" areas of our country, will continue to grow in complication and bitter disputes.

Another geological container of surface water is known as *diffused surface water.*

---

17. Joseph Dellapenna, "Developing a Suitable Water Allocation Law for Pennsylvania," *Villanova Environmental Law Journal* 17, no. 1 (2006).

Diffused Surface Water

"Diffused" surface water is water that runs across the surface of the land due to either rainfall, snow melt, condensation, or other atmospheric conditions *before* the water enters a watercourse to become surface water or enters the ground to become groundwater. Diffused surface water use by impoundment or diversion can create conflict. Professor Ronnert Reis aptly discussed this in 1967:

> Undoubtedly the major problem regarding surface water exists where one party seeks to prevent such water from entering his land (or to remove it therefrom). When the conflicting landowners are both private citizens, American courts have dealt with the problem in three different ways. Perhaps these best can be labeled the common law approach, the civil law approach, and the reasonable use approach. According to the common law approach, surface water is considered a common enemy and anyone is permitted (without liability) to take any steps necessary to prevent it from coming onto or remaining on his land. According to the civil law approach of dominant and servient estates, both parties are required to allow the water to flow in its natural course and cannot take any preventive measures. Under this approach one may not interfere with the natural flow of surface water to the detriment of another's interest. Under the reasonable use approach, liability exists only when the interference with the flow of surface water is unreasonable in light of all of the surrounding circumstances. This approach seeks to deal with each case individually and does not attempt to set up any absolute standards.[18]

The ownership of diffused surface water varies across the nation by state, but its conjunctive relationship to surface and groundwater is undisputed at least among water scientists. In most states, a landowner uphill of his neighbor may not divert water into a stock pond if the diversion interferes with natural diffused flow to the detriment of another person's interest. However, in states like Texas, the uphill landowner *may* capture diffused surface water in a new stock pond even if it deprives the downhill neighbor of this water. Even if the uphill owner in Texas diverts the diffused surface water in total into a stock pond, keeping it from a watercourse or entry into the groundwater below, this uphill owner may do so without any liability.

The third geological container, and currently the one most important to life, is *groundwater*.

---

18. Ronert I. Reis, "Connecticut Water Law: Judicial Allocation of Water Resources" (1967), *Special Reports* 3, Connecticut Institute of Water Resources, https://opencommons.uconn.edu/ctiwr_specreports/3.

Groundwater

According to the United States Geological Survey (USGS), *groundwater* is defined as "water that exists underground in saturated zones beneath the land surface."[19] The USGS's "saturated zones" could also be referred to as "pools" of water underground.

An interesting follow-up to the *waters of the state* definition is the number of states that include groundwater as a water of their state. According to the Environmental Council of the States, "Twenty-eight state definitions include 'groundwater' or 'underground water' as a water of their state; (AK, AL, AR, CA, CT, FL, IL, KY, LA, MD, MA, MI, MN, MS, MT, NY, ND, OH, OR, RI, SC, SD, UT, VT, VA, WA, WI, WY)."[20]

A historic ownership concept came to America with the English settlers known as the *absolute ownership rule*, often referred to as the *English rule* or the *absolute dominion rule*. This rule was established under English common law, which is nonstatutory.[21] In brief, the property owner owns the soil beneath his property and the groundwater it contains. Under this concept, landowners have the unlimited right to withdraw the water found beneath their land. The English rule was established by a court ruling in Wigan, England, in 1843 from the case *Acton v. Blundell*.[22] This court held that groundwater was part of the soil beneath the land following the ancient right that a landowner owned ground beneath to the center of the earth in a conical shape and everything within that cone.[23] I discuss *Acton v. Blundell* in further detail in the following pages.

The National Agricultural Law Center at the University of Arkansas Division of Agriculture Research and Extension provides the generally accepted modern definition of the *absolute ownership doctrine* in water, also known as the *absolute dominion rule*. Accordingly, they detail the doctrine as follows:

> Under the Absolute Dominion Rule, also called the "Absolute Ownership Rule" or the "English Rule," a landowner may use as much ground water as possible. The rule does not take into account impacts on neighboring users, and, as a result, one owner could monopolize the entire aquifer without incurring liability.

---

19. https://www.usgs.gov/faqs/what-groundwater?qt-news_science_products=0#qt-news_science_products.

20. https://www.aswm.org/pdf_lib/ecos_feb_2009_definitions_of_waters_of_the_state.pdf.

21. The generally accepted brief definition of *common law* is "a system of laws based on customs and court decisions rather than on written laws made by a parliament. Common law forms the basis of the legal system in the UK, US, and various other countries" (from the *Cambridge Dictionary*). "English common law" simply refers to common law as it exists in England.

22. 152 E.R. 1223 (Eng. 1843).

23. Adell L. Amos, David Getches, and Sandra Beth Zellmer, *Water Law in a Nutshell*, 5th ed. (St. Paul, MN: West Academic, 2015), 227.

> This doctrine creates an incentive to pump as much water as possible because of the lack of concern of incurring penalties from a neighboring user. Most states have rejected this doctrine, as malicious withdrawals of water could not be enjoined. The states that do continue to follow this doctrine allow for remedies for willful injury. States following this doctrine are Connecticut, Georgia, Indiana, Louisiana, Maine, Minnesota, Massachusetts, Mississippi, Rhode Island, Texas, and Vermont.[24]

Groundwater rights are owned by the state in thirty-nine states but owned by the private individual or entity based on overlying land ownership in eleven states. As an example of one state's definition of *groundwater*, in the Texas Water Code, Chapter 36, Section 36.001, groundwater is defined in subsection (5) as "water percolating below the surface of the earth."[25] This groundwater is most often held in aquifers but can be held in smaller pools. The distinction between an aquifer and a pool of underground water is not significant to my efforts here, but the Texas definition that describes the water as percolating is significant in many states' laws. In fact, some U.S. legal scholars have claimed "percolating" groundwater to be different from "stratum" groundwater in arguments over who should own the groundwater.[26] As in my state-by-state analysis of surface water rights, I will also discuss the variations in groundwater ownership and its definition.

Acton v. Blundell[27] established not only in England but also in many parts of the United States the idea of nonliability for groundwater withdrawal by one neighbor if he or she extracts so much groundwater that another neighbor is harmed. This concept is commonly known as the *rule of capture*, a phrase severely hated phrase in many places. A fine quote from *Acton*:

> Each owner has an equal and complete right to the use of his land, and to the water which is in it. Water combined with the earth, or passing through it, by percolation, or by filtration, or chemical attraction, has no distinctive character of ownership from the earth itself; not more than the metallic oxides of which the earth is composed. Water, whether moving or motionless in the earth, is not, in the eye of the law, distinct from the earth. The laws of its existence and progress, while there, are not uniform, and cannot be known or regulated. It rises to great heights and moves collaterally, by influences beyond our apprehension. These influences are so secret, changeable, and uncontroulable [*sic*], we cannot subject them to the regulations of law, nor build upon them a system of rules, as has been done with streams upon the surface. Priority of enjoyment does not, in like cases, abridge the natural rights of adjoining proprietors.[28]

---

24. "Water Law: An Overview." https://nationalaglawcenter.org/overview/water-law/
25. Texas Water Code, Chapter 36, Section 36.001 (5).
26. Hugh Buck.
27. *Acton v. Blundell*, 152 E.R. 1223 (Eng. 1843).
28. Ibid.

Professor Reis, in support of my conclusion that the English rule of no liability has been modified across the nation in most states, wrote about the preceding section of *Acton v. Blundell*, "As one can easily discern from the above, the court's decision was subject to two primary factors: (1) their failure to differentiate ground water from the land in which it flows and (2) their lack of scientific knowledge regarding the nature of ground water and the pattern by which it moves. As scientific knowledge in this area began to increase, the Acton rule was gradually modified in Connecticut."[29]

Another case in the nineteenth century that addressed liability between neighbors in the use of groundwater in the United States, *Frazier v. Brown*,[30] was decided by the Supreme Court of Ohio, which held,

> In the absence of express contract and a positive authorized legislation, as between proprietors of adjoining land, the law recognizes no correlative rights in respect to underground waters percolating, oozing, or filtrating through the earth; and this mainly from considerations of public policy: (1) Because the existence, origin, movement, and course of such waters, and the causes which govern and direct their movements, are so secret, occult and concealed that an attempt to administer any set of legal rules in respect to them would be involved in hopeless uncertainty, and would be practically be impossible. (2) Because any such recognition of correlative rights would interfere, to the material detriment of the commonwealth, with the drainage of agriculture, mining, the construction of highways and railroads, with sanitary regulations, building, and the general progress of improvement in works of embellishment and utility.[31]

In several states such as Texas, groundwater is owned by the surface landowner, but this ownership is often a matter of ongoing controversy in much of the public's eyes. In other states with no comprehensive groundwater regulations, ownership is not mentioned, but these states allow unlimited withdrawals without any liability, making the practical matter of ownership insignificant.

Another fundamental concept in groundwater law is the *restatement (second) of torts rule*.

The Restatement (Second) of Torts Rule

Ohio and Wisconsin adopted the restatement (second) of torts rule in their water codes. According to the National Agricultural Law Center, "The Restatement's rule is seen as a merger of the Absolute Dominion Rule and

29. Reis, "Connecticut Water Law."
30. *Frazier v. Brown*, 12 Ohio St. 294 (1861).
31. Ibid.

the Reasonable Use rule." Section 858 of the Restatement (Second) of Torts states,

Liability for Use of Groundwater:

1. A proprietor of land or his grantee who withdraws groundwater from the land and uses it for a beneficial purpose is not subject to liability for interference with the use of water by another, unless
   a. the withdrawal of groundwater unreasonably causes harm to a proprietor of neighboring land through lowering the water table or reducing artesian pressure,
   b. the withdrawal of groundwater exceeds the proprietor's reasonable share of the annual supply or total store of groundwater, or
   c. the withdrawal of the groundwater has a direct and substantial effect upon a watercourse or lake and unreasonably causes harm to a person entitled to the use of its water.[32]

This concept incorporates beneficial use, reasonable use, and equitable share for all and even recognizes the conjunctive relationship of groundwater to surface water. Upon examination of this basic tort idea, Ohio and Wisconsin may very well be leading the United States in at least a justice-based idea of water rights being a common for all. This tort concept also recognizes the *correlative rights* of people using groundwater.

The Correlative Rights Doctrine

Correlative rights in groundwater, or in so many areas of our human interactions, require people to limit their use of common sources to a reasonable amount. If groundwater is considered a "common," then one user must limit their use to meet the requirement of equitable sharing between neighbors. The simplest way to allocate between neighbors is by basing the proportions on the amount of land owned. But this method overlooks the uses of each sharing party, the future uses of each sharing party, and many, many other factors. For example, in 1903 the California Supreme Court rejected the extant absolute dominion rule and extended the American or reasonable use rule to require sharing groundwater between landowners above the water. Water law scholars Anthony Dan Turlock and Jason Anthony Robison wrote of the California situation, "All overlying owners have correlative rights to an equitable share of a ground water basin."[33] In Texas recently there has been discussion of

32. "Water Law: An Overview."

33. Anthony Dan Turlock and Jason Anthony Robison, *Law of Water Rights and Resources*. Environmental Law Series (Eagan, MN: Thomson Reuters, 2018), 190.

"fair share" concepts in groundwater to offset the absolute dominion rule in the state. Considering the historical legislative and judicial decisions in Texas, a recognition of correlative rights in groundwater, other than the limitations against waste, deliberate malice toward a neighbor, and causing subsidence on a neighbor's land, is likely not to become the law anytime soon.

According to the National Agricultural Law Center,

> The Correlative Rights Doctrine distributes water on an equitable basis among landowners and allows off-tract uses, although these uses are subordinate to on-tract uses. Like the Absolute Dominion Rule, the Correlative Rights Doctrine determines rights in groundwater based on ownership of land. The difference, however, is that landowners overlying the same aquifer are limited to a reasonable share of the aquifer's total supply, rather than having an absolute right to groundwater or an unlimited right to pump.
>
> This doctrine was first recognized in California in *Katz v. Walkinshaw*, 74 P. 766 (Cal. 1903). The court held that in times of shortages an overlying owner must limit withdrawals to a "fair and just proportion" of the underlying supply. Thus, when two users are both exporting water, the court would use the doctrine of prior appropriation. Finally, in disputes between an overlying landowner and an exporter, the overlying landowner receives a reasonable share of the water, even if the overlying owner is junior to the exporter. The states that apply this doctrine include: Arkansas, California, Iowa, Minnesota, Oklahoma, and Vermont. Nebraska follows a combination of this doctrine and the Reasonable Use doctrine.[34]

Because surface water has been fully allocated, especially in the West, over the past fifty years, coupled with our continuing thirsty and growing population, groundwater today has become more important than ever. Desalination could relieve the pressure on groundwater in the future, but its cost in both money and potential environmental damage might make it a solution of last resort. To better understand the new reliance on groundwater for our near future, as well as the change in the decades- if not centuries-long public attitude to its ownership and regulation, Blake W. Griggs, consulting professor for the Bill Lane Center for the American West at Stanford University, wrote in 2014,

> In a surface water system, the relationship between water rights, the state, and the public is clearly apparent. The diversion of water from an upstream tributary diminishes the flow of both near and distant rivers "by a certain amount," and that diversion affects the owners of downstream rights and the public accordingly. The same goes for upstream diversions of alluvial groundwater. In either hydrologic situation, upstream diversions can become sufficiently damaging to

34. "Water Law: An Overview."

> downstream interests such that the state itself takes legal action. Importantly, it does so on behalf of all of its citizens, and not just its water rights owners. The state as a whole is more than a mere agent or trustee for its private water rights owners. Yet the groundwater revolution complicated this relationship.[35]

I have written and spoken extensively over the past fifteen years about groundwater policy as the increasingly most serious issue in Texas and everywhere in the United States west of Interstate 35. Since 2015, I have been actively involved in changing Texas law and policy to wake up the public to the significance of groundwater in our future. For example, in 2015, after two years of volunteer work heading a personally financed ad hoc committee to modify the mandatory seller's disclosure notice in Section 5.008 of the Texas Property Code to require, for the first time in over sixty-five years at the time, sellers of single-family properties to inform potential buyers whether or not the property for sale was located in a groundwater conservation district,[36] the bill became law on January 1, 2016. Shortly thereafter I wrote and published a history of the Groundwater Conservation Act of 1949 in the *Panhandle*

---

35. Blake W. Griggs, "Beyond Drought: Water Rights in the Age of Permanent Depletion," *Kansas Law Review* 62 (2014). Professor Griggs also served as special assistant attorney general for the state of Kansas.

36. HB 1221–2014–16. Porter was a private sponsor and author of HB 1221 providing live testimony at the House Natural Resources Committee Hearings and the Senate Business and Commerce Committee Hearings (the only witness). Noted by Porter, "HB 1221 was my idea and over a two-year period I gathered a committee of attorneys and water experts to draft the bill, then presented the bill to the Texas Association of Realtors, the Texas Alliance of Groundwater Districts, the Texas Water Conservation Association and countless numbers of other trade associations and groups including the State Bar of Texas. I received unanimous support from political groups and trade associations representing over 250,000 members. The bill was signed into law by Governor Abbott on June 17, 2015, effective January 1, 2016. It amended the Texas Property Code Section 5.008 to include a question requiring the seller of a residential property in Texas to disclose their knowledge about the property being in the jurisdiction of a groundwater conservation district, the local regulatory agency over groundwater in Texas. Over the first ten years of this revision, over 39,000,000 participants in residential real estate transactions will be forced to answer or read this question. I testified in both the House and the Senate committees to support the bill." From the capitol archives in Austin:

HOUSE COMMITTEE REPORT

Natural Resources Committee

March 18, 2015–2:00 PM or upon adjournment

For:

Porter, Charles (Self; Austin Board of Realtors)

Sledge, Brian (Co-Chair, TWCA Groundwater Legislative Stakeholders Committee; Lone Star GCD; Prairielands GCD; Upper Trinity GCD; and Barton Springs-Edwards Aquifer GCD) And HB 1221—Senate Committee Report, Business & Commerce

May 5, 2015–9:00 AM

FOR:

Porter, Charles (Self; Austin Board of Realtors), Austin, TX

Sledge, Brian Attorney (Co-Chair, TWCA Groundwater Legislative Committee; Prairielands GCD; Lone Star GCD; Upper Trinity GCD; Barton Springs Edwards Aquifer Conservation District; North Texas GCD), Austin, TX

Plains Historical Review.[37] Groundwater is the single-most significant natural resource of the West.

The United States' current situation in groundwater policies is discussed by the Water Systems Council, a nationwide nonprofit organization focused on private water wells:

> Population growth, drought, increasing demand and other factors may lead to a reexamination of groundwater ownership rights in the coming years. The current trend has been away from the Absolute Ownership doctrine, towards a Reasonable Use or Correlative Rights approach, and towards state statutes regulating groundwater withdrawal. However, Individual rights should be considered when determining "reasonableness." Recent widespread droughts have increased the tension between private property rights in groundwater and the public's right in water. Although the property right may be regulated, like the right to use land is regulated, too much regulation results in a taking of private property for public purposes without just compensation. Another trend in the years since the prior edition of this booklet is the increasing recognition of a "regulatory taking" of groundwater rights—situations where government regulation of groundwater unlawfully infringes on groundwater rights. Policy makers should be admonished to remember the limits of their authority to regulate the right to use water. States do not "own" the water.[38]

Yet another natural scientific fact that must be considered in any workable, credible water policy is that all three geological containers always relate to one another conjunctively.

The Three Geological Containers Exist Conjunctively

Water is the ultimate example of an element of nature that exists in a *conjunctive* state. Surface water, diffused surface water, and groundwater are, have been, or will be in union with one another ultimately; water exists in a conjunctive relationship in all three geological containers all the time. Diffused surface water feeds both surface water and groundwater. Groundwater feeds surface water both in the underflow and via natural springs. As water flows downhill above or below ground, the containers feed and deplete each other

37. Charles Porter, "'Of Urgent Concern': What Prompted House Bill 162, the Groundwater Conservation Act of 1949," January 2018 in the *Panhandle Plains Historical Review* 88 (2017), West Texas A & M University.

38. "Founded in 1932, the Water Systems Council (WSC) is the only national nonprofit organization with programs solely focused on private water wells and small, shared wells serving more than 13 million households nationwide (US Census American Housing Survey 2015). WSC is committed to ensuring that Americans who depend on wells have safe, reliable drinking water and works to educate well owners, consumers, and policymakers at the local, state and federal levels about water wells and the importance of protecting America's groundwater resources" (from https://www.watersystemscouncil.org/about-wsc).

visibly and invisibly. This conjunctive relationship is a key concept that must be grasped in order to understand water rights in the United States. This law of nature, when applied to water ownership, complicates the debate since even with modern technology we cannot yet "see" clearly underground.

The Texas Legislature, between sessions in 2018 and 2020, included in the charter of the state House and Senate interim natural resources committees a request to investigate revising groundwater management to recognize the conjunctive relationship between surface water and groundwater in the 2019 and the 2021 legislative sessions. Not only did no mention of the idea of conjunctive relationships in groundwater and surface water arise at all in any committee hearings in 2019 and 2021, but there was nothing even mentioned in a recommendation from the interim committees to respond to the inquiries. Yet another inescapable fact often overlooked in water policy is that water ignores political boundaries.

Water Ignores Political Boundaries

Setting workable public water policy based upon surface political boundaries and not upon the boundaries of the common pool of water in a given river basin, watershed, or underground aquifer is problematic. The water one user draws from a common pool affects the other users of that common pool, much as when one is sharing a milkshake with a sibling using separate straws simultaneously (the users' rights are correlative obviously). "Water ignores political boundaries" is a concept prudent policymakers must keep in mind. The convenience of establishing autonomous county-based entities to regulate groundwater according to jurisdictions set along existing county boundaries without recognition that the aquifer being managed is shared with neighboring counties leads to mismanagement of the resource, intense competition, and public disgust with and distrust of the water policy. Our use and misuse of water also follows the *conjunctive relationship theory*.

Other Fundamental Concepts Nationwide: The Conjunctive Relationship of Fresh Water to Sanitary Sewage and Storm Sewage

A mistake made by policymakers is to put primary focus on the segment of water policy involving fresh water, either surface water, diffused surface water, or groundwater. But just as the three geological containers relate to each other conjunctively, *a complete water policy must consider the three most significant impacts of the human interface with water: fresh water, sanitary sewage water, and storm drainage water*; the infrastructure of water systems in the United States is made up of all three. We deliver fresh water throughout our municipal and privately owned water systems; we send the freshwater to millions of taps inside our structures where it is used for drinking, cooking, laundry, irrigation for landscaping, bathing, cleaning, and flushing our toilets. As we use this fresh water, we flush our toilets and deliver other wastewater into the system, which is eventually treated at a water treatment plant, then returned either to surface water as effluent or, at times, to the municipal supply system. This water is referred to as *sanitary sewage*, a term that is an oxymoron: in no way is human wastewater sanitary. Just think of the millions of gallons of human wastewater generated 24/7/365 in any major American city.

The conjunctive relationship of fresh water and sanitary sewage is obvious. If the infrastructure that usually shares underground ditches is damaged, this conjunctive relationship can cause sickness or even death.

Storm drainage is the diffused surface water that flows from the hydrologic system over roofs, streets, industry, parking lots, and open fields. The millions of miles of underground and aboveground storm drainage in the United States are amazing. Most of these storm drainage systems deliver the runoff water into surface streams, many without any detention or filtration. Just take a look at the early runoff from any rain from our streets; it is a conglomeration of crankcase oil and other fluids from our automobiles, filth and trash from the streets and sidewalks, and at times even raw human sewage from leaking sanitary sewage plants. While this book's focus is on water rights and laws and not environmental regulations, it must be kept in mind at all times that water rights and laws have a natural interrelationship with sanitary sewage and stormwater drainage.

A farmer's right to use water for irrigation from a surface stream can be seriously harmed by untreated human sewage from leaking sanitary sewage plants upstream. In the same way, a farmer's herbicides and fertilizers can seriously damage those municipal water systems downstream. Groundwater is impacted as well by sanitary sewage and storm drainage including industrial and agricultural uses.

Uses of Water Also Define Water Rights

Across the nation, *domestic and livestock* use is generally protected and rarely requires a permit from any regulatory agency. Surface and groundwater use for personal use in our homes and gardens and to water our livestock is normally exempt from permit across the United States. The definition of domestic and livestock use varies from state to state and even by county in some states. Domestic and livestock use comprises about 10 percent of all water usage in the country.

The other and most significant use of water, both surface and groundwater, is for irrigation of crops. Agribusiness west of the Mississippi is inextricably linked to irrigation. While "dry-land" farming—that is, farming without irrigation, dependent on moisture from rain and other sources—is still practiced, most long-term successful and sustainable agribusiness must have irrigation. Except in rare situations, irrigation requires permits from some regulatory agency. Irrigation uses about 60 percent of our water in the United States.

The balance of our water is used by municipalities and for industrial use. Across the nation, municipal and industrial use comprises about 20 percent of our water use. In almost all states, municipal and industrial use requires a permit of some kind from a regulatory agency. Shocking to many people is the fact that municipalities do not have priority over private uses, especially in the western United States.

In Texas, for example, a prior-appropriation-based surface water rights state, the earliest appropriated water right is first-in-time/first-in-right regardless of the type of ownership. In a major Texas Supreme Court ruling, even in times of drought to protect the health, safety, and welfare of people in municipalities, the prior-appropriation water right still prevails. The case was styled *Texas Farm Bureau v. Texas Commission on Environmental Quality* (the agency responsible for the administration of surface water rights in Texas). The ruling sent a strong warning to municipalities with junior surface water rights: find other sources because the farmer with the senior water right gets the water first over any junior water right holder. This ruling troubles some since, according to many sources, almost 90 percent of Texans live in a municipality; it seems to send the public the message from the ancient creed "every man for himself and God for us all" when it comes to Texas surface water policy.

No doubt, at any one point in time, less water may be used for domestic and livestock purposes and more for irrigation and municipal and industrial purposes; the ratios are dynamic, but for decades the norm has been 10 percent domestic and livestock, 60 to 70 percent irrigation, and 20 to 30 percent municipal and industrial.

Statistical Constants of Water

Two very important constants about water hold another key to beginning to understand water and its human-water interface. Each time, anywhere on earth, it rains one inch, 27,154 gallons fall on one acre of ground. Using this constant, a calculation may be made for the amount of water a person could collect from their roof. In Austin, a city that "averages" thirty inches of rain in a "normal" year (there's no normal year in Texas due to millennia of recurring droughts), a single-story, two-bedroom, two-garage home with a four-inch and twelve-inch pitch roof could, according to this constant, capture sixty thousand gallons of water a year. Of course, this rainfall does not come in equal amounts in regular intervals. Adequate storage is the key to capturing roof water, or diffused surface water.

The other constant that so readily tells the opposing sides to an out-of-district water transfer is that one acre-foot of water contains 325,581 gallons of water. How does this simple definition indicate the sides in a water dispute? The side that wants to transfer water out of district advertises that we are only moving ten acre-feet a year to another area. The opposition advertises, no, you are moving 3,255,810 gallons a year to another area, a huge amount of water. Guess what? Both sides are advertising the exact same amount of water. Water policy mostly deals in acre-feet, not gallons.

Two other "constants" should be kept in mind. There is only one amount of water on our planet; it is just held in different states of existence. This is referred to as the one *hydrologic cycle*. Additionally, water ignores political boundaries; this must be kept in mind when governments are tempted to establish the jurisdictional boundaries of water based on existing political boundaries.

Chapter Two

Ownership of Water

Does It Really Matter?

Does ownership really matter in water? Ownership in real property includes three basic rights:

1. The right to exercise sole discretion of the use of the property
2. The right to enjoy the income or sales proceeds of the property
3. The right to sell or rent all or any portion of the property

The idea of ownership in real property also retains the right to exclude someone from the property. But even in the states where absolute dominion is the base legal concept over groundwater, for example, sole discretion over the use, sole discretion over the income or sales proceeds, or sole discretion to sell or rent the water is limited. And of course, there is absolutely no physical way to exclude someone from access to another's groundwater if the water lies in an aquifer or shared pool. Surface water across the United States is owned by the individual states; the only right a person has to use surface water is referred to as a *usufruct*—the right to use water but without any ownership in it.

Does an individual really own something if a statute or government regulatory entity retains final say over the use or sale of the property? Even in groundwater in the absolute dominion states, there usually are either statutes, court precedents, or regulatory agencies with final say; violation of the law and regulatory agency is subject to fines and even physical restraint from using the water. In states like Texas, where the law and regulatory agencies allow transfer of a water right in either surface or groundwater, oftentimes the permit process is so convoluted, capricious, and expensive that effectively the enjoyment of the ownership of the right is not in the sole discretion of the owner. In Texas, no matter the law and its support by the courts, the political will of the people is these days generally against the transfer of groundwater out of the "area" by lease or sale. If the people can't stop the permit if required, they usually can so limit the amount of water transferred that it renders practical challenges to the profitability of the venture. If the people can't stop an economically feasible permit for transfer of groundwater out of their district, the people's next battleground is to stop any pipeline built to move the water by simply eliminating the right-of-way for the pipeline. If some owner of groundwater finds a way to enjoy eminent domain authority, even then, the right-of-way fights often take so many years that the end user by lease or purchase of the groundwater might not financially be able to delay their receipt of the water; therefore the transaction falls apart. So does one really "own" the groundwater in these examples?

In Texas again, there are areas with few if any regulatory rules over individual uses of groundwater. Texas has a limited and confusing group of local groundwater conservation districts with permitting authority over the groundwater in their jurisdiction. Not all of Texas is under the jurisdiction of a groundwater conservation district, however. Whether in the jurisdiction of a government entity or not, except for the occasional needs of drillers during Texas's short-lived recurring oil and gas exploration booms, end users won't drive up in a truck and haul the water they are buying by sale or lease. Without a pipeline to deliver the water, the only use of the water is for domestic and livestock purposes or agricultural purposes on the landowner's site. Certainly, the groundwater could be processed on site for bottled water, industrial purposes, or other economic uses, but the fair market value of the water is quite limited by the demand for the final product and the cost of production.

There are other considerations when discussing the question of who owns the water in any given state. Ownership of water across the United States is not truly absolute, is it? How can true absolute ownership be held in surface water or groundwater when both are subject to varying and at times overwhelming and confusing federal, state, and local regulations? The very difficult issue today that our courts face and will certainly face more so in the future is determining which governmental body has primary jurisdiction over water in any geological container in any given state or region. It is my experience that the rules and regulations concerning water rights in individual states of each of the three primary government entities often overlap and at times contradict each other. In general, our U.S. Constitution clearly states that when there is a conflict between federal and state law, the federal law takes precedent. While on the surface this might be obvious, in the real world of day-to-day workings in water rights, the concept of federal authority is strongly and actively resisted in every state from time to time, or in a state like Texas, always. The simple fact to keep in mind when reading this book is that ownership of surface or groundwater is rarely a simple matter

Hudson River at West Point

to determine. Texas again tired of the disputes over groundwater ownership even though the courts for decades made such ownership clearly to lie in the landowner above the groundwater. In 2011, for once and for all, the Texas

Legislature added a statute that established ownership of groundwater to lie in the realm of the surface landowner.[1]

In our country, the Constitution requires just compensation for "takings" of private property. One way in which a government entity may owe just compensation to a private property owner is by so restricting the property by laws and regulations that the "investment-backed economic opportunity" is taken from the owner.[2] Claims of "takings" are being made in lawsuits over water permitting and authority to do so. Recent claims against regulatory authorities in Texas have focused on the taking of the property owner's investment-backed expectations and economic opportunity by an overreaching regulatory authority. The argument generally is not over the right to regulate; the significant issue is the amount that the owner will be compensated. In water rights issues, determining the fair amount of compensation due the owner can be very complicated.

If groundwater in a given state is determined to be private property, what is the fair market value of the groundwater right, and what challenges do appraisers and others face when attempting to value the water?

1. Senator Troy Fraser's SB 211, effective January 1, 2016.

2. Daniel R. Mandelker, "Investment-Backed Expectations: Is There a Taking?," *Washington University Journal of Urban and Contemporary Law* 31 (January 1987): 3–43. "In *Penn Central Transportation Co. v. City of New York* Justice Brennan added a new factor to the judicial lexicon of the taking clause. A taking may occur, he stated, when legislation frustrates 'distinct investment-backed expectations.' Although Justice Brennan stated that investment-backed expectations are but one factor in the application of a taking clause that has no 'set formula,' they add yet another complexity to the doctrinal muddle of taking law."

Chapter Three

Problems in Determining the Fair Market Value of Water

Land adjacent to flowing water is obviously the most valuable in our state; the better the water and the water right, the more valuable the land. In this chapter, I use Texas as the geographical location for my discussion of water valuation.

An early example of the value of water in Texas can be found in the historical record. On November 19, 1879, George W. Brackenridge, pioneer San Antonio banker, University of Texas regent, and donor of the "Brackenridge" tracts in Austin and San Antonio, completed an inspection of several sections of land in Kimble County owned by his land-speculating brother Thomas. His enthusiasm about the land was based upon its water: "We arrived on this place last evening from a survey of the Seventeen Sections [10,880 acres] of your land in the northern portion of this County and I found it to far exceed my expectations." He described "an abundance of water" on several of the tracts and said that tract nineteen had "all the water there is in that section in [a] splendid spring."

Toward the end of the letter, Brackenridge made a prophetic statement: "You must be careful not to dispose of those sections on which the water is unless the other goes with it, as the water renders the land valuable."

Nothing was truer then, and nothing is truer now.

Considering that the "norm" for Texas is drought or "soon-to-be-back-in-drought," the troublesome consequence of water scarcity, outside the most obvious—the ability of an area to sustain life—will be a decrease of land values, leading to a weakened ad valorem tax base, inevitably making Texas a less attractive home for new people and industry. Our ad valorem tax base across the state underlies the funding of our most cherished public services and societal values.

Water is fast becoming the battleground between the basic ways of life in Texas, rural and urban. The cities are thirsty for water, and the source they seek to quench this thirst is, in many cases, the groundwater held by rural neighbors. If an urban area pumps away a rural neighbor's groundwater, land values in the rural area drop subsequently, diminishing its ad valorem tax base. Without a corresponding increase in tax rate, which always ignites heated debate, our most valued civic services, such as public schools and hospitals, could suffer. Since almost 90 percent of Texans now live in urban areas, we simply cannot, and likely will not, allow any urban area to decline even if that urban area's only available new water resource comes from adjacent rural groundwater. Competition over water is a zero-sum game: if one gains, another loses. The choice between urban and rural life is one no legislature or court should have to make, but without fully funded, comprehensive, long-term, statewide water planning respecting all the stakeholders' needs, there could very well be a winner and a loser. The cities will rightly do their duty and act to protect their citizens by gathering rural groundwater in any manner legally possible. Statewide water policy must be written such that it enhances and protects both urban and rural ways of life in Texas. The market value of water at the everyday level is easily determined. We quickly understand the price of water when we read and pay our water bills or buy bottled water. The market value of a water right is not as obvious. The fair market value of a water right is based upon comparable sales of existing water rights, judicial rulings, and government contracts. Over the years, a tepid marketplace has developed for the sale of surface and groundwater rights. Comparable sales and leases of today's water rights are discoverable; some of the groundwater conservation districts (GCDs) and the Edwards Aquifer Authority in particular post for sale or lease notices by holders of water rights in their jurisdictions. Some real estate appraisers are now able to give reasonably well-supported valuations of water rights based upon confirmed comparable sales, always the best indicator of fair market value.

A significant and notable indication of a more sophisticated valuation aspect of water rights came in a court ruling in 2010. The judge offered the market value not only of groundwater rights per acre-foot but also the added incremental value of market classification of the land in the matter as an irrigated farm as opposed to a nonirrigated farm.

Many Texans, when asked, profess confusion about how to determine their water rights, what government entities regulate water, and, of utmost importance, the market value of the water they own. Everyone feels as if their water right has value, but few have experienced the sale of that water. There is no Multiple Listing Service available, as in residential property sales, to instantly find true and reliable comparable sales in water transactions. There is no Blue Book for guidelines as to value as exists for automobiles. To begin the process of sale of a water right, first a buyer, seller, or lender must gain a fundamental understanding of who owns the water, what regulations, if any,

Pedernales River, Texas

apply to allow the transfer of that water to the purchaser or lessee, and what process is required to close a sale or lease of the water right. A thorough investigation must be undertaken to determine the credible and defendable fair market value of water. This is especially challenging no matter the methodology used. The commonly heard saying that "water is the next oil" is fundamentally flawed. Water is an all but real-time renewable resource and is to be conserved and ideally allocated fairly; oil is a resource that is only renewable over millennia and is to be mined by the highest bidder. Certainly, water has real value; it has been said that "water renders the land its value," and nothing could be truer, especially in most farm and ranch real estate transactions. To begin to discover an answer to credible and defendable valuation of water and water rights, it is important to first understand some basics about water, ownership, and regulations.

WATER VALUATION METHODOLOGIES AND CHALLENGES

The three traditional and widely accepted methods or approaches to determining the fair market value of real property are the *replacement cost*, also known as the *cost approach*; the *sales comparison approach*; and the *income capitalization approach*, or the capitalization of the net operating income stream generated from operation of the property. One other significant method may prove very useful in the determination of credible water valuations: valuations offered in rulings and judgments of our courts. All four should be considered to determine the value of a water right.

The generally accepted short definition of *fair market value* is the price a buyer and seller will arrive at to consummate the sales transactions with neither party being under duress. A more thorough definition of fair market value, however, is more appropriate to use in estimating the value of water or a water right. Academics William B. Brueggeman and Jeffrey D. Fisher offer the best and most comprehensive definition of fair market value as follows:

> Market value is a key consideration when *financing or investing in* [emphasis added] income-producing properties. It is defined as follows:
>
> "The *most probable price* [emphasis added] which a property should bring in a competitive and open market under all conditions requisite to a fair sale, the buyer and seller acting prudently and knowledgably, and assuming the price is not affected by undue stimulus. Implicit in this definition is the consummation of a sale as of a specified date and the passing of title from seller to buyer under conditions whereby:
>
> 1. Buyer and seller are typically motivated;
> 2. Both parties are well-informed or well-advised, and acting in what they consider their best interests;
> 3. A reasonable time is allowed for exposure in the open market;
> 4. Payment is made in terms of cash in United States dollars or in terms of financial arrangements comparable thereto; and,

5. The price represents the normal consideration for the property sold unaffected by special or creative financing or sale concessions granted by anyone associated with the sale."[1]

The definition developed by Brueggeman and Fisher is the most appropriate for use in water valuation due to the depth of analysis it contemplates. The basis of my reasoning is important to fully understand.

First, the term *most probable price* makes a very specific and realistic point that must always be kept in mind when offering any fair market valuation of water because water valuation is not like traditional real property valuation. The value of water is accompanied by so many variables that any value or price opined should be given only as "most probable." Coupled with the qualifier of "most probable" is the equally significant idea that all water transactions, maybe more so than in traditional real estate transactions, are the epitome of "time is of the essence" transactions. Buyers of water or water rights, especially agricultural operators growing fragile crops, factor the timeliness of the actual delivery of the water purchased heavily into the price they agree to pay. The statement "Implicit in this definition is the consummation of a sale as of a specified date" in the Brueggeman and Fisher definition refers to this "time is of the essence" concept. Water valuation is greatly influenced by time. Around the world the market for water is so dynamic that significant changes often occur in very short periods of time.

Second, our preferred definition includes the idea that the buyer and seller are both acting prudently and knowledgeably, an idea that experience shows is rare in water transactions. Buyers and sellers of water rights today in Texas are faced with the arduous task of self-education in the intricacies and complexities of water rights and regulations, knowledge that is simply not readily available from any one source. For example, with one hundred different GCDs, each having a unique set of rules and regulations, coupled with the widely variable nature of water resources around the state, acting "knowledgeably" is a difficult goal to accomplish and takes on a new urgency.

Water policies change often and are highly complicated by several mitigating factors such as permitting processes, the overlapping jurisdictions between federal and state agencies, especially in surface water, and by the wide variances in rules and regulations of the GCDs. Complicating the groundwater conservation district challenges is that experience has shown that the ways in which GCD boards grant permits for groundwater transfer can be quite inconsistent and unpredictable at times. Any water valuation must include a realistic assessment of the impact of any regulatory permitting

1. William B. Brueggeman and Jeffrey D. Fisher, *Real Estate Finance and Investments*, 14th ed. (New York: McGraw-Hill Irwin, 2011), 296.

process, the cost in time and money to discover feasibility information, and the conflicting doctrines and practices of the regulatory agencies involved.

Third, Brueggeman and Fisher's "undue stimulus" refers to the widely accepted concept of "duress" on either party. "Undue stimulus" not only takes into account the idea that parties could be under personal duress but also includes notions such as the case of an oil exploration company that must have water for hydraulic fracturing at the exact time it is needed and not a minute later. During the normal conditions of drought west of Interstate 35 in Texas, duress and undue stimulus are much more likely to enter into a water valuation equation. Any valuation must be adjusted for the drought conditions at the time of the valuation in order to more credibly meet the "most probable price" goal of the valuation opinion.

Fourth, Brueggeman and Fisher's reasonable time of exposure to the market is another challenge in water market valuation, especially in groundwater transfers. What constitutes a "reasonable time" in a proposed groundwater transaction can vary greatly from GCD to GCD; in a proposed surface water transaction, "reasonable time" can vary by watermaster and geographical region, river authority jurisdiction, and the level of the backlog of overall Texas Commission on Environmental Quality surface water application processing. The exposure to a broad group of potential buyers or lessors usually does influence the most probable price attainable. Traditionally it is not easy to discover water rights for sale or lease, so it is incumbent on the seller or lessor, more so than in other real property transactions, to find a path to full exposure of their offerings in order to reach as vast a market of buyers or lessees as possible.

Fifth, Brueggeman and Fisher's normal "consideration" without creative financing is highly germane to water valuation. One important element that requires an adjustment in the most probable price of a water right is any impact "creative" financing could have on the eventually agreed price. Very short-term loans without longer-term loan take-out commitments skew agreed-upon prices. Loosely underwritten seller or lessor financing does the same, as do any other nontraditional underwriting criteria. Typical lenders in water rights acquisitions face first and foremost the challenge of understanding the basics of water rights in order to begin to properly underwrite and assess the risk of any water-related loan. Their underwriting process must be prepared to meet the stringent requirements of the eventual audits from government agencies or other assessors of risk, especially by bank deposit insurers such as the Federal Deposit Insurance Corporation. It is highly likely that federal Office of the Comptroller of the Currency bank auditors will not immediately understand water rights transactions; most of their experience is in more traditional real estate loan valuation. Keep in mind also that the vast majority of real estate–related loans over the past decade have been underwritten to allow the loans to be sold in the secondary market. It is very unlikely that any loan made to acquire a water right will be easily sold into a secondary market. Likewise, it is unlikely that a water right loan could be "securitized" as more recent real estate loans have been, constituting a real-time damper on financing any water right acquisition. An even more basic aspect influencing the ability to find financing for a water project or right is the simple question of whether enough water will be present at the water's source to fulfill the long-term obligations of volume in any water contract.

Yet another complication to these four methodologies to arrive at fair market valuation of water is the chemical and geological nature of the subject water itself. For example, in the traditional valuation of real estate, scientific investigation is usually limited to physical inspections of the land and improvements and defects thereto. However, valuation of water requires at the least a chemical analysis of the quality of the water. The reliability, availability, and amount of the water to be sold must also be reasonably estimated based on scientific testing at the source of the water. The natural fact that all three geological containers of water are constantly in motion and are subject to drainage in many ways can greatly influence the long-term reliability of the availability of the water source. Most groundwater does not lie in a bathtub-like formation; the amount and accessibility can be affected in many ways. For example, aquifer level can be impacted by pressure changes that are difficult if not impossible to observe or predict. Gaining the confidence of the buyer, lessee, or lender as to the reliability of the source water in volume and quality just might be the most basic hurdle in fair market valuation.

Demand for a water right is fickle, as well as highly dependent upon rainfall amounts, the immediate varying needs of water buyers, and at times strange local politics. Most people forget that "demand" has two dependent elements in order to be "effective": desire for the product or good welded to the ability to pay for the product or good. In many areas of our state, the ability of any community to pay for water can be quite limited, even though there is strong desire and/or need. State Comptroller Susan Combs's 2012 report titled "Your Money and Local Debt" found that many local governments in Texas were deeply in debt. Our conclusion drawn after reading Combs's well-researched report was simple: many local governments in Texas simply cannot afford any more debt; nor should they seek it, even if they desperately need water.

HOW CAN IT BE DETERMINED IF A WATER MARKET EVEN EXISTS?

The most critical consideration, more so in water valuation than traditional real property valuation, is whether or not the water sold or leased is truly deliverable both legally and/or politically. In order for a water transaction to be consummated, the water must be delivered to the buyer. Accordingly, the three groups of questions below offer a starting place to determine if a potential market for the water actually exists in any given area.

1. Questions about transferability and deliverability.
    - Would the ability to transfer and/or deliver the water to the buyer from surface rights or groundwater rights be a factor in the "value" of the water?
    - Will the state or local rules allow the water right to be sold and delivered to the end user?
    - Will the local rules allow the water to be sold or leased and transferred out of its current geographical or political district and in what quantity?
    - Will the local people "revolt" against the transfer of the water out of their area or district and cause expensive delays in permitting, making the potential sale or lease infeasible and imprudent?
    - Is acquisition of the right-of-way for a delivery pipeline possible both at a reasonable cost and in a timely manner to fulfill any potential sale or lease contract?
    - Can a distribution system be installed, including lift stations to compensate for geographical challenges with adequate ingress and egress to and from the source of the water? Can physical operations and maintenance of the producing equipment be accomplished in a timely manner so as to fulfill a sale or lease contract?
2. Questions about the quality and use of the water.
    - What is the ultimate use of the water? Use of the water has a great impact on its market value. Use of the water for a corn crop or other agribusiness purposes surely influences the market value and generally indicates a lower value for the water. Of course, this varies from crop to crop and varies geographically. Use for bottled water or other industrial uses certainly influences the market value of the water and generally indicates a higher value for the water.
    - Is the use "beneficial"?
    - Is the use of the type that will not cause subsidence?
    - Has the water been tested for salts, pollution, or other hazardous conditions?
    - Is the desired amount of water available over the economic life of the user's desired project?
    - Is there any chance that the water could be damaged by neighboring parties' current or future use?
    - Are there geographical features that disrupt production of the water?

- Are there other water sources available that could be produced by competitors of better quality or more inexpensively?
- Are there other water users now or in the future whose permitted use could deplete the common pool of water in the area?
- Would it be less expensive for an interested user/producer to acquire his or her own surface water or groundwater instead of purchasing the subject water?

3. Questions about market demand, depth, and absorption.
   - Will the market be able to absorb the amount of water offered for sale or lease?
   - Can the water be delivered in a timely manner to meet current demand?
   - How "deep" is the demand: How many buyers are there who meet the "ability to buy or lease" the water?
   - What legal and physical factors must be considered if the water is being sold or leased to a municipality?
   - Are any comparable sales transactions discoverable by the buyer or seller?

These groups of questions are a sample starting list that must be asked and answered by both buyer and seller before considering purchase or sale of any water right. There are surely many other questions that might need to be considered as determined by the uniqueness of any certain water sale or lease.

If the answers to the three groups of questions above indicate the proposed water transaction is feasible, then prudent value experts should next use all four aforementioned valuation methodologies (replacement cost, also known as cost approach; sales comparison approach; income capitalization approach, or capitalization of the net operating income stream generated from operation of the property; and valuations offered in rulings and judgments of our courts) to generate a complete picture of fair market value.

Chapter Four

Right-of-Way Acquisition

The Oft-Ignored Key to Water Policy

As mentioned before, one of the key elements in credible water valuation is the availability of a system of delivery to the end user or purchaser of the water. No doubt, water can be trucked around the country, but only rarely in emergency situations, and surely not as the marketable norm for water sales from source to purchaser. The norm is, of course, via underground pipeline. Pipelines can be built inside negotiated easements gained from landowners. However, oftentimes landowners will not agree to granting the easement for the pipeline. In these cases, the exercise of eminent domain by a government entity is likely the only way the pipeline can be built. Fortunately, we live in a nation in which government entities cannot take private property unless the "take" provides just compensation to the private property owner.

According to Tiffany Dowell Lashmet, attorney-at-law and associate professor and extension specialist in agricultural law at Texas A&M University, "Eminent domain is the power of the government or someone acting upon power granted by the government to take private property for public use. The power of eminent domain is recognized in both the United States and Texas Constitutions. The Fifth Amendment of the United States Constitution provides that private property may not be taken for public use without just compensation. Article I, Section Seventeen of the Texas Constitution,[1] likewise, prohibits the taking, damaging or destruction of property for public use without adequate compensation being made."[2]

The battles over just compensation across the nation are ubiquitous and never-ending; these disputes between the condemner (entity exercising its

1. Most state constitutions have similar language.

2. Tiffany Dowell Lashmet, "Eminent Domain in Texas (Part 1)—What Is It?," *Texas Agriculture Law Blog*, March 17, 2014, https://agrilife.org/texasaglaw/2014/03/17/eminent-domain-in-texas-part-1-what-is-it.

eminent domain authority) and the property owner over fair market value fill the court records in every community.

Lashmet continues,

> Condemnation is the exercise of the power of eminent domain. Thus, when the government or a person/entity authorized to use eminent domain takes property, it engages in condemnation.
>
> There are three elements of eminent domain under Texas law:
>
> 1. The actor must be the state or a private entity authorized to condemn;
> 2. the property must be taken for public use; and
> 3. the landowner must receive adequate compensation for the condemned property.[3]

Few if any landowners desire their property to be "taken" in condemnation. In states, such as Texas, with very favorable oil and gas statutes, the oil and gas condemner may proceed with their pipeline construction, and the only argument is over the amount of money to be awarded the property owner. The will of the people in fighting oil and gas pipelines sometimes prevails, but generally the pipeline will be installed and operating with few delays in construction other than those caused by weather.

Water pipelines generally always meet the basic criteria for eminent domain. A water provider can at times collaborate with some government agency with eminent domain authority. There can be little argument that water pipelines from wet areas or water-rich areas to dry areas or water-challenged areas serve the public good. Again, the controversy arises over the just compensation owed the landowner. Generally, water pipelines do not have the suprafavorable process that oil and gas pipelines have in some states, but as the climate warms, this could be easily changed by statute.

The skill and attitude of the right-of-way seeker can make a tremendous difference in acquiring the water pipeline right-of-way. First of all, the product—water—is not hazardous to health like oil and gas product pipelines. Second, a smart right-of-way seeker will not allow "straight-line" paths of the proposed pipeline to prevail over less sensitive paths. Landowners are generally less troubled over pipeline easement across the front of their property, especially for water pipelines. Where landowners get riled up is when the right-of-way seeker splits the property, causing all kinds of disruptions. An example of a smart water pipeline right-of-way acquisition is the way in which the Vista Ridge pipeline from Burleson and Lee counties in Texas to San Antonio was planned; the pipeline followed existing roads and generally stayed on the frontage of properties along the way. Over three

---

3. Ibid.

A livestock tank in Wilson County, Texas

thousand private landowners in Burleson and Lee counties leased or sold their groundwater to the pipeline company, which in turn sold the water to the San Antonio Water System. It is my understanding that the pipeline traversed over 450 private properties with few arguments. The offers to gain the easements were fair, and disruptions to the private property owners' ways of life were few. The entire delivery system was installed in under five years.

An idea I have floated for years is not to seek perpetual easements from landowners via either negotiation or eminent domain but to acquire fifty-plus-year ground leases. This time period usually meets the requirements of any lending institution and usually represents the economic life of the pipeline. The landowner then gains back the land after the fifty-year term ends. The smart acquirer of the easement right-of-way will negotiate "bumps" in the rent paid the landowner over time, may allow the landowner to freely add water to the pipeline, and will offer adequate maintenance of the pipeline corridor with acceptable landscaping to minimize the impact on the landowner.

Since permitting of water transfers can be quite controversial, the opponents to groundwater (when privately owned) transfers out of their area can actually lose the permit battle but defeat the economics of the proposed water transfer by joining together to delay or defeat the water transport pipeline. Delay the pipeline long enough, and the end user will likely find other sources as *time is of the essence* especially in water transactions. Opponents that gather together and demand such a high price of acquisition of the right-of-way can kill the water transfer project as well. Usually, unless there is some eminent domain authority available to the acquirer of the right-of-way for the water pipeline, the project is doomed from the start.

My personal experience with right-of-way acquisition in Texas, having testified as an expert several times, has taught me that controversial widening of freeways via eminent domain and other public projects can take as many as *ten years* to complete. My decades of water rights research have taught me that most end users simply will not be able to wait ten years to bring a new water source via long-range pipelines.

But the future of water policy in the United States should not ignore two significant ideas. The most important and critical idea is that for the good of the country and all of its people, water should be moved and shared between wet areas (generally east of the one hundredth meridian) and the dry areas of our country. In order to physically allow this to happen, we need a water "grid" similar to the electricity grid nationally. It is my opinion that water is equally important to the life of our nation as electricity and defense. We simply cannot, should not, and will not abandon dry areas of our nation.

Chapter Five

Duties and Obligations of Real Estate License Holders in Water Rights

Texas is my example for a typical state's duties and the obligations of real estate license holders and water rights as it has one of the most stringent sets of rules and regulations in the United States. Why should Texas real estate license holders become familiar with Texas water rights and laws?

- To be "scrupulous and meticulous," to "avoid misrepresentation, in any wise, by acts of commission or omission," to "be informed on . . . state and local issues," and to "exercise judgment and skill in the performance of the work" (Canons of Professional Ethics—Rules of the Texas Real Estate Commission [TREC])
- To know what defects or latent defects a seller needs to disclose (Section 1101.652 [b] [3] of the Texas Real Estate License Act)
- To be cognizant of the defects or latent defects in properties, especially in rural areas
- To be geographically competent in the market in which you are practicing real estate brokerage (Texas Real Estate Commission Rule 531.4)

. . . and water is fundamental to the value of most real estate in Texas, the United States, and frankly the world as a whole.

Do real estate license holders need to be experts in the intricate laws of water rights in Texas or their individual state? Certainly not; however, license holders must have a working knowledge of basic water rights concepts in order to be competent; must know if a groundwater conservation district, the Texas Commission on Environmental Quality (TCEQ), the Environmental Protection Agency (EPA), or the U.S. Army Corps of Engineers has any authority over the surface or groundwater of a property, just as a competent agent knows the potential impact zoning may have on a property; and must be able to advise the client to seek special expertise when purchasing property that could potentially have water rights as a significant issue.

The statutes and rules a real estate license holder in Texas must follow are some of the most stringent in the United States. In 2019, the Texas Legislature further increased the duties of real estate agents to include "geographic competency," meaning knowledge of water in most of Texas is a key part of the agent's competency.

TREC §531.3 was amended on August 12, 2019, to make clear that license holders must be knowledgeable about local market issues, water rights included, in the geographic area in which they work and about the characteristics involved in the specific type of property being sold or leased. Penalties for violating this requirement were added to §535.191, with a range of $500 to $3,000.

22 TAC §531.3 Competency
The proposed amendments clarify the definition of competency to conform with recent changes to §535.2, Broker Responsibility, which requires brokers to ensure their sponsored agents have geographic and property type competence

Rule Number:
22 TAC §531.3

Rule Name:
Competency

Proposed Date:
Monday, May 6, 2019

Adopted Date:
Monday, August 12, 2019

From TREC Agenda Materials, August 12, 2019

Changes to 535.2 (i):

A broker who sponsors sales agents or is a designated broker for a business entity shall maintain, on a current basis, written policies and procedures to ensure that:

1.Each sponsored sales agent is advised of the scope of the sales agent's authorized activities subject to the Act and is competent to conduct such activities, including competence in the geographic market area where the sales agent represents clients.

AGENDA ITEM 17 ADOPTED RULE ACTION FROM THE AUGUST 12, 2019, MEETING OF THE COMMISSION CHAPTER 531 CANONS OF PROFESSIONAL ETHICS AND CONDUCT §531.3.

Competency §531.3 Competency. It is the obligation of a license holder [real estate agent] to be knowledgeable and competent as a real estate brokerage practitioner. The license holder must [agent should]:

(1)be informed on local market issues and conditions affecting [the] real estate in the geographic area where a license holder provides services to a client [business and pledged to continuing education in the intricacies involved in marketing real estate for others;;]

(2)be informed on national, state, and local issues and developments in the real estate industry; [and]

(3)exercise judgment and skill in the performance of brokerage activities [the work]; and

(4)be educated in the characteristics involved in the specific type of real estate being brokered for others.

From TREC Agenda Materials, August 12, 2019

An agent now has to be cognizant of water rights and the regulations impacting the rights in the geographic area in which they practice. It is somewhat easier to assist your clients on water rights matters in major cities and other municipalities, but in rural areas and for properties with surface water frontage, a working knowledge of water rights and regulations is critical to a real estate agent's duty of competency. Texas requires sellers of single-family residences to disclose known defects about the property being sold. Defects in water must be disclosed if *actually* known.

DISCLOSURE DUTIES OWED BY SELLERS TO BUYERS

The land-buying public statewide is becoming more cognizant about defects in water rights. For almost two decades, any defect actually known to the seller and the real estate agents has had to be disclosed to potential purchasers of single-family homes.[1] Nondisclosure of defects involving access to water and water rights by the sellers and/or their real estate agents potentially creates substantial liability for civil damages in lawsuits. Sellers' and real estate agents' duties are similar as to disclosure of all known defects.

After 1993 in Texas, the concept of "caveat emptor," or "let the buyer beware," disappeared in single-family residential transactions. Sellers of single-family residential properties, whether represented by a real estate agent or not, are required to disclose *known* defects to any potential buyer while the buyer is making the decision to purchase the property. The 73rd Texas Legislature added section 5.008, "Seller's Disclosure of Property Condition," to the Texas Property Code effective January 1, 1994: "A seller of residential real property comprising not more than one dwelling unit located in this state shall give to the purchaser of the property a written notice as prescribed by this section."[2] From this revision to the property code came a myriad of locally developed seller's disclosure notices, the birth of the home inspection industry, and, of course, hundreds of lawsuits.

Seller's disclosure notice forms are required, at a minimum, to include this line to disclose information about the water source of the property for sale: "Water Supply: City: Well: MUD Co-op:."

Not all farms and ranches have single-family residences, but if a single-family residence is on the property, any defect in the water system or any well's water quality or working status, permit status, or any other known defect must be disclosed to a potential purchaser.[3] Typical plaintiff's petitions involving nondisclosure of defects include claims under the Texas Deceptive Trade Practices Act, as well as claims of common law fraud, fraud in the

1. Texas Property Code, Section 5.008.
2. Ibid.
3. Ibid.

inducement, negligent misrepresentation, and civil conspiracy many times even in situations where there is no single-family home on the property. A prudent seller, agent, or buyer keeps in mind that the source and availability of water to any property are absolutely critical items that must be fully and truthfully disclosed.

Other questions on the minimum statutory seller's disclosure notice form that could involve water conditions include the following:

- Are you (seller) aware of any item, equipment, or system in or on the property that is in need of repair?[4]
- Are you (seller) aware of . . . any notices of violations of deed restrictions or governmental ordinances affecting the condition or use of the property?[5]
- Are you (seller) aware of . . . any condition on the property which materially affects the physical health or safety of an individual?[6]

Any pertinent water-related issues must be disclosed in the answer to any or all of these questions, and supporting documents should be provided to the purchaser prior to making a commitment to buy.

DISCLOSURE DUTIES OWED BY REAL ESTATE AGENTS IN TEXAS

The duties of disclosure of defects for real estate agents are even broader in some ways than the seller's duty to disclose. Any and all actually known defects must be disclosed by the agent even if the seller has disclosed them.[7] Disclosures of latent defects are not considered confidential information in Texas or elsewhere in the United States.

Real estate agents' duties to disclose known defects in water are found in the Texas Occupations Code, in the Rules of the Texas Real Estate Commission, and if the agent chooses to join the National Association of Realtors (NAR), in NAR's Code of Ethics.

First, a real estate licensee's duty to disclose defects is found in the Texas Occupations Code, Chapter 1101, also known as the Real Estate License Act, specifically Section 1101.652 (b) (3) and (4). In short, TREC may revoke an agent's license if the agent fails to disclose to a potential purchaser structural or other latent (hidden) defects *known* to the agent. In fact, this duty

4. Ibid.
5. Ibid.
6. Ibid.
7. Texas Occupations Code, Chapter 1100, Section 1101.652 (b) (3) and (4).

to disclose applies to all types of real estate, not just single-family homes, a fact many agents in Texas still fail to recognize. Note that the key word in 1101.652 (b) (3) is *known*. Most attorneys who defend agents in disclosure lawsuits correctly demand proof of the accused agent's *actual knowledge* of any alleged defect.

The Texas courts have also ruled over the years that license holders have no duty to investigate defects and only have a duty to disclose their actual knowledge of any defect. Here are the cases that discuss the conclusion that a license holder's duty is to disclose *actual* knowledge.

1. *Kubinsky v. Van Zandt Realtors*, 811 S.W.2d 711, 715 (Tex. App.—Ft. Worth 1991, writ denied). "Further, an agent or broker only has a duty to disclose latent defects *known* [emphasis added] to the agent or broker."
2. *Pfeiffer v. Ebby Halliday Real Estate, Inc.*, 747 S.W.2d 887, 889 (Tex. App.—Dallas 1988). "An agent or broker has no duty to undertake an inspection of the property to determine if latent defects exist or make an inspection for possible defect." Also, "An agent or broker has no duty to disclose what someone claims they should have *known* [emphasis added]." Also, "Therefore, unless *known* [emphasis added], the agent or broker has no duty to disclose latent defects to a buyer." Also, "We decline to impose a 'common knowledge' requirement upon Ebby Halliday when the legislature has incorporated an actual *knowledge* [emphasis added] requirement in 17.46 (b) (23)."
3. *Sherman v. Elkowitz*, 130 S.W.3d 316 (Tex. App. 2004). "Consequently, the broker would have a duty to come forward only if he had any reason to believe the seller's disclosures were false or inaccurate." Also, "Finally with regard to the Shermans' contention that Elkowitz himself admitted that he was required to disclose 'all matters relating to the property,' what Elkowitz actually testified to was, 'As a realtor—as a listing agent, I have to disclose any defects I am made aware of to all parties involved.' This testimony, that Elkowitz was obligated to disclose defects he was 'aware of,' is consistent with the listing broker or agent's general duty to disclose known defect to potential purchasers. See *Kubinsky*, 811 S.W. 2d at 715."

Each of these cases appeared, at one time or another, in TREC legal/ethics required courses. In TREC ethics manual *MCE Legal Update*, Edition 5.0, Chapter 3, "Case Studies," the first case reviewed was referred to by them as *Boehl v. Boley*, 2011 WL 238348 (Tex. App.—Amarillo, 2011). In the text box TREC wrote, "To prevail on a case alleging the failure to disclose a known defect, the plaintiff must prove the defendant had actual *knowledge* [emphasis added] of the defect."

In TREC *Legal Update* manual, Edition 4.0, January 2010, TREC reviewed another case referred to by them as *Sutton v. Ebby Halliday*, 279 S.W.3d 481 (TX2009). According to TREC in this edition of the manual, "At trial the court noted that judgment required a finding that the defendants had actual knowledge of the defective condition of the property."

If the license holder has actual knowledge of a defect in the water, water rights, or regulatory characteristics of the water associated with any real property, then that license holder has the duty to disclose the defect. However, the license holder does not have any to duty to investigate, does not have a constructive (or "should have known") duty. If a member of the National Association of Realtors, the license holder is actually barred from providing advice or interpretations in areas outside the license holder's area of expertise.[8]

Plaintiff attorneys, on the other hand, feel the agent's conduct should be judged upon not only what the agent knew but also what they heard, thought, said, did, decided, and failed to do. Many plaintiff attorneys would also like to see "known" changed to "should have known" in 1101.652 (b) (3).

"Should have known" is considered constructive knowledge, which is deemed to be actual knowledge in Texas.[9]

The next place agents' disclosure duties are outlined is found in the Rules of the Texas Real Estate Commission, codified as Title 22, Chapter 531, of the Texas Administrative Code and titled "Canons of Professional Ethics and Conduct for Real Estate Licensees." These duties are organized under the general headings of fidelity, integrity, and competence. Under this code

---

8. Article 2. Realtors® shall avoid exaggeration, misrepresentation, or concealment of pertinent facts relating to the property or the transaction. Realtors® shall not, however, be obligated to discover latent defects in the property, to advise on matters outside the scope of their real estate license, or to disclose facts which are confidential under the scope of agency or non-agency relationships as defined by state law. (Amended 1/00).

See also Article 11: The services which REALTORS® provide to their clients and customers shall conform to the standards of practice and competence which are reasonably expected in the specific real estate disciplines in which they engage; specifically, residential real estate brokerage, real property management, commercial and industrial real estate brokerage, land brokerage, real estate appraisal, real estate counseling, real estate syndication, real estate auction, and international real estate.

REALTORS® shall not undertake to provide specialized professional services concerning a type of property or service that is outside their field of competence unless they engage the assistance of one who is competent on such types of property or service, or unless the facts are fully disclosed to the client. Any persons engaged to provide such assistance shall be so identified to the client and their contribution to the assignment should be set forth. (Amended 1/10).

9. *Black's Law Dictionary*, 6th ed.: "If one by exercise of reasonable care would have known a fact, he is deemed to have had constructive knowledge of such fact." In Texas, constructive knowledge is actual knowledge.

of ethics, effective since 1976, an agent is deemed to be a fiduciary[10] for the client. Fiduciary duty, per the code of ethics, means that the agent must place his or her clients' interests above that of the agent and that the agent be *scrupulous and meticulous*[11] when performing the work. The agent must also avoid misrepresentation by acts of commission or omission,[12] must be informed on market conditions affecting the real estate business,[13] must be informed on national, state, and local issues and developments in the real estate industry,[14] and must exercise judgment and skill in the performance of the work.[15] If the real estate agent fails to inquire about the water rights and conditions of a property, the agent may violate some or all of these duties in the statutory code of ethics.

ADDITIONAL DUTIES OWED BY REAL ESTATE AGENTS IN TEXAS

The fiduciary duty is greater for those holding the senior license status of broker[16] according to rules section 535.2 (b):

A real estate broker has the very highest fiduciary obligation to the agent's principal and is obliged to convey to the principal all information of which the agent has knowledge and which may affect the principal's decision.[17]

The significance of this fiduciary duty is further mentioned in the rules as follows under section 535.156, "Dishonesty; Bad Faith; Untrustworthiness":

a. A licensee's relationship with the licensee's principal is that of a fiduciary. A licensee shall convey to the principal all known information which would affect the principal's decision on whether or not to make,

10. 22 TAC 531.1. "A real estate broker or salesperson, while acting as an agent for another, is a fiduciary. Special obligations are imposed when such fiduciary relationships are created." A relationship of trust and confidence is built between client and agent; therefore the agent serves in a fiduciary capacity.

11. *Texas Real Estate Commission Ethics MCE Instructor's Manual*, p. 1. "Scrupulously is defined as acting in strict regard for what is considered right or proper; punctiliously [paying great attention to detail or correct behavior] exact; painstaking. Meticulously is defined as marked by extreme or excessive care in the consideration of details; careful. Therefore, one can conclude by these definitions that the licensee must perform his or her duties in a way that exhibits a knowledge of what is right and appropriate under the circumstances and with care about details."

12. 22 TAC 531.2.

13. 22 TAC 531.3.1.

14. 22 TAC 531.3.2.

15. 22 TAC 531.3.3.

16. There are two types of licensees in Texas, real estate broker and real estate salesperson. The broker status is the senior status; the salesperson must have a sponsoring broker, and the broker is responsible for the authorized acts of the sponsored salesperson. A salesperson may eventually become a broker under the procedures of the Real Estate License Act.

17. Rules of the Texas Real Estate Commission, 535.2 (b).

accept or reject offers; however, if the principal has agreed in writing that offers are not to be submitted after the principal has entered into a contract to buy, sell, rent, or lease property, the licensee shall have no duty to submit offers to the principal after the principal has accepted an offer.

b. The licensee must put the interest of the licensee's principal above the licensee's own interest. A licensee must deal honestly and fairly with all parties; however, the licensee represents only the principal and owes a duty of fidelity to such principal.
c. A licensee has an affirmative duty to keep the principal informed at all times of significant information applicable to the transaction or transactions in which the licensee is acting as agent for the principal.
d. A licensee has a duty to convey accurate information to members of the public with whom the licensee deals.[18]

All of these additional duties definitely apply to the water circumstances on any property. Section 535.156 is especially applicable to water rights; agents must make an effort to provide their clients with "significant information," and what is more significant than information about a tract of land's water and water rights?

DUTIES FOR MEMBERS OF THE NATIONAL ASSOCIATION OF REALTORS: THE NAR CODE OF ETHICS AND STANDARDS OF PRACTICE

There is an additional code of ethics that applies for some real estate agents. Real estate agents who choose to join the National Association of Realtors pledge themselves to honor NAR's Code of Ethics. The NAR Code of Ethics also recognizes the obligation of agents to disclose defects in properties, which of course includes the circumstances of water of a property. In 2001, NAR added a sentence to Article 1 of its Code of Ethics and Standards of Practice for Realtors, clearly stating that information about defects is *not* considered confidential. This provision makes clear that the agent is not at risk of violating loyalty to his or her client under NAR's Code of Ethics when the agent discloses defects. Disclosure of defects is a nationally recognized duty of members of the National Association of Realtors. Agents may owe fiduciary duty to their client, but Article 1 of the Code of Ethics still requires the agent to treat all parties to the transaction honestly.[19] Therefore, NAR

18. Ibid., 535.156.
19. Code of Ethics of the National Association of Realtors.

agrees with Texas law that all actually known defects such as those pertaining to water on a property must be disclosed.

CIVIL LIABILITY FOR NONDISCLOSURE OF KNOWN DEFECTS

The only safe and prudent practice for sellers and real estate agents is to disclose *anything and everything actually known* about any defect in a single-family residence or any other property for sale or lease, including defects in water rights. The potential monetary damage to unwitting sellers and agents who fail to disclose known defects can be, and many times are, quite substantial. Agents who conspire with sellers to hide defects should be held especially liable for damages and severely sanctioned by the real estate commission.

The path to civil damages for a real estate agent flows from the way in which an agent can lose his or her license by negligent behavior and failing to meet duties owed under the statutes. Negligence in Texas is failure to meet the ordinary standard of care.[20] However, real estate agents have duties that exceed the ordinary standard of care as outlined in the statutes. The Texas Occupations Code, Chapter 1101, section 1101.652 (b) (1), states that an agent who acts negligently or incompetently could have their license suspended or revoked by TREC. Since civil damages stem from negligence, if the agent is negligent under the license act, then the agent is/could be liable for monetary damages.

There is a most fundamental value and ethical concept we hold dear in the United States: *the public has a right to rely upon the representations of agents, and these representations must be accurate and true*. Prudent agents and sellers disclose all defects in writing, prior to offering the home for sale, to help purchasers assess their risk while they are making their decision to purchase. In Texas, amazingly, verbal disclosure is still allowed, but it is more correct behavior to keep everything in writing. Remember, the new purchaser will have to disclose defects when they sell the home in the future, so buyer's agents acting dutifully will assist their buyers in careful review of the disclosures before committing to purchase the property. Buyer's agents should always recommend to their client that they should *consult an attorney*[21] or a licensed inspector, engineer, or any other appropriate consultant.

20. *Negligence* means "the failure to use ordinary care, that is, failing to do that which a person of ordinary prudence would have done under the same or similar circumstances or doing that which a person of ordinary prudence would not have done under the same or similar circumstances."

21. In bold print on each and every contractual document promulgated by TREC: "Consult an Attorney."

Understanding the complex issues about water on a property, whether the agent represents the buyer or the seller, is a clear duty owed by the agent. Does this mean the agent and seller must know the law like an attorney or the science of water like a hydrological engineer? No, but the agent must be *cognizant of the water circumstances* on any property and advise the client, whether buyer or seller, and the public to seek the help of appropriate professionals to assess the water rights, access, availability, quality—all the water features and issues of a property. In most rural properties, water is so critical to the value of the land that any prudent agent will first seek to understand what water rights exist so as to fully inform the potential buying public of the property's features. A property with verifiable water rights will be easier to market and of course is likely to bring the highest price to the seller. Water status should be one of the first areas of a property's features to be investigated by real estate agents, sellers, and buyers.

EXAMPLES OF UNIQUE DISCLOSURES ABOUT WATER AND WATER RIGHTS

If the property is located in the jurisdiction of a GCD, an example of a defect that must be disclosed is a water well that does not have a required permit or that has been abandoned and not plugged. Other examples of required disclosures would be a well in which the pump is not working properly, a well dug too close to a septic field, or a well in which the water is "salty" or "brackish."

Another subtle example of a water defect that should be disclosed is found where a home is located adjacent to a running creek. Assume a well serves this home. The source of the water may not be groundwater, as one would normally think, but the unseen underflow of the running or at times "dried-up" creek. "Dried-up" creeks and streams many times have underflow, sometimes very shallow underflow.[22] The close proximity of the well to the creek in the photograph below requires a prudent and careful person to seek guidance from the Texas Commission on Environmental Quality to be sure it is not in the underflow. The TCEQ is the agency of jurisdiction for surface water and any water *flowing*[23] underground in a defined channel. If the source is the underflow of the creek, then the water is owned by the state, not the

22. An example of this is a hand-dug, rock-lined, twelve-foot-deep water well I found in 2010 on the banks of Leon Creek near the back entrance to Old Dominion in Bexar County. The well likely dates to the nineteenth century since it was just below the Aue "Castle" in Leon Springs. During the droughts when Leon Creek dried up, the settlers dug this well in the flood plain in order to have drinking water.

23. Percolating water underground is considered groundwater and is owned by the surface owner and managed by local groundwater conservation districts, which is the subject of later portions of this book.

landowner as would be the case with groundwater. Even if the well is used for domestic and livestock purposes, which could be exempt from permit, the fact that the source of the water in this well is actually from state-owned water drawn without a permit is a potential defect that must be disclosed to a potential purchaser. Is it a defect which might cause liability to fall upon the seller if not disclosed? Yes. Will a purchaser sue for damages based upon the nondisclosure of this water well's true source? It depends, but they may have a strong cause of action for nondisclosure.

Of course, anyone diverting a flowing stream, since the water in the stream is owned by the state, should seek the approval of or a permit from the TCEQ, even if the use more than likely meets exemptions such as domestic and livestock use or wildlife management. All aspects of the diversion should be disclosed, especially if it was done without a permit relying on an exemption.

As the price of real property increases and, with it, the costs of ownership, such as ad valorem taxes, insurance, and normal maintenance costs, consider this question: Would you want to buy a home on that bubbling creek and take the risk that the TCEQ might put you on notice that you have no right to use the water from the well serving your home? Worse still, would you want to risk the high fines applicable for using the underflow state water without a permit or water right? Of course not. The scenario described above indicates clearly that modern real estate investment requires much more in-depth research than ever before in order to adequately assess the risk of purchase and ownership.

A prudent buyer, seller, and/or real estate agent should seek assistance from the TCEQ to be sure all wells close to any stream comply with regulations. It is always best to ask the TCEQ before diverting any water from a stream, even if the use meets exemptions from permitting.

As technology improves in the science of hydrology, which enables us to better understand groundwater and underflow of streams, creeks, and rivers, it is reasonable to predict that more claims for defects involving water will be pursued under the statutes. Why? Because defects concerning water have the potential to severely diminish real property value. Of equal importance, once a defect is known by the new owner, disclosure of the defect will continue to be an obligation in future sales until cured. Even then, it is advisable to disclose the defect and any corrective actions taken.

Another example of a potential defect that is not normally considered occurs when a seller has rights to divert water from a stream or river for irrigation. The seller may very well have an appropriative right to divert and use the water, but the amount of water permitted could be curtailed by acts of the river authorities or watermasters. For example, assume the seller has a thirty-acre-foot appropriative right to divert water from the Concho River for irrigation, but the Concho River watermaster has not approved the full volume, which has been the case along this river for many years. If the approved volume is only fifteen acre-feet, then this should be disclosed to a potential purchaser.

Offering the property by marketing the full right of thirty acre-feet must be modified with a statement of actual allowed diversions. A measure of damage in a subsequent lawsuit could be $82,500, which is the result of fifteen acre-feet (thirty acre-feet in right less fifty acre-feet actually granted) at the market rate of $5,500. Add in the possibility that the property could no longer be considered "an irrigated farm," as in the Bragg case, and the damages could increase. Certainly, there are many other unique water issues that require disclosure.

Just as water is essential to life, water rights are essential in the everyday real estate transactions of Texans. As Texas grows and water becomes an even more valuable commodity, the need for sophistication in water rights will become increasingly critical to everyone. As of December 30, 2022, the EPA and the US Army published the revised Waters of the United States (WOTUS) rules. What new disclosures will the prudent license holder need to make to clients and customers in the wake of this yet-again revised set of definitions of the jurisdictions of the EPA and the US Army in regulating our waters? The following chapter discusses WOTUS in great detail; Appendix C contains the fact sheets released to the public about the newly revised WOTUS rules. This federal administration's revision of these highly significant rules will have long-lasting intended and *unintended* consequences for private property rights.

Chapter Six

The Federal Government versus the States

The Best Example Is Known as "WOTUS"

The most significant and soon to be highly controversial question in today's surface rights study concerns who has jurisdiction over a state's surface waters, the individual state government or the federal government. The answer is confusing and ultimately will be up to the federal courts—both the state and federal governments have jurisdiction over any individual state's surface water at some level, but the *extent* to which each governmental entity has jurisdiction over the state's water is of growing concern and sure to erupt into a hotly debated issue.

The Waters of the United States (WOTUS) is the best example of the supralegal authority of the federal government over state law. The Clean Water Act (CWA) of 1972 proposed waters of federal jurisdiction, but ongoing disputes began in defining the boundaries of federal and state jurisdiction. A landmark case involving the CWA's jurisdictions was argued in 2001 in *SWANCC v. United States*, followed by other court rulings that continued to confuse the issue of jurisdiction. The current definition of federal jurisdiction over the waters of the United States is found in the federal code, reprinted below exactly as published:

§ 120.2 Definitions.

For the purposes of this part, the following terms shall have the meanings indicated: Navigable waters means waters of the United States, including the territorial seas.

Surface water in Wyoming

I. Waters of the United States:

A. Jurisdictional waters. For purposes of the Clean Water Act, 33 U.S.C. 1251 et seq. and its implementing regulations, subject to the exclusions in paragraph (2) of this section, the term "waters of the United States" means:

1. The territorial seas, and waters which are currently used, or were used in the past, or may be susceptible to use in interstate or foreign commerce, including waters which are subject to the ebb and flow of the tide;
2. Tributaries;
3. Lakes and ponds, and impoundments of jurisdictional waters; an
4. Adjacent wetlands.

B. Non-jurisdictional waters. The following are not "waters of the United States":

1. Waters or water features that are not identified in paragraph (A) (1), (2), (3), or (4) of the above;
2. Groundwater, including groundwater drained through subsurface drainage systems;
3. Ephemeral features, including ephemeral streams, swales, gullies, rills, and pools;
4. Diffuse stormwater run-off and directional sheet flow over upland;
5. Ditches that are not waters identified in paragraph (1) (i) or (ii) of this definition, and those portions of ditches constructed in waters identified in paragraph (1) (iv) of this definition that do not satisfy the conditions of paragraph (3) (i) of this definition;
6. Prior converted cropland;
7. Artificially irrigated areas, including fields flooded for agricultural production, that would revert to upland should application of irrigation water to that area cease;
8. Artificial lakes and ponds, including water storage reservoirs and farm, irrigation, stock watering, and log cleaning ponds, constructed or excavated in upland or in non-jurisdictional waters, so long as those artificial lakes and ponds are not impoundments of jurisdictional waters that meet the conditions of paragraph (3) (vi) of this definition;
9. Water-filled depressions constructed or excavated in upland or in non-jurisdictional waters incidental to mining or construction activity, and pits excavated in upland or in non-jurisdictional waters for the purpose of obtaining fill, sand, or gravel;
10. Stormwater control features constructed or excavated in upland or in non-jurisdictional waters to convey, treat, infiltrate, or store stormwater run-off;
11. Groundwater recharge, water reuse, and wastewater recycling structures, including detention, retention, and infiltration basins and ponds, constructed or excavated in upland or in non-jurisdictional waters; and
12. Waste treatment systems.

II. Definitions. In this section, the following definitions apply:
   A. Adjacent wetlands. The term adjacent wetlands refers to wetlands that touch at least at one point or side of, a water identified in paragraph (A) (1), (2), or (3) of this definition;
      1. Are inundated by flooding from a water identified in paragraph (A) (1), (2), or (3) of this definition in a typical year,
      2. Are physically separated from a water identified in paragraph (A) (1), (2), or (3) of this definition only by a natural berm, bank, dune, or similar natural feature; or
      3. Are physically separated from a water identified in paragraph (A) (1), (2), or (3) of this definition only by an artificial dike, barrier, or similar artificial structure so long as that structure allows for a direct hydrologic surface connection between the wetlands and the water identified in paragraph (1) (i), (ii), or (iii) of this definition in a typical year, such as through a culvert, flood or tide gate, pump, or similar artificial feature. An adjacent wetland is jurisdictional in its entirety when a road or similar artificial structure divides the wetland, as long as the structure allows for a direct hydrologic surface connection through or over that structure in a typical year.
   B. Ditch. The term ditch means a constructed or excavated channel used to convey water.
   C. Ephemeral. The term ephemeral means surface water flowing or pooling only in direct response to precipitation (e.g., rain or snow fall).
   D. High tide line. The term high tide line means the line of intersection of the land with the water's surface at the maximum height reached by a rising tide. The high tide line may be determined, in the absence of actual data, by a line of oil or scum along shore objects, a more or less continuous deposit of fine shell or debris on the foreshore or berm, other physical markings or characteristics, vegetation lines, tidal gages, or other suitable means that delineate the general height reached by a rising tide. The line encompasses spring high tides and other high tides that occur with periodic frequency but does not include storm surges in which there is a departure from the normal or predicted reach of the tide due to the piling up of water against a coast by strong winds, such as those accompanying a hurricane or other intense storm.
   E. Intermittent. The term intermittent means surface water flowing continuously during certain times of the year and more than in direct response to precipitation (e.g., seasonally when the groundwater table is elevated or when snowpack melts).

F. Lakes and ponds, and impoundments of jurisdictional waters. The term lakes and ponds, and impoundments of jurisdictional waters means standing bodies of open water that contribute surface water flow to a water identified in paragraph (A) (1) of this definition in a typical year either directly or through one or more waters identified in paragraph (A) (2), (3), or (4) of this definition. A lake, pond, or impoundment of a jurisdictional water does not lose its jurisdictional status if it contributes surface water flow to a downstream jurisdictional water in a typical year through a channelized non-jurisdictional surface water feature, through a culvert, dike, spillway, or similar artificial feature, or through a debris pile, boulder field, or similar natural feature. A lake or pond, or impoundment of a jurisdictional water is also jurisdictional if it is inundated by flooding from a water identified in paragraph (A) (i), (ii), or (iii) of this definition in a typical year.

G. Ordinary high-water mark. The term ordinary high-water mark means that line on the shore established by the fluctuations of water and indicated by physical characteristics such as a clear, natural line impressed on the bank, shelving, changes in the character of soil, destruction of terrestrial vegetation, the presence of litter and debris, or other appropriate means that consider the characteristics of the surrounding areas.

H. Perennial. The term perennial means surface water flowing continuously year-round.

III. Prior converted cropland. The term prior converted cropland means any area that, prior to December 23, 1985, was drained or otherwise manipulated for the purpose, or having the effect, of making production of an agricultural product possible. EPA and the Corps will recognize designations of prior converted cropland made by the Secretary of Agriculture. An area is no longer considered prior converted cropland for purposes of the Clean Water Act when the area is abandoned and has reverted to wetlands, as defined in paragraph (3) (xvi) of this definition. Abandonment occurs when prior converted cropland is not used for, or in support of, agricultural purposes at least once in the immediately preceding five years. For the purposes of the Clean Water Act, the EPA Administrator shall have the final authority to determine whether prior converted cropland has been abandoned.

A. Snowpack. The term snowpack means layers of snow that accumulate over extended periods of time in certain geographic regions or at high elevation (e.g., in northern climes or mountainous regions).

B. Tidal waters and waters subject to the ebb and flow of the tide. The terms tidal waters and waters subject to the ebb and flow of the tide mean those waters that rise and fall in a predictable and measurable rhythm or cycle due to the gravitational pulls of the moon and sun. Tidal waters and waters subject to the ebb and flow of the tide end where the rise and fall of the water surface can no longer be practically measured in a predictable rhythm due to masking by hydrologic, wind, or other effects.

C. Tributary. The term tributary means a river, stream, or similar naturally occurring surface water channel that contributes surface water flow to a water identified in paragraph (1) (i) of this definition in a typical year either directly or through one or more waters identified in paragraph (1) (ii), (iii), or (iv) of this definition. A tributary must be perennial or intermittent in a typical year. The alteration or relocation of a tributary does not modify its jurisdictional status as long as it continues to satisfy the flow conditions of this definition. A tributary does not lose its jurisdictional status if it contributes surface water flow to a downstream jurisdictional water in a typical year through a channelized non-jurisdictional surface water feature, through a subterranean river, through a culvert, dam, tunnel, or similar artificial feature, or through a debris pile, boulder field, or similar natural feature. The term tributary includes a ditch that either relocates a tributary, is constructed in a tributary, or is constructed in an adjacent wetland as long as the ditch satisfies the flow conditions of this definition.

D. Typical year. The term typical year means when precipitation and other climatic variables are within the normal periodic range (e.g., seasonally, annually) for the geographic area of the applicable aquatic resource based on a rolling thirty-year period.

E. Upland. The term upland means any land area that under normal circumstances does not satisfy all three wetland factors (i.e., hydrology, hydrophytic vegetation, hydric soils) identified in paragraph (3) (xvi) of this definition, and does not lie below the ordinary high water mark or the high tide line of a jurisdictional water.

F. Waste treatment system. The term waste treatment system includes all components, including lagoons and treatment ponds (such as settling or cooling ponds), designed to either convey or retain, concentrate, settle, reduce, or remove pollutants, either actively or passively, from wastewater prior to discharge (or eliminating any such discharge).

G. Wetlands. The term wetlands means areas that are inundated or saturated by surface or ground water at a frequency and duration sufficient to support, and that under normal circumstances do support, a prevalence of vegetation typically adapted for life in saturated soil

> conditions. Wetlands generally include swamps, marshes, bogs, and similar areas.[1]

The complicated and at times ambiguous language of section 120.2 continues to cause friction among stakeholders, the public, and even within the Environmental Protection Agency (EPA). EPA regional offices can operate within broad discretion in their interpretations, which can significantly concern agribusiness and other private interests. After several fights in the federal courts during the Barack Obama administration over the waters of the United States issue, which resulted in permanent stays of enforcement of new rule interpretations, the Donald Trump administration administratively relaxed the EPA's interpretations of the rules, quieting the issue for a few years. The Joe Biden administration has taken steps to revert to the previous Obama EPA interpretations with possibly more zeal, resulting in new concerns for many in the country.

According to the EPA, as of August 6, 2021, "waters of the United States" will be addressed again based on President Biden's Executive Order #13990, as summarized on the EPA website:

> Executive Order 13990 on Protecting Public Health and the Environment and Restoring Science to Tackle the Climate Crisis (Jan. 20, 2021) directed the EPA and Army "to immediately review and, as appropriate and consistent with applicable law, take action to address the promulgation of Federal regulations [including the Navigable Waters Protection Rule (NWPR)] and other actions during the last four years that conflict with these important national objectives."
>
> The order also specifically revoked Executive Order 13778 of February 28, 2017 (Restoring the Rule of Law, Federalism, and Economic Growth by Reviewing the "Waters of the United States" Rule), which resulted in promulgation of the NWPR.
>
> The order provides that "[i]t is, therefore, the policy of my Administration to listen to the science; to improve public health and protect our environment; to ensure access to clean air and water; to limit exposure to dangerous chemicals and pesticides; to hold polluters accountable, including those who disproportionately harm communities of color and low-income communities; to reduce greenhouse gas emissions; to bolster resilience to the impacts of climate change; to restore and expand our national treasures and monuments; and to prioritize both environmental justice and the creation of the well-paying union jobs necessary to deliver on these goals."
>
> In conformance with Executive Order 13990, the agencies reviewed the NWPR. See also Fact Sheet: List of Agency Actions for Review. The agencies

1. 40 CFR § 120.2—Definitions.

have completed their review of the NWPR and determined that the rule must be replaced.[2]

Below are further quotes from the EPA website on the issue:

"Waters of the United States" is a threshold term in the Clean Water Act and establishes the scope of federal jurisdiction under the Act. Clean Water Act programs, including Water Quality Standards, TMDLs, and sections 311, 402, and 404 address "navigable waters," defined in the statute as "the waters of the United States, including the territorial seas."

The Clean Water Act does not define "waters of the United States" rather, *it provides discretion for EPA and the U.S. Department of the Army to define "waters of the United States' in regulations* [emphasis added]."

Since the 1970s, EPA and the Department of the Army have defined "waters of the United States" by regulation. In the mid-1980s, both agencies promulgated a definition of "waters of the United States."

Three Supreme Court decisions have addressed the definition of "waters of the United States." In 1985, in *United States v. Riverside Bayview Homes, Inc.*, the U.S. Supreme Court deferred to the Corps' assertion of jurisdiction over wetlands adjacent to a traditional navigable water, stating that adjacent wetlands may be regulated as waters of the United States because they are "inseparably bound up" with navigable waters and "in the majority of cases" have "significant effects on water quality and the aquatic ecosystem" in those waters.

In Solid Waste Agency of Northern Cook County v. U.S. Army Corps of Engineers (SWANCC) in 2001, the Court rejected a claim of federal jurisdiction over non-navigable, isolated, intrastate ponds that lack a sufficient connection to traditional navigable waters, noting that the term "navigable" must be given meaning within the context and application of the statute. The Court held that the use of "isolated" non-navigable intrastate ponds by migratory birds was not by itself a sufficient basis for the exercise of federal regulatory authority under the Clean Water Act. In 2001 and again in 2003, the agencies developed guidance to address the definition of "waters of the United States" under the Clean Water Act following the SWANCC decision.

The Court most recently interpreted the term "waters of the United States" in Rapanos v. United States in 2006. A four-Justice plurality stated that "waters of the United States" "include[] only those relatively permanent, standing or continuously flowing bodies of water 'forming geographic features' that are

2. https://www.epa.gov/wotus/intention-revise-definition-waters-united-states.

described in ordinary parlance as 'streams[,] . . . oceans, rivers, [and] lakes,'" and "wetlands with a continuous surface connection" to a "relatively permanent body of water connected to traditional interstate navigable waters." In a concurring opinion, Justice Kennedy took a different approach, concluding that "to constitute 'navigable waters' under the Act, a water or wetland must possess a 'significant nexus' to waters that are or were navigable in fact or that could reasonably be so made." He stated that adjacent wetlands possess the requisite significant nexus if the wetlands "either alone or in combination with similarly situated lands in the region, significantly affect the chemical, physical, and biological integrity of other covered waters more readily understood as 'navigable.'" The four dissenting Justices, who would have affirmed the court of appeals' application of the agencies' existing regulation, concluded that the term "waters of the United States" encompasses all tributaries and wetlands that satisfy either the plurality's standard or Justice Kennedy's. Following Rapanos, in 2007 and again in 2008, the agencies developed additional guidance for implementing the "waters of the United States" definition.

The agencies amended their regulations defining "waters of the United States" in 2015 in the Clean Water Rule: Definition of "Waters of the United States." The two federal district courts that reviewed the merits of the 2015 Clean Water Rule found that the rule suffered from certain errors and issued orders remanding the 2015 Clean Water Rule back to the agencies. Multiple other federal district courts preliminarily enjoined the 2015 Clean Water Rule, such that more than half of the states continued to implement the 1980s regulations and not the 2015 Clean Water Rule. The 2015 Clean Water Rule was repealed by the 2019 Rule, which reinstated the 1980s regulations, implemented consistent with the U.S. Supreme Court cases and applicable guidance. The following document related to the 2015 Clean Water Rule is provided for informational purposes only.

Federal Register Notice—Clean Water Rule: Definition of "Waters of the United States"

The agencies replaced the 2019 Rule with the Navigable Waters Protection Rule in 2020.[3]

The extent of and the actual use of the discretion of the EPA and the U.S. Department of the Army has not been disclosed yet, and many stakeholders are already quite concerned about the extent of the discretion in promulgating new rules. On June 9, the EPA released a statement of intent to revise the definitions of the waters of the United States; it is clear the revision will be a significant goal of the agency and the army with unknown consequences for private interests, state interests, and even local interests. A summary paragraph clearly declares the EPA's intent:

3. https://www.epa.gov/wotus/about-waters-united-states.

Intention to Revise the Definition of "Waters of the United States"

> On June 9, 2021, the U.S. Environmental Protection Agency and the Department of the Army announced their intent to revise the definition of "waters of the United States." This process includes two rulemakings: a foundational rule to restore longstanding protections, and an anticipated second rule that builds on that regulatory foundation. The forthcoming rule will propose to restore the regulations defining "waters of the United States" in place for decades until 2015, updated to be consistent with relevant Supreme Court decisions. The agencies will also pursue a second rulemaking process that further refines and builds upon that regulatory foundation.[4]

The EPA and the army announced a revision to the rules on December 30, 2022. According to Ariel Wittenberg and Hannah Northey of E&E News's *Greenwire*, "The new rule would give federal protection to large waterways, like interstate rivers and streams and wetlands that are *adjacent* to them."[5] The layman is concerned with the distance from federal protected waters and would ideally be able to look to one source to clearly define by distance which a property is within the jurisdiction of the EPA and the army. Continuing with the comments of Wittenberg and Northey, "The final rule does not include any distance requirements for adjacent wetlands to be protected by the Clean Water Act, but explains that protected wetlands must be 'reasonably close such that the wetland can modulate water quantity or quality' in another protected waterway."

The Biden administration decided against setting distance limits in the rule, it says, because wetlands' effect on downstream waters "depends on regional variations in climate, landscape and geomorphology."

"While bright-line rules (for example, wetlands that are more than a specific number of feet from a jurisdictional water are not 'adjacent') are easiest to understand and implement, convenience is not the only goal the agencies must consider in administrating the Clean Water Act," the rule states.

It explains that "a more nuanced approach is required" because a wetland's impact on larger waterways can vary by region and climate.

Wetlands are considered adjacent if they are connected to those larger waterways with "relatively permanent" surface water connections, or if they have a "significant" hydrologic or ecological "nexus" to those protected tributaries." But without clear distance rules or boundaries in place, the regional EPA/army offices will be able to act within a wide range of discretion to define the limits of their jurisdiction, rightly generating fear in the minds of astute real estate agents, potential buyers of property, and agribusiness

4. https://www.epa.gov/wotus/intention-revise-definition-waters-united-states.
5. https://www.eenews.net/articles/biden-wotus-rule-revives-decades-old-protections.

operations, to name only a few of the concerned parties. The complete EPA/army fact sheet issued on December 30, 2022, is attached as Appendix C. Here's the direct link for further information: https://www.epa.gov/wotus.

It is certain that these "finalized" rules will cause strong controversy among many political groups and likely many of the states. Most certainly, several federal courts will be involved in assessment and analysis of the complaints sure to come against the rule's "finalized" revisions. An extensive 238-page economic analysis offered by the EPA/army is found here: https://www.epa.gov/system/files/documents/2022-12/2022_WOTUS%20EA_FinalRule_508.pdf. A 564-page "Technical Support" report is found here: https://www.epa.gov/system/files/documents/2022-12/TSD-FinalCombined_508.pdf.

In response to the original EPA definition of the waters of the United States, stakeholder groups wrote thousands of pages airing their opinions, with many more thousands to come for sure. For example, according to the Environmental Council of the States, "Twenty-six states include 'any (or) all surface waters' within definition of 'waters of the state'; (AK, AR, CA, CO, CT, FL, HI, IL, KS, LA, ME, MD, MO, MT, NY, ND, OH, OR, RI, SD, UT, VA, WA, WV, WI, WY)."[6] These states apparently wanted to make clear their statutory individual laws of what waters they control.

On December 30, 2022, the new definitions were published by the EPA/U.S. Army Corps of Engineers. On January 18, 2023, the National Association of Realtors and other major stakeholders filed a lawsuit (Case 3:23-cv-00020) in federal court challenging the new definitions. The definitions became law on February 28, 2023 (sixty days after posting in the *Federal Register*). Twenty-five states filed similar lawsuits in federal courts across the country on or about January 23, 2023.

My book, *Public Water Policies: The Ultimate Weapons of Social Control* (2018), is dedicated to discussing the ways in which governments and regulatory agencies can use water policies to control their respective societies. This new WOTUS rule is a prime example of a device in which the U.S. government can potentially exercise significant control over the people and their enterprises.

6. https://www.aswm.org/pdf_lib/ecos_feb_2009_definitions_of_waters_of_the_state.pdf.

Chapter Seven

The Path through the Maze

The world of water rights and regulations in the United States has morphed into one of the most complex, and at times contradictory and confusing, sets of public policy directives in history. Each state's water rights and regulations are unique; even the states with similar policies seem to vary infinitely from the neighboring states. Overlying each state's policies is the bludgeon of federal regulations concerning water regulations and policies that change like a chameleon with each new administration. This situation has created general confusion and in most cases a maze that rivals any created by man. There is a basic set of procedures to follow to at least begin on a path to some ultimate outcome, and I propose it now. I try to make the path as generic as possible for any neophyte and even some more sophisticated players as well.

The path I recommend that could be used in each and every state is as follows:

1. Begin to research the court cases involving water issues in your region and specific area. Why? The attorneys who are trying these cases have to be experts on water issues. Your first step in any water work is to *consult an attorney with courtroom experience in water issues.* Anyone seeking a water use permit or trying to discover and understand their individual property rights in water simply must bring an attorney on their team. Water permitting, discovery, and eventual disclosure of water rights requires an attorney's advice. The attorneys who work in water issues and participate in the court disputes simply are the first source to research. *Most of the more qualified water rights attorneys often present at law conferences—both papers and speeches with PowerPoint decks—and many of these conferences are academically reviewed.* Again, the reason one looks to these sources is to discover the attorneys to interview about how you can meet the goals you may have concerning the water rights of your property or properties you are considering purchasing or selling.

2. Go to the website of each and every regulatory agency that has any jurisdiction over your property and its water resources. Download each and every document prepared by the state agency for public distribution first. Some state agencies do an exceptional job of sharing information about water rules and regulations with the public; some do not. Generally, the state agencies across the country make a sincere effort to share at least the basic information about water rights with their constituencies.

The other local agencies involved with water rights and use permitting are many and vary across the individual states. It is generally easier to navigate through water rights in smaller states like Rhode Island than in a state like Texas simply because of either the lack or the wide range of geographic diversity across the state's lands. In researching water rights locally, it is always best to go visit the office(s) in person. Remember to be patient, polite, and respectful—those who follow these three principles at all times with governmental agencies will stand out and be helped with ease as compared to so many others who feel entitled to the immediate time of an agency staff member.

3. Dependent upon the geological container of water you are investigating, seek the help of a hydrogeologist. This task is especially true in groundwater issues. The hydrogeologist is equally as key a team member as the attorney in a similar way a real estate developer needs a civil engineer. As complex and odd as water rights are and can be, an inquirer needs to look at the chosen site from all professional disciplines—that is, take an interdisciplinary approach to water rights investigations. Just like trying to find the appropriate attorney by looking into court cases and journal articles, follow the same path with hydrogeologists. Hydrogeologists often testify as expert witnesses in court cases, often testify in legislative committee hearings, participate in professional conferences, and write peer-reviewed articles; those hydrogeologists who participate in their profession in these ways are likely the most qualified to assist you in your search.

Definitely do not call the local Environmental Protection Agency/U.S. Army Corps of Engineers office without the assistance of your attorney and/or your hydrologist. The new waters of the United States rules are open to regional interpretations. *Be very careful in all relations with these offices while the revisions are being implemented.*

4. Look closely at your title insurance policy or, in the case of your efforts to buy a property, the commitment for title insurance. Look to be sure that a water right has not been severed to a third party. Remember, just as you can sever your mineral rights and sell them away from the surface, you can severe and sell your water rights as well. These severed rights are scary as they will become the dominant estate over the surface landowner and dependent upon the holder of the executive rights to the determination of the use of the rights, severed water rights can cause significant problems for the surface landowner.

5. If your water source is groundwater, seek the advice of local water well drillers. In most states, water well drillers must provide a report of the results of any well they drill. The water well drillers will not be involved in the well permitting process, only the actual drilling. Just because a well driller will drill a well for you, that does not mean the well is permitted properly—*the water well drillers are not responsible for permitting the well.*

6. Visit the closest United States Geological Survey (USGS) office. The USGS, in many areas of the country, has water science centers that often, but not always, have older sample electric logs of wells drilled in the area. The staff hydrogeologists can be very helpful in the physical characteristics of the area's water resources.

7. Talk to any agricultural extension office in your area. For example, in Texas, we have the Agri-Life Extension Service, which has agents in each county; hence the old name of "county agent" was the representative to assist with agricultural activities. The water resources of the area, as the key to agriculture, will be well known to the local county agent. Take advantage of the opportunity these wonderful public servants offer everyone.

8. Talk to the local real estate brokerage industry, especially those experienced in farm and ranch properties. No one knows better about the water resources of any property than an experienced farm and ranch broker. "Water renders the land its value" is a motto they all know.

9. Visit the local feed and seed stores along with the agricultural implement dealers; the center pivot irrigation providers or irrigation pump suppliers are great sources too. Since these folks are in the agribusiness supply industry, they know all about the good, the bad, and the ugly of their area's water sources.

10. Visit the neighbors on all sides of the property in question. Neighbors have already experienced water problems. Their perspective is an eyewitness to the immediate area's water resources and problems.

11. Consider the following checklists that offer a more detailed path to guide your initial research. I use Texas as an example for regulatory agencies for surface (Texas Commission on Environmental Quality) and groundwater (groundwater conservation districts), but you can modify the checklists to include the agencies in your state.

Surface Water Right Disclosure Worksheet*	**Comments**
(It is strongly recommended that you consult an attorney or hydrologist.)	
https://www.tceq.texas.gov/permitting/water_rights/wr-permitting/wrwud	
Who owns the water right?	
TCEQ water right file number?	
TCEQ classification of right?	
Priority date of water right?	
Temporary water permit from TCEQ?	
Expiration date of temporary water permit from TCEQ?	
Diversion point and brief description?	
Location of diversion (attach map)?	
Delivery system - Pump? Canal?	
Volume of water permitted to be diverted?	
Water Use Reports (Amounts) filed at TCEQ?	
Use - Domestic and Livestock?	
Use - Irrigation?	
Meter present?	
Meter records available?	
Water Right Deed available? From owner possibly.	
Water Right Deed filed of record? From county real property records.	
Any water leases to others? From owner or possibly real property records.	
Past or pending TCEQ violations? From TCEQ files.	
Type of crops irrigated in past?	
Type of crops irrigated currently?	
Please attach copies of any and all available documents.	
**This disclosure sheet is to be used for preliminary research purposes only.*	
Ask for enough time in the purchase contract to seek the advice of and attorney	
and hydrologist to determine the details of any surface water right!	
By Charles Porter, PhD ALL RIGHTS RESERVED	

Surface water detailed path for questions to ask

Groundwater Water Right Disclosure Worksheet from Owner* *(It is strongly recommended that you consult an attorney or hydrologist.)*	**Comments (or Unknown)**
Does the landowner own 100% of the groundwater right?	
Is the property subject to GCD (regulatory agency) jurisdiction?	
GCD or other regulatory agency contact information?	
GCD or agency website?	
Single family residence on property?	
Swimming pool on property?	
Existing well(s) on property? How many?	
Any abandoned wells on property? How many? Covered?	
Pump type (submersible, deisel or electric)?	
Water Quality Report Available?	
Use - Domestic and Livestock?	
Use - Irrigation?	
Use - Other?	
Iirrigation permit number/copy/authorized volume?	
Transfer permit and volume?	
Is the well registered at the GCD? Registration Number?	
Are there volume meters present?	
Volume allowed to be pumped per day?	
Meter records available?	
Well driller's name and contact information?	
Distance from septic system?	
Depth of well(s)?	
Any past or present violations of GCD rules?	
Any current leases of water to others?	
Crops irrigated currently?	
Crops irrigated in past?	
Type of irrigation system - Center Pivot? Canal? Drip?	
Knowledge of past contested permit hearings?	
Past or pending lawsuits involving the property?	
Any current permit in process?	
Any current contested permit hearing?	
Please attach copies of all documents mentioned above that are in your possession. **This disclosure sheet is to be used for preliminary research purposes only. Ask for enough time in the purchase contract to seek the advice of and attorney and hydrologist to determine the details of any groundwater right!* ***By: Charles Porter, PhD ALL RIGHTS RESERVED***	

Groundwater detailed path for questions to ask

Above all else, keep close notes in a journal-like fashion and be patient with yourself as you research water. You are looking for the availability of the water, the quantity of water available, the quality of the water, the cost of the water, the most recent sales of water rights or leases of water, and others' experiences in water use permitting at the local level. There's no one go-to source available to the public even in the smaller states. You will need to function as a project manager in order to learn about your water's characteristics and issues. If you are buying a property, be sure and negotiate enough time to thoroughly investigate the property's water. What's a reasonable time for investigation? It would be wise to seek at least thirty days to investigate the water of the property with a full return of the earnest money should the results of your feasibility study fall short of your goals. If your goal depends upon acquiring a permit for your particular water use, it is wise to make the purchase contract contingent upon full permit approval. Of course, these ideas are fully negotiable, but water is so important to any kind of future property use that, without it, the property's value is questionable.

Chapter Eight

A View of the Future

I wish sincerely that I could offer an optimistic view of the future of water in the United States, but tell-yourself-the-truth practice points to a negative conclusion. The Joe Biden administration made its position known on December 30, 2022, with a major revision to the Waters of the United States (WOTUS), indicating a possible expanding jurisdiction of the federal government over local water policy. The future surely holds years of court cases to determine the boundaries of state and federal water jurisdiction. Sadly, there will be many areas in which these jurisdictions overlap, causing property owners and their activities and transactions much consternation and expense.

Climate change is here and is frightening. The consequences of climate change for agriculture became most obvious to all and continue to be reported daily across the country. Texas and California growers have suffered terribly over the past few years of horrific drought. California growers have been bulldozing almond groves, piling up dead fruit trees, and losing billions of dollars as their drought continues into, many say, the seventh year.[1]

In December 2022, the *Dallas Morning News* published an article headlined "Texas' Worst Drought in a Decade Could Rival 2011 Economic Losses," summarizing the impact the drought could have on the state economy. According to this article, experts are predicting a loss of $2.1 billion in economic activity for cotton producers, not including the losses covered by crop insurance.[2]

This astutely written article illustrates the consequences of the extended drought in Texas and could serve as a reporting form for agriculture across the western United States. Just substitute a state's name for Texas, a crop for

---

1. Since the author's final edit of this book, California's drought has been temporarily ended by the so-called atmospheric river. Whether or not this welcome relief lasts long enough to recover some of the billions of dollars of losses California's agricultural community has suffered is yet to be determined.

2. Alexandra Skores, "Texas' Worst Drought in a Decade Could Rival 2011 Economic Losses," *Dallas Morning News*, December 16, 2022, https://dallasnews.com/business/economy/2022/12/16/texas-worst -drought-in-a-decade-could-rival-2011s-economic-losses.

Pedernales River, Texas

cotton, and interviews and reports from that state's agriculture department or comptroller of accounts, and the results will be similar. Past agricultural practices must be radically changed or else.

Other areas of the United States are experiencing drought-related disruption, which is especially noticeable on the Mississippi River. This most significant river is experiencing record low water levels, so low in fact that barge traffic was greatly reduced in 2022. These barges carry huge amounts of agricultural products from the breadbasket of the United States to the port of New Orleans. Grain, heavy equipment, and other bulk commodities are barged efficiently not only in cost but also in physical transport in the strong downward current of the river. The Mississippi River's watershed drains some 1.2 million square miles of the United States, normally creating a massive current of water. Thousands of barges are backed up at various points along the river, creating a nightmare for moving products and eventually contributing significantly to inflationary economic problems. Traveling through the Midwest of the United States, any doubtful denier of global warming will surely register the most obvious consequence of climate change.[3]

3. "Record Low Water Levels on the Mississippi River in 2022 Show How Climate Change Is Altering Large Rivers," *The Conversation*, December 14, 2022, https://theconversation.com/record-low-water-levels-on-the-mississippi-river-in-2022-show-how-climate-change-is-altering-large-rivers-193920.

The most prolific areas of California's vegetable fields are now suffering due to the severe drought such as farmers are experiencing in the Westlands Water District. The San Joaquin Valley is in trouble—irrigated water has been restricted to farmers due not only to the drought but also to competing environmental goals at the state level. As the Midwest is experiencing, the California agribusiness, all but totally dependent upon irrigated water from canal systems, is suffering at a level few could have anticipated twenty years ago. The results of climate change are just as visible there; I've seen it in person. I've seen the plowed-under fields, the bulldozed almond groves, the economic devastation of drought exacerbated by global warming.[4]

According to the *Huffpost* on December 15, 2022, "The nation's largest water supplier [the Metropolitan Water District] declared a drought emergency for *all* of Southern California, clearing the way for potential mandatory water restrictions early next year that could impact 19 million people." The *Huffpost* article goes on to say, "State officials recently announced that water agencies like Metropolitan will only get 5% of their requested supplies for the start of 2023 due to lower reservoir levels."[5]

Similar conditions are being experienced in the Rio Grande Valley as the flow in the Rio Grande in this highly productive agricultural area of Texas is so restricted that reservoirs along and adjacent to the river are drying up. Like in California, without irrigation from the Rio Grande, the agribusiness in the "Valley" will "dry" up, with disastrous economic and social implications. Not only is the Rio Grande in Texas experiencing the challenge of a U.S. immigration that is shattered, now the extended drought in Texas, New Mexico, and northern Mexico is piling pain on all municipal services.[6]

To round out the most current brief report of the West, only those who have no access to television, radio, the internet, or social media could have avoided the deluge of reports on the extended drought's driven-by-climate-change consequences for the Colorado River, Lake Mead, Lake Powell, and the entire basin. The disaster throughout the entire basin is beginning to destroy all life and livelihood. There is little relief on the horizon.[7]

I see few, if any, practical solutions offered to the problem of global warming. The vast majority of reports are about scaring us about climate change;

4. "Some of America's Biggest Vegetable Growers Fought for Water. Then the Water Ran Out," *NPR*, December 15, 2022, https://www.npr.org/2022/12/15/1139932893/some-of-americas-biggest-vegetable-growers-fought-for-water-then-the-water-ran-o. I visited California for many weeks over the past five years and observed firsthand the nightmare the farming community is facing.

5. "Drought Emergency Declared for All of Southern California," *Huffpost*, December 15, 2022, https://www.huffpost.com/entry/drought-emergency-california_n_639aad84e4b0804966b3ad22.

6. "Drifting toward Disaster: The (Second) Rio Grande," *Texas Observer*, December 2022, https://www.texasobserver.org/rio-grande-water-drifting-toward-disaster.

7. Joshua Partlow, "Officials Fear Complete Doomsday Scenarios for Drought-Stricken Colorado River," *Washington Post*, December 1, 2022, https://www.washingtonpost.com/climate-environment/2022/12/01/drought-colorado-river-lake-powell.

okay, we all get the message. How do we divert the path to worse warming and planet destruction without destroying our economy? How do we change centuries of lifestyle patterns? These may be the questions of the century.

What do we need to do in relation to the severe water challenges resulting from climate change? It's really quite simple:

- Build water pipelines to move water from wet to dry areas.
- Build desal plants to desalinate ocean water and brackish groundwater. The technology is not new or rocket science; it's all about political will.
- Reward users of water who practice conservation with tax breaks and other incentives.

However, without far-reaching thinking about the entire process of moving and sharing water across our nation, we will face huge problems in agriculture beginning now.

Irrigation is essential, and it uses 60 percent of all our water. Some better-designed irrigation systems are already dropping that usage percentage. Bringing desal water to irrigators at a reasonable price could free up surface and groundwater being used by farmers now. Smarter crop selection can help as well; support for the development of new varieties of crops adapted for drier conditions should be funded as an emergency, just like we funded Covid-19 vaccinations.

But the key to solving this water crisis is to begin *now* to acquire the right-of-way for pipelines to move water so everyone in our country gets a fair chance at it. The other steps, such as electric automobiles, more water conservation, alternative energy sources, and lifestyle changes, are admirable goals and certainly should be pursued vigorously.

But water must be our key focus now, *right now*, to give everyone in the United States a fair chance to life. Life does not exist without water.

Appendix A

Briefs on Water Regulations and Regulatory Agencies State by State

In order to keep this book under three thousand pages, all I can offer is the most basic gateway to water rights in each state. There is no consistency in their documentation; there is no one go-to source for information. Above all else, the URL locations of their websites change like wind direction without notice. However, the briefs are useful as a beginning point in water rights research in each state. You will find great detail in several of the state briefs such as Texas and New York as indicative of regional water rights and regulations concepts.

Always keep in mind that any water rights issues such as permitting, use of water from any of the three geological containers, reservation of water rights, and any other research *must* include working with a water law attorney who practices water law in the specific state. Not every lawyer in every state will have the appropriate experience in the water laws and processes in that state; it is a very unique area of legal practice. As mentioned before, the first place to begin searching for an experienced water lawyer in your state is to look for the authors of law journal and other peer-reviewed articles germane to your needs. All pending water use permits in any state are open records; hence the attorneys mentioned in those permits likely are quite experienced in water law in that state. Your state agricultural agency's local representations or "county agents" are good resources for recommendations in your search for an experienced local water law attorney. Expect to pay your attorney a retainer, expect to pay legal fees in excess of $250 per hour, and expect to need to hire a hydrologist who will support you and the attorney you hire in the process of permitting your particular use or in assisting you in making your decision to purchase a property with water rights.

As of March 20, 2023, the new Waters of the United States (WOTUS) definitions have become effective, even though the major lawsuit mentioned before is pending. A federal judge, Jeffrey Brown, just issued a preliminary injunction against the effective date of the new WOTUS as it applies to Texas and Idaho. This likely will not be the only injunction across the nation.

There is also congressional action to quash the new definitions of WOTUS recently underway in the US House of Representatives, but the action is symbolic only as President Joe Biden has already announced he will veto any action taken by either house of Congress concerning his administration's new definitions of WOTUS.

There is a real possibility that any property you own or are considering purchasing with any type of water right may now come under the jurisdiction of the U.S. Army Corps of Engineers (Corps) and the U.S. Environmental Protection Agency (EPA). A federal resource for beginning your search to see if a jurisdictional determination of your property's relationship to WOTUS has already been made by the Corps of Engineers is found at https://watersgeo.epa.gov/cwa/CWA-JDs.

CLEAN WATER ACT–APPROVED JURISDICTIONAL DETERMINATIONS

This website presents information on approved jurisdictional determinations (JDs) made by the Corps and the EPA under the Clean Water Act since August 28, 2015. Users are able to search, sort, map, view, and download approved JDs from both agencies using different search parameters (e.g., year, state, watershed). Corps-approved JD forms can be found on the Corps JD public interface.[1]

You will discover that the 168,335 jurisdictional determinations mentioned in the caption to the website do not necessarily represent the total number already made by the Corps. For example, if you insert Brazos for the Brazos River in Texas, links to six registered jurisdictional determinations are shown, but inside these six links, there can be many more watercourses that have jurisdictional determinations shown in an Excel spreadsheet. The website also does not yet include the future jurisdictional determinations that will be made under the new WOTUS definitions. *Be very careful in your communications with the Corps and the EPA. I strongly advise you to seek the assistance of an attorney in all matters involving these agencies!*

1. https://watersgeo.epa.gov/cwa/CWA-JDs.

THE NORTHEAST

New York, Connecticut, Rhode Island, Delaware, Maine, New Hampshire, New Jersey, Maryland, Massachusetts, Vermont, Virginia, West Virginia, and Pennsylvania

"New York State is fortunate to have plentiful water resources. The preservation and protection of these resources is vital to New York's residents and businesses, who rely on these resources for drinking water supplies and to support agriculture, manufacturing and other industries and recreation in the state. Aquatic and terrestrial flora and fauna are also dependent on these critical resources to maintain healthy populations. Good policy and sound natural resource management practices are critical to assuring long-term supplies of water to meet these needs now and into the future."[2]

The New York State Assembly aptly describes the water availability of the Northeast section of the United States as having plentiful water resources. Since New York is the most populated area of the Northeast, I begin my analysis of this section of the United States with New York and Connecticut.[3]

New York
Most Significant Issue in Water

New York's most significant water-related issue is water quality due to human sanitary sewage, coupled with storm drainage issues due to transportation and miles of impervious cover in the cities. The conjunctive relationship between sanitary sewage water, stormwater, and fresh drinking water is a challenge in the densely populated cities.

New York is a party to the Great Lakes Compact, an agreement between eight states and two Canadian provinces fronting on the Great Lakes that outlines the parties' relationships to the lake system. In 1900, New York adopted the *reasonable use* rule for groundwater use in the judicial opinion rendered in *Forbell v. City of New York*, 164 N.Y. 522. The statutes in New York comprehensively regulate the use of groundwater and surface water. Some attorneys claim New York codified the *correlative rights* doctrine in groundwater as well, but others claim uncertainty in that regard.

The first place to find any state's primary right to regulate water is its definition of "waters of the state" or "waters." In New York, it is found in the statute quoted below:

2. New York State Assembly, 2011.

3. My son and daughter-in-law live in South Salem, New York. When I visit, I spend each early morning in Connecticut. Other than a small sign, almost unnoticeable, these states seem to be connected invisibly.

> (ENV Section 15–0107) "Waters" shall be construed to include lakes, 8 bays, sounds, ponds, impounding reservoirs, springs, wells, rivers, streams, creeks, estuaries, marshes, inlets, canals, the Atlantic Ocean within the territorial limits of the State of New York, and all other bodies of surface or underground water, natural or artificial, inland or coastal, fresh or salt, public or private, which are wholly or partially within or bordering the state or within its jurisdiction.[4]

A layman's reading of New York's definition of waters reveals that the state owns and claims jurisdiction over *all* water resources. Frankly, for the everyday citizen, this one definition may be as much as they need to know before embarking on their chosen water use plan. Since the state owns the water, it is obvious that before using the water for any purpose, one needs to search for and contact local and state agencies to understand the rules and any permitting process.

In most states, domestic and livestock uses are exempt from permit; however, many states and/or local regulatory agencies require registration of groundwater wells even if exempt from permitting. But domestic and livestock uses historically only use 10 percent of the total groundwater use; irrigation continues to use 60 percent around the nation and the world.

To complicate matters, some states have clear definitions of what comprises domestic and livestock use, but some states' definitions are murky at best or nonexistent at worse. In Texas, for example, groundwater is privately owned and regulated by local—at today's count, one hundred—groundwater conservation districts. However, my own recent study revealed that each district's rules define domestic and livestock differently. Making things even more complicated, not all of Texas's groundwater is regulated by a district; roughly 30 percent of the state has not chosen to create a district to regulate local groundwater use.

Surface Water

Surface water is owned by the state of New York. Permits are required for six uses of surface water:

1. Potable purposes (public supplies)
2. Agricultural irrigation
3. Multipurpose public projects
4. Supply of water to other states
5. Withdrawals exceeding one hundred thousand gallons per day (gpd)
6. Transportation of water by vessel

4. http://public.leginfo.state.ny.us.

The agency responsible for permitting water uses in New York is the Division of Water of the Department of Environmental Conservation (DEC).

New York's Water Resources Law (ECL Article 15, Title 15) requires all water withdrawal systems with the capacity to withdraw one hundred thousand gallons per day or more ("threshold volume") to obtain a water withdrawal permit. The capacity is determined by totaling all groundwater and/or surface water sources independently of how they are plumbed or their designation, such as for redundancy, and so forth.[5] Systems exceeding the threshold volume (with some exceptions) must obtain a water withdrawal permit and report water use annually.[6]

According to a report by the New York Department of Environmental Conservation, New York surface water follows the basic concept of "riparian rights." The unnamed author of the report wrote, "For many years, New York's water laws have generally followed a legal approach known as riparian rights, which gives all users with access to water resources a right to 'reasonable' use of water, recognizing that where one user's taking of water begins to adversely affect another user's ability to obtain water, no one user has the right to an unreasonable portion of the total available resource."[7]

Professors Sorrell Negro and Keith S. Porter of Cornell Law School agree that New York has abundant water resources: "From the Catskills to the Adirondacks, from the Great Lakes to Lake Champlain, and from the Susquehanna to Long Island, New York is a water-rich state. New York enjoys abundant water resources with high quality surface and ground water resources."[8]

Approximately nine billion gallons of water are withdrawn each day from the lakes, rivers, streams, estuaries, and groundwaters of upstate New York (this excludes Nassau and Suffolk counties). Uses include public supply, thermoelectric power generation, agriculture, commercial/industrial, recreational, and more. Thermoelectric power is by far the most significant of all water use categories, accounting for about 66 percent of total water withdrawn. Public water supply accounts for the next-largest use at 25 percent. Less than 5 percent of water used is for industrial purposes. Agricultural water use comes to less than 1 percent of statewide water use.[9]

---

5. https://www.dec.ny.gov/lands/55509.html.
6. Ibid.
7. "Regulating Water Withdrawals in New York: The Water Resources Protection Act," Hudson Valley Regional Council, November 2015, https://hudsonvalleyregionalcouncil.org/wp-content/uploads/2015/11/Regulating-Water-Withdrawal-in-NY-s.pdf: "This Project has been funded in part by a grant from the New York State Environmental Protection Fund through the New York Department of Environmental Conservation."
8. S. Negro and K. S. Porter, "Water Stress in New York State: The Regional Imperative," *Journal of Water Law* 20 (2009): 5.
9. https://www.dec.ny.gov/lands/67073.html.

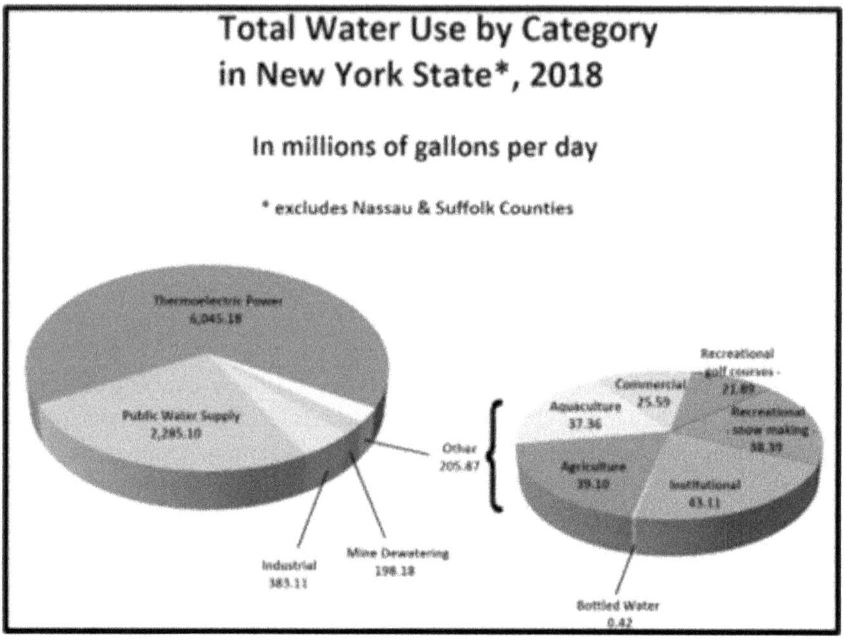

Figure A.1. Water use in New York in 2018.
Source: https://subscriber.politicopro.com/eenews/f/eenews/?id=00000186-ff00-d959-adcf-ffc273a80000

Groundwater

New York claims groundwater is owned by the state. In *Ivory v. International Business Machines, Corp.* (2014), the state appellate court ruled that "groundwater does not belong to the owners of real property, but is a natural resource entrusted to the state by and for its citizens." The court cited Navigation Law #170 as the source of its opinion and relied upon the following section of that law:

> The legislature finds and declares that New York's lands and waters constitute a unique and delicately balanced resource; that the protection and preservation of these lands and waters promotes the health, safety and welfare of the people of this state; that the tourists and recreation industry dependent on clean waters and beaches is vital to the economy of this state; that the state is the trustee, for the benefit of its citizens, of all natural resources within its jurisdiction; and that the storage and transfer of petroleum between vessels, between facilities and vessels, and between facilities, whether onshore or offshore, is a hazardous undertaking and imposes risks of damage to persons and property within this state.[10]

10. https://codes.findlaw.com/ny/navigation-law/nav-sect-170.html.

The court in *Ivory* declared, by reference to the section above, that the state is trustee of all the natural resources of the state for the benefit of all its citizens. An argument could be made as to jurisdiction in a claim that groundwater is owned by the overlying landowner, but there appears to be no record of this claim made to date. While unsaid in writing by the agency, domestic and livestock use of the waters (surface and groundwater) of New York is allowed without permit as long as withdrawals do not exceed one hundred thousand gallons per day. Some agricultural uses are exempt from permit also according to New York's Department of Environmental Conservation rules below:

> Withdrawals for agricultural purposes that were registered or reported their annual water usage reported to DEC prior to February 15, 2012. Although a permit is not required, these withdrawals must be reported annually to DEC. In addition, it is important to note that agricultural facilities that were not registered prior to February 15, 2012 or did not submit annual water usage to DEC by that date must apply for a permit.[11]

The water withdrawal regulations (6 NYCRR Part 601) define "agricultural purposes" as "farming for crops, plants, vines, trees, and the keeping, grazing, or feeding of livestock for sale of livestock or livestock products, and the on-farm processing of crops, livestock, and livestock products." Note that multiple noncontiguous parcels of land under the ownership or control of the same person are generally considered to be one agricultural facility.[12] Agriculture in 2018 used 36.38 million gallons per day (from both surface and groundwater sources), or 18 percent of "other uses" in the state. Of the total usage of water in the state, agriculture used less than half a percent of total water usage in 2018. This is obviously because rainfall and snowmelt are in adequate amounts to allow "dry land" farming or farming without irrigation, quite differently than in the states west of the one hundredth parallel.

---

11. https://www.dec.ny.gov/lands/86935.html#Exemptions.

6 CRR-NY 601.9

NY-CRR

Official Compilation of Codes, Rules and Regulations of the State of New York Title 6. Department of Environmental Conservation Chapter V. Resource Management Services Subchapter E. Water Regulation Part 601. Water Withdrawal Permiting, Reporting and Registration (Exclusive of Long Island Wells Regulated under Part 602 of This Title)

601.9 Permit exemptions.

The following actions with respect to a water withdrawal system are exempt from the permit requirements of this Part:

(a) withdrawals for agricultural purposes that have been registered or their annual water usage reported pursuant to the requirements of ECL article 15, title 16 or title 33 as of February 15, 2012. These withdrawals are subject to the annual reporting requirements of section 601.5 and the registration requirements of section 601.17 of this Part.

12. Ibid.

But even with abundant water availability, New York faces future water challenges. Between climate change and rising ocean waters, as well as an increasing population that creates a need for more sanitary sewage treatment, safer storm drainage, and continued diligence in regulating and enforcing industrial and agricultural pollution, New York could face a future drought that potentially would likely lead to water shortages.

An example of a current serious problem is New York City's older design of a shared sanitary sewer and storm drainage system. At times of heavy rains, untreated sanitary sewage (human waste from simply the flushing of toilets) often flows into surface waters.

More than half of New York City has a combined sanitary sewage/storm drainage system. This system is overwhelmed during times of heavy rains. According to the New York City Environmental Protection website,

> About 60 percent of New York City has a combined sewer system. In a combined sewer system, there is a single pipe that carries both stormwater runoff and sewage from buildings. This mix of stormwater and sewage is usually sent to a wastewater treatment plant.
>
> During heavy rainstorms, combined sewers receive higher than normal flows. Treatment plants are unable to handle flows that are more than twice the design capacity. When this occurs, a mix of stormwater and untreated sewage discharges directly into the City's waterways. These events are called combined sewer overflows (CSOs). We are concerned about CSOs because of its effect on water quality and the recreational use of local water bodies.[13]

Certainly, there are local, state, and federal laws and regulations long in place that address pollution of surface water. However, the physical and fiscal reality of enforcement of such laws and regulations in a city as densely populated as New York City in many ways makes it all but impossible to protect surface waters. How does a city the size of New York shut down millions of toilets in public places and private homes and offices during times of "heavy" rains? Is it even possible to replace the hundreds of miles of underground sanitary/storm drainage systems without a total disruption of daily life and the economic life of the city? If the money to do so could be found and appropriated, is the city willing to endure decades of torn up streets and plumbing restructuring and repair?

Regulatory Agency Responsible for Water Rights

Department of Environmental Conservation: Division of Water
New York State Department of Environmental Conservation

13. https://www1.nyc.gov/site/dep/water/combined-sewer-overflows.page.

625 Broadway
Albany, NY 12233–0001
(518) 402-8044
http://www.dec.ny.gov

Connecticut

According to the Connecticut Department of Energy and Environmental Protection, "Connecticut is fortunate to be a 'water rich' state, with more than 5,800 miles of rivers and streams. (This distance is roughly the equivalent of the U.S.-Canada and U.S.-Mexico borders combined!) These waters include large rivers (e.g. the lower Connecticut River) to much smaller, babbling brooks. Connecticut is also home to four federally designated Wild and Scenic River Systems—the Eightmile River, the lower Farmington River and Salmon Brook, the West Branch Farmington River, and the Wood and Pawcatuck River systems."[14]

Connecticut follows the "absolute ownership rule" in groundwater. However, the Connecticut Supreme Court has held that a property owner's ability to use underlying groundwater does not allow him to pollute it. The Connecticut Supreme Court reiterated in several rulings that the absolute ownership rule does not apply to surface water. In Connecticut, as in several other states that follow the absolute ownership doctrine for groundwater, one cannot take groundwater with malicious intent against a neighbor. Of course, defining and proving malicious intent is impossibly subjective.

According to the Water Systems Council,

> Although the property owner owns the groundwater under his land, a number of state laws and regulations affect groundwater use. For example, a local health department must test a private well before it can be used for drinking, bathing, or other domestic uses; the state Well Drilling Code requires that wells produce a certain yield; and state environmental laws recognize a "public trust" in the state's air, water and other natural resources.
>
> The landmark case establishing absolute ownership in Connecticut is Roath v. Driscoll (20 Conn. 533 (1850)), involving a situation where an excavation made on one person's property affected the water level on his neighbor's land. The Connecticut Supreme Court, after finding that the first property owner did not intend to harm his neighbor when he excavated the land, held that he had a right to do so. "Each owner has an equal and complete right to the use of his land, and to the water which is *in it*" (italics in original), the Court held. "Water combined with the earth, or passing through it, by percolation, or by filtration,

14. Connecticut Department of Energy and Environmental Protection.

> or chemical attraction, has no distinctive character of ownership from the earth itself; not more than the metallic oxides of which the earth is composed."[15]

Clearly the intent of this court was to confirm groundwater was owned by the surface landowner. Pursuant to the General Statutes of Connecticut, Title 22a, Environmental Protection, Chapter 4461, Water Resources, "'Waters' means all tidal waters, harbors, estuaries, rivers, brooks, watercourses, waterways, wells, springs, lakes, ponds, marshes, drainage systems and all other surface or groundwater streams, bodies or accumulation of water, natural or artificial, public or private, which are contained within, flow through or border upon the state or any portion thereof."[16]

Noted in Chapter 4461 above, at first glance, it appears the waters of Connecticut include groundwater, but note the phrase used is "groundwater streams," or groundwater that runs in an underground river or underground watercourse. This does not refer to groundwater, water that percolates from the earth's surface and collects in pools or aquifers.

Regulatory Agency Responsible for Water Rights

Connecticut Department of Environmental Protection: Water
No address or phone number available. https://www.ct.gov/Deep/site/default.asp.

Pennsylvania

Article I, Section 27, of the Constitution of the Commonwealth of Pennsylvania, titled Natural Resources and the Public Estate, makes a fundamental statement about water in the state: "The people have a right to clean air, pure water, and to the preservation of the natural, scenic, historic and esthetic values of the environment. Pennsylvania's public natural resources are the common property of all the people, including generations yet to come. As trustee of these resources, the Commonwealth shall conserve and maintain them for the benefit of all the people."[17]

This section, similar to other state constitutions, uses the word "shall" instead of "may," creating a duty, not a choice, for the trustee, the commonwealth, to honor and obey. The natural resources of Pennsylvania, including

---

15. "Who Owns the Water? A Summary of Existing Water Rights Laws," Water Systems Council, 2003, http://nationalaglawcenter.org/wp-content/uploads/2017/03/Who-Owns-the-Water-2016-Update-FINAL.pdf.

16. General Statutes of Connecticut, Title 22a, Environmental Protection, Chapter 4461, Water Resources, Sec. 22a-367. Definitions.

17. Article I, Section 27, of the Constitution of the Commonwealth of Pennsylvania, titled Natural Resources and the Public Estate.

all the water, are owned by the state as trustee for the people. There is no comprehensive legal or institutional approach to water use in the state; water use is governed by common law. Common law is made by the courts, and disputes are based on particular facts guided by general principles and legal precedent (stare decisis), not hydrology. As legal precedents are set by each decision, provisions concerning water use may be modified, refined, or reversed by subsequent cases. Litigation is expensive, time-consuming, stressful, and unpredictable between private litigants.[18]

Pennsylvania water law includes rulings on four basic geological containers: surface water, diffused surface water, groundwater in subterranean streams, and percolating groundwater.[19] There is no absolute ownership of water by individuals or entities other than the commonwealth. Property law and tort law create the water law in the state. As in other states, the landowner may only gain usufructuary rights, or the right to use the water. These rights cannot be severed from the land.[20]

Surface Water

Pennsylvania follows the riparian rights doctrine. In order to gain a riparian right, one must own land appurtenant to a stream. The riparian then has a right to make use of the water that flows, but the right holder has no ownership or property right in the water. There is no right to withdraw a specific amount—no quantification. All rights to use the water depend on equal, correlative rights of other riparians to use the common resource.[21]

The riparian may withdraw all water necessary for household and domestic use. Domestic use includes drinking, bathing, cooking, laundry, and livestock use. Domestic use has the highest priority in any conflict. This is similar to the situation in Texas, a prior appropriative state. The first priority in Texas is given the domestic and livestock user. All other withdrawals in Pennsylvania are subject to reasonable use. Withdrawals cannot harm others unreasonably. There can be extraordinary uses but diversions off land are prohibited. Public water suppliers have eminent domain power. The public has a priority right to navigation over all domestic uses.[22]

18. Pamela Bishop, "A Short Review of Pennsylvania Water Law."
19. In Texas, all groundwater is considered by common law to be "percolating."
20. Ibid.
21. Ibid.
22. Ibid.

Groundwater

Pennsylvania percolating groundwater law allows the landowner above to withdraw all groundwater beneath his or her land of natural and ordinary uses, or beneficial uses. The "doctrine of a reasonable user" applies—if the water withdrawn is used for a lawful purpose, there is no liability owed a neighbor for withdrawal. However, if the withdrawal use is malicious or negligent and causes foreseeable harm to a neighbor's use, then there could be liability to the withdrawing party.[23]

In 1940, the Pennsylvania Supreme Court officially rejected the English absolute ownership rule and adopted what is referred to as the "rule of reasonableness." According to the Water Systems Council, the Pennsylvania legislature has not attempted to modify it by statute.[24] The court ruled in 1940, "While there is some difference of opinion as to what should be regarded as reasonable use of such waters, the modern decisions are fairly harmonious in holding that a property may not concentrate such waters and convey them off his land if the springs or wells of another are impaired. . . . In the absence of precedent in our own State we adopt this view as the proper interpretation of the law."[25]

Under percolating groundwater law, off-land use is unreasonable and unlawful per se if it interferes with other users who may be entitled to damages or an injunction. In Pennsylvania, as in Texas's "rule of capture" concept, the deepest well with the biggest pump often gets the groundwater. There is no quantification of a percolating groundwater right.[26]

The Water Resources Planning Act of 2002 requires registration of all withdrawals exceeding ten thousand gallons per day for both surface and groundwater. However, political subdivisions are prohibited from allocating water resources.[27]

There are a number of interstate compacts, such as the Delaware River Basin Compact, which requires a project review for withdrawals of one hundred thousand gallons per day or more, again applicable to both surface and groundwater. The compact created the Southeast Pennsylvania Groundwater Protected Area, which regulates withdrawals of ten thousand gallons per day or more. The Susquehanna River Basin Compact also requires project reviews for withdrawals of one hundred thousand gallons per day or more and is also applicable to surface and groundwater and consumptive uses of twenty thousand gallons per day or more. If there is a conflict with municipalities,

23. Ibid.
24. Water Systems Council, 49.
25. Ibid.
26. Bishop, "A Short Review."
27. Ibid.

the Susquehanna River Basin Compact preempts any municipal regulation of water.[28]

As Pennsylvania fronts on the Great Lakes, it is subject to the Boundary Waters Treaty of 1909 between the United States and Canada. This treaty has jurisdiction over applications of use, obstruction, or diversion of boundary waters. Pennsylvania is also subject to the Great Lakes Basin Compact, which created the Great Lakes Commission in 1986 via the Water Resources Development Act of 1986, amended in 2000. Under this compact, no diversion or export of water from the Great Lakes Basin or tributaries can be made without approval by eight Great Lakes governors.[29]

Pennsylvania is also a party to the Great Lakes Charter of 1985, which is described as a good faith agreement between eight states and two provinces (in Canada). The parties agreed to prior notice and consultation for diversions/consumptive uses exceeding five million gallons per day. This charter is dynamic and in continual review by the parties.[30]

The Great Lakes–St. Lawrence River Basin Sustainable Water Resources Agreement of December 2005 is also a good faith agreement of eight states and two Canadian provinces. It created a regional body of governors and premiers.[31]

Regulatory Agency Responsible for Water Rights

Department of Environmental Protection: Office of Water Management
Southwest Regional Office: (412) 442-4000
Northwest Regional Office: (814) 332-6945
North-Central Regional Office: (570) 327-3636
South-Central Regional Office: (717) 705-4700
Southeast Regional Office: (484) 250-5900
Northeast Regional Office: (570) 826-2511
Regional Permit Coordination Office: (717) 772-5987
https://www.dep.pa.gov/Business/Water/Pages/default.aspx

Rhode Island

Rhode Island defines "groundwater" as water found underground that completely fills the open spaces between particles of soil and within rock formations and "surface water" as any waters of the state that are not groundwaters.

---

28. Ibid.
29. Ibid.
30. Ibid.
31. Ibid.

Rhode Island also defines "waters of the state" or "the waters" as all surface water and groundwater of the state of Rhode Island, including all tidewaters, territorial seas, wetlands, and land masses partially or wholly submerged in water, and both inter- and intrastate bodies of water that are, have been, or will be used in commerce, by industry, for the harvesting of fish and shellfish, or for recreational purposes. Here's an exact quote from the statutes: "'Waters' means all surface waters including all waters of the territorial sea; tidewaters; all inland waters of any river, stream, brook, pond, or lake; and wetlands, as well as all groundwaters."

Most disputes in Rhode Island involve the relationship of private land ownership and oceanfront property. Rhode Island's regulatory agency, the Water Resources Board, appears to be prompt in response to water use permitting by private landowners.

Regulatory Agency Responsible for Water Rights

Water Resources Board
RI Division of Statewide Planning
235 Promenade Street, Suite 230
Providence, RI 02908
http://www.wrb.ri.gov

Delaware

The word "water" is not in the Delaware Constitution.[32] The most basic water policy in Delaware requires a permit for any withdrawal of groundwater or surface water.[33] Delaware follows the reasonable use rule for groundwater.[34]

Delaware defines "waters of the state" as follows: "'Waters of the state' means all the tidal waters under the jurisdiction of the state where the lunar tide regularly ebbs and flows and all nontidal waters under the jurisdiction of this state except for nontidal waters contained in aquacultural facilities registered with the Department of Agriculture."[35]

Regulatory Agency Responsible for Water Rights

1. Department of Natural Resources and Environmental Control: Water Resources Division Office of the Secretary: (302) 739-9000 http://www.dnrec.delaware.gov/Pages/Portal-old.aspx

---

32. https://delcode.delaware.gov/constitution/constitution.pdf.
33. 7 Del. Code Ann. § 6003(a)(3).
34. "Who Owns the Water?"
35. http://delcode.delaware.gov/title3/c004/index.shtml.

2. Division of Soil and Water Conservation http://www.dnrec.delaware.gov/swc/Pages/WebReorg.aspx

New Hampshire
Surface Water

In 2011, Jennifer Rowden of the New Hampshire Department of Environmental Services presented "Who Owns the Water: Exploring How Public Trust Affects NH's Lakes and Rivers" at the New Hampshire Water & Watershed Conference. Similar to the definition of waters of the state, according to Rowden, "State Water Jurisdiction includes all natural bodies of fresh water [which] are state-owned public waters, and are held in trust by the state for public use. . . . [T]he state retains its existing jurisdiction over those bodies of water located on the borders of the state over which it has exercised such jurisdiction." New Hampshire has jurisdiction over the public waters via "police powers" to protect the people and property within the state. New Hampshire defines "reasonable use" of state waters to include boating, fishing, swimming, and "other lawful and useful purposes." Rowden opined that riparian landowners' rights are greater than those of the public generally, including the right to "use and occupying waters adjacent to their shore for recreational purposes." New Hampshire's riparian rights are also incidental rights, meaning shorefront property may build a dock, as long as it does not unreasonably interfere with the public's use of the water. Landowner rights are always subject to the state's rights to control them reasonably for public purposes; yet, of course, the state can only take away rights if a landowner is compensated. Pursuant to the Shoreland Protection Act, New Hampshire has an interest in protecting those waters and has the jurisdiction to control the use of the public waters and the adjacent shoreland for the greatest public benefit.[36]

Groundwater Rights

The Groundwater Protection Act in New Hampshire is the fundamental policy doctrine for groundwater. According to Rowden, "Groundwater is a shared resource in New Hampshire. Therefore, the question of 'who owns groundwater' may better or more practically be restated as who has the right to use water and how much? New Hampshire's water rights system is based on common law (law that is based on historic court decisions opposed to

---

36. https://campus.plymouth.edu/cfe/wp-content/uploads/sites/127/2011/03/H_Rowden_2011-Watershed-Conference-Public-Trust-in-NH.pdf.

written codified law). New Hampshire's common law with respect to water use is governed by the doctrine of reasonable use."[37]

The New Hampshire Department of Environmental Services (NHDES) is responsible for administering all water policies in the state. According to its website, concerning groundwater, "Water use in New Hampshire is governed by common law, statutes that provide water rights to particular entities, and statutes that NHDES administers. The statutes administered by NHDES help to ensure that the uses of the state's water resources are understood and do not adversely interfere with other water uses or resources."[38]

The NHDES at one time issued this well-written and explanatory statement about its definition of reasonable use as it applies to all New Hampshire water: "'Reasonable use' is generally taken to mean that one property owner's water use may not unreasonably interfere with the water use of another property owner, regardless of which use was established first. 'Reasonable use' is a mixed question of fact and law, and the standard may change over time—so what was once reasonable may over time become unreasonable."

The statement that reasonable use is a dynamic standard, adapting over time in response to the everchanging relationship of water use demands, climate conditions, and public will, is a significantly true and insightful observation that is applicable to all states with reasonable use policies.

The unknown writer of this lost publication astutely continues to discuss another significant aspect of water: "Because the movement of groundwater does not respect municipal boundaries, it makes sense that the state is the entity that can regulate or restrict groundwater use." That water ignores political boundaries is a cornerstone of my water policy lectures, classes, and presentations. All of my students in water rights classes learn the importance of this cornerstone of water policy each time they enter my classroom.

According to the NHDES,

> New Hampshire's Groundwater Protection Act (RSA 485-C) is intended to ensure that new "large" groundwater withdrawals (those that exceed 57,600 gallons over any 24-hour period) do not adversely impact the quality or quantity of groundwater or water resources such as neighboring wells, wetlands, streams, rivers and lakes. Since August 1998, any proposed "large" groundwater withdrawal must undergo a comprehensive permitting process to demonstrate that other water users or water resources (lakes, rivers and wetlands) would not be adversely impacted. The permitting process includes public notification, two public hearings, extensive field testing and assessment of data, and development of an environmental monitoring, reporting, and mitigation plan. It is important to note that RSA 485-C does not replace common law with respect to water

37. New Hampshire Department of Environmental Services (www.des.nh.gov).
38. https://www.des.nh.gov/water/groundwater.

rights; rather, common law coexists with the statute. This means that landowners developing a groundwater withdrawal of any amount have a right to reasonable use of the water under common law, that large new groundwater withdrawals are regulated under RSA 485-C, and that civil cases may be brought to the courts to resolve conflicts when the water rights of another land owner are unreasonably impacted by any withdrawal.[39]

Regulatory Agency Responsible for Water Rights

New Hampshire Department of Environmental Services
29 Hazen Drive
Concord, NH 03302–0095
(603) 271-3503
www.des.nh.gov

Maine

Maine is a water-rich state with ample rainfall and moisture year-round. The Maine Department of Environmental Protection is the key agency responsible for water regulations and their enforcement in the state. The following is the department's statement about rivers and streams: "Like lakes and ponds, Maine is blessed with an abundance of rivers and streams. The primary sources for all Maine rivers are the smaller brooks and streams, which often begin in the mountains. Fed by underground springs or from rain and melting snow, brooks and streams flow downhill, merge to become larger streams, and eventually all become rivers flowing to the sea. A variety of important aquatic animals and plants live along the entire course."[40]

As in other New England coastal states, Maine's water regulations are complex due to the inclusion of seashore waters. Maine's Section 3–38 §361-A defines "waters of the state" as "any and all surface and subsurface waters that are contained within, flow through or under, or border upon this state or any portion of the state, including the marginal and high seas, except such waters as are confined and retained completely upon the property of one person and do not drain into or connect with any other waters of the State, but not excluding waters susceptible to use in interstate or foreign commerce, or whose use, degradation, or destruction would affect interstate or foreign commerce."[41]

---

39. https://www.des.nh.gov/organization/commissioner/pip/factsheets/dwgb/documents/dwgb-22-13.pdf.
40. https://www.maine.gov/dep/water/rivers-streams/index.html.
41. http://www.mainelegislature.org/legis/statutes/38/title38sec361-a.html. (PL 1997, c. 794, Pt. A, §11 [AMD].)

Surface Water

Maine defines surface water as "fresh surface water," which "means all waters of the State other than estuarine and marine waters and ground water" [PL 1985, c. 698, §2 (AMD)]. Surface water is owned by the state of Maine.

In recognition of riparian rights, landowners may use the state water for "working it" within the rules and regulations:

> §651. Milldams and canals
>
> Any man may on his own land erect and maintain a watermill and dams to raise water for working it, upon and across any stream not navigable; or, for the purpose of propelling mills or machinery, may cut a canal and erect walls and embankments upon his own land, not exceeding one mile in length, and thereby divert from its natural channel the water of any stream not navigable, upon the terms and conditions and subject to the regulations hereinafter expressed.
>
> §652.—diversion of water
>
> Any person, authorized to erect and maintain a watermill and dams on a stream not navigable and to divert the water of such stream from its natural channel by a canal not exceeding one mile in length for the purpose of propelling mills or machinery under section 651, may so divert such waters without said limitation to one mile, provided he is the owner of the land on which the canal is to be located or has the consent of the owners thereof, and provided he is the owner of all riparian rights on said stream between the point of diversion and the point at which the waters are returned to the stream, upon the terms and conditions, and subject to the regulations under this chapter. Under this section, "canal" shall include excavations in the ground and closed flumes, penstocks, pipelines and other appropriate means of conveying water from the point of diversion to the point of return to the stream.[42]

Groundwater

Maine defines groundwater as "all the waters found beneath the surface of the earth which are contained within or under this State or any portion thereof, except such waters as are confined and retained completely upon the property of one person and do not drain into or connect with any other waters of the State" [PL 1979, c. 472, §9 (NEW)].

> §404. Ground water rights

42. http://legislature.maine.gov/legis/statutes/38/title38ch5sec0.html.

1. Definitions. As used in this section, unless the context indicates otherwise, the following terms have the following meanings.
   A. "Beneficial domestic use" means any ground water used for household purposes essential to health and safety, whether provided by individual wells or through public supply systems.
   B. "Ground water" means all the waters found beneath the surface of the earth.
   C. "Preexisting use" means any use which was undertaken by a public water supplier, a landowner or lawful land occupant or a predecessor in interest of either of them, at any time during the period of 3 years prior to the commencement of the use which resulted in the interference.
2. Cause of action created. Subject to the limitations of subsection 3 and except as provided by Title 23, section 652, a person is liable for the withdrawal of ground water, including use of ground water in heat pump systems, when the withdrawal is in excess of *beneficial domestic use for a single-family home and when the withdrawal causes interference with the preexisting beneficial domestic use of ground water by a landowner or lawful land occupant* [emphasis added] [PL 1987, c. 491, §4 (NEW)].[43]

Who Owns Groundwater in Maine?

According to the Maine Rural Water Association and the Maine Water Utilities Association, groundwater rights in Maine are as follows:

> Maine property owners (including water utilities and water bottlers) obtain groundwater rights through land ownership. Under the common law in Maine, an owner of land also owns the groundwater beneath the land. However, these rights are not absolute; one cannot extract water from their land in a manner than negatively affects one's neighbors right to the water under their property. This rule has defined property rights in Maine for generations. Like other property owners, water utilities have relied on this common law to gain rights to groundwater for their customers and to protect groundwater though land ownership. Changing this long-standing doctrine would greatly affect existing property rights and interfere with the ability of water utilities to protect the groundwater they provide their customers.[44]

---

43. http://www.mainelegislature.org/legis/statutes/38/title38sec404.html.
44. https://mwua.org/wp-content/uploads/2020/01/GW-availability-ownership-and-rights-in-Maine-2-11-19.pdf. From a February 11, 2019, joint publication of the Maine Rural Water Association and the Maine Water Utilities Association.

Groundwater rights are gained through land ownership, but there is liability for withdrawal of groundwater that affects your neighbor; therefore, the rule of capture as found in Texas does not apply in Maine.

Most-Active Water Issues in Maine

Many stakeholder groups have been and remain quite concerned about private water bottlers such as Nestlé, owner and operator of Poland Spring bottled waters. Many Maine citizens, who contend that they will suffer the future consequences of Nestlé's groundwater withdrawal, complain the permit process for Nestlé has not allowed their concerns to be aired.[45]

Maine citizens are also actively concerned about industrial users of water, which recently includes proposed or ongoing mining operations. Water quality, not the amount of water available, is the emphasis in Maine. The permitting process is not well defined on public websites; therefore, consultation with local attorneys and hydrologists is essential.

Regulatory Agency Responsible for Water Rights

Maine Department of Environmental Protection
17 State House Station
32 Blossom Lane
Augusta, ME 04333–0017
(207) 287-7688
https://www.maine.gov/dep/index.html

Vermont

"'Waters' [in Vermont] means any and all rivers, streams, brooks, creeks, lakes, ponds or stored water, and groundwaters, excluding municipal and farm water supplies."[46]

Regulatory Agency Responsible for Water Rights

Vermont Agency of Natural Resources
1 National Life Drive, Davis 2
Montpelier, VT 05620–3901
(802) 828-1294

---

45. "Maine Activists Protest Nestle's Potential Sale of Poland Spring Water to Private Equity Firm," *Bangor Daily News*, February 12, 2021.
46. http://www.leg.state.vt.us/statutes/fullsection.cfm?Title=10&Chapter =037&Section=00902.

https://anr.vermont.gov

New Jersey

"'Waters of the state' means, but shall not be limited to, the waters of the Atlantic Ocean for three nautical miles eastward from the shores of this state; all navigable and non-navigable tidal and non-tidal, rivers, bays, streams, and inlets; and any other water within the jurisdiction of the state."[47]

Surface Water

In New Jersey, surface water is owned by the state. New Jersey follows riparian principles of surface water rights. Like their neighboring states, New Jersey has ample natural water resources. The state of New Jersey provides the best comment about their riparian water law: "Riparian rights have a long and somewhat checkered history in New Jersey. It is a subject that for too long has been difficult for most people to understand because of developing and shifting administrative policy, technical jargon, and unnecessarily complicated statutes. The result is that riparian land management is understood by very few that it most directly affects. In fact, there is an absence of general agreement concerning the meaning of essential terms."[48]

This astute comment could apply across the United States, not only to riparian rights but to all water laws in all states.

Groundwater

In New Jersey, "ground water" means the portion of water beneath the land surface that is within the "saturated zone." "Saturated zone" means the zone in which all the subsurface voids in the rock or soil are filled with water.

Who Owns Groundwater in New Jersey?

It is unclear who owns groundwater in New Jersey, but different court rulings indicate the state follows a correlative rights doctrine along with the American rule of reasonable use. Using their definition of "waters of the state," then groundwater is likely to be claimed as owned by the state.

According to the Water Council,

---

47. http://www.njleg.state.nj.us.

48. Lewis P. Goldshore, *New Jersey Riparian Rights Handbook* (State of New Jersey County and Municipal Government Study Commission, 1979).

New Jersey's common law rule for percolating groundwater remains unclear. Early cases applied the American rule (Meeker v. East Orange, 77 N.J.L. 623, 638 (E. & A. 1909)). However, some authorities interpret Meeker as adopting the Correlative Rights rule (Woodsum v. Pemberton Twp., 172 N.J. Super. 489, 502, 504, 412 A.2d 1064 (Law Div. 1980), aff'd on other grounds, 177 N.J. Super. 639, 427 A.2d 615 (App. Div. 1981), citing Hanks, Eva M. and John L. Hanks, The Law of Water in New Jersey: Groundwater, 24 Rutgers L. Rev. 621, 649 (1970)). Correlative Rights protect all users, including transporters. When reviewing all cases, it appears as if New Jersey uses the Reasonable Use rule.[49]

Most-Active Water Issues in New Jersey

Currently the most-active water issues in New Jersey involve water quality standards. According to *NJ Spotlight News*, "Four New Jersey towns and an investor-owned water supplier are suing 3M, DuPont and other makers of PFAS—so-called forever chemicals—saying the companies knew their products would contaminate drinking water but continued to sell them, and must now pay for their cleanup."

Regulatory Agency Responsible for Water Rights

Department of Environmental Protection: Division of Water Supply and Geoscience
P.O. Box 420
Trenton, NJ 08625
(609) 777-3373
https://www.state.nj.us/dep/watersupply/g_reg.html

Maryland

"'Waters of the state' includes: both surface and underground waters within the boundaries of the state subject to its jurisdiction; that portion of the Atlantic Ocean within the boundaries of the State; the Chesapeake Bay and its tributaries; all ponds, lakes, rivers, streams, public ditches, tax ditches, and public drainage systems within the state, other than those designed and used to collect, convey, or dispose of sanitary sewage; and the floodplain of free-flowing waters determined by the department on the basis of the 100-year flood frequency."

---

49. "Who Owns the Water?"

Surface Water and Groundwater

Surface and groundwater are owned by the state in Maryland. Maryland follows the American rule of reasonable use in both surface and groundwater. Permits for any use of surface or groundwater must be obtained. The only exemptions from permits are "(1) use for water for domestic purposes other than for heating and cooling, (2) use of water for agricultural purposes, if the average annual water use is less than 10,000 gallons per day, and (3) Use of groundwater at an average annual water use of 5,000 gallons of water per day or less."[50]

The U.S. Department of Energy's Regulatory and Permitting Information Desktop (RAPID) Information Tool Kit offers no summary of Maryland's water rights.

Most Significant Issue in Maryland Water

Chesapeake Bay is the focal point of Maryland's water issues. The issues are quite basic: chemicals in the water from past industrial or other operations and stormwater drainage into the bay.

Regulatory Agency Responsible for Water Rights

Department of the Environment: Water Information Center
1800 Washington Blvd.
Baltimore, MD 21230
(410) 537-3000
https://mde.maryland.gov/programs/water/Pages/index.aspx

Massachusetts

"Waters" and "waters of the commonwealth" mean "all waters within the jurisdiction of the commonwealth, including, without limitation, rivers, streams, lakes, ponds, springs, impoundments, estuaries, coastal waters, and groundwaters."[51]

---

50. 2010 Maryland Code, Environment, Title 5—Water Resources, Subtitle 5—Appropriation or Use of Waters, Reservoirs, and Dams, Section 5-502—Permit to appropriate or use State waters.

51. http://www.mass.gov/legis/laws/mgl/gl-21-toc.htm; https://www.aswm.org/pdf_lib/ecos_feb_2009_definitions_of_waters_of_the_state.pdf.

Surface Water and Groundwater

Surface water is owned by the state, but groundwater follows the absolute dominion rule and is owned by the landowner. In 1985, Massachusetts enacted legislation that placed amounts of groundwater in excess of 100,000 gallons a day, 36.5 million gallons per year, or 113 acre-feet a year under the governance of the state.

Most Significant Issue in Massachusetts Water

The most significant issue in Massachusetts water in 2021 is pollution of urban drinking water from polyfluoroalkyl substances (PFAS) and pesticides. According to NBC 10 Boston, "PFAS are a group of man-made chemicals often found in drinking water, but people are also exposed through consumer products and food. The family of chemicals has been used since the 1950s to manufacture stain-resistant, water-resistant and non-stick products."[52]

Regulatory Agency Responsible for Water Rights

Department of Environmental Protection: Water, Wastewater, and Wetlands
Headquarters Boston Office: (617) 292-5500
https://www.mass.gov/orgs/massachusetts-department-of-environmental-protection
Water Resource Authority: http://www.mwra.com

Virginia

"'State waters' means all water, on the surface and under the ground, wholly or partially within or bordering the Commonwealth or within its jurisdiction, including wetlands. Such waters are a natural resource which should be regulated by the Commonwealth. 'Wetlands' means those areas that are inundated or saturated by surface or groundwater at a frequency and duration sufficient to support, and that under normal circumstances do support, a prevalence of vegetation typically adapted for life in saturated soil conditions. Wetlands generally include swamps, marshes, bogs and similar areas."[53]

The U.S. Department of Energy's RAPID Information Tool Kit offers no summary of Virginia's water rights.

---

52. https://www.nbcboston.com/news/local/high-levels-of-toxic-chemicals-found-in-water-supplies/2388163.
53. http://leg1.state.va.us/000/cod/TOC6201000.HTM.

Surface Water and Groundwater

Virginia follows the American rule of reasonable use in both surface and groundwater. According to Virginia's Groundwater Act of 1973,

> The General Assembly hereby determines and finds that, pursuant to the Groundwater Act of 1973, the continued, unrestricted usage of ground water is contributing and will contribute to pollution and shortage of ground water, thereby jeopardizing the public welfare, safety and health. It is the purpose of this Act to recognize and declare that the right to reasonable control of all ground water resources within this Commonwealth belongs to the public and that in order to conserve, protect and beneficially utilize the ground water of this Commonwealth and to ensure the public welfare, safety and health, provision for management and control of ground water resources is essential.[54]

Most Significant Issue in Virginia Water

Recently, an environmental group in Virginia known as the Environmental Working Group tested tap water in several areas in Northern Virginia that allegedly contain toxins known as "forever chemicals."[55] The regulatory investigations are ongoing at this time.

Regulatory Agency Responsible for Water Rights

Department of Environmental Quality
1111 East Main Street, Suite 1400
Richmond, VA 23219
https://www.deq.virginia.gov/Programs/Water.aspx

West Virginia

"'Water resources,' 'water,' or 'waters' means any and all water on or beneath the surface of the ground, whether percolating, standing, diffused or flowing, wholly or partially within this state, or bordering this state and within its jurisdiction, and includes, without limiting the generality of the foregoing, natural or artificial lakes, rivers, streams, creeks, branches, brooks, ponds (except farm ponds, industrial settling basins, and ponds and water treatment facilities), impounding reservoirs, springs, wells, and watercourses."[56]

---

54. Code of Virginia § 62.1–254. Findings and purpose.
55. https://www.ewg.org/areas-focus/toxic-chemicals/pfas-chemicals.
56. http://www.legis.state.wv.us/WVCODE/22c/code/WVC%2022%20C -%20%201%20%20 -%20%20%203%20%20.htm.

The U.S. Department of Energy's RAPID Information Tool Kit offers no summary of West Virginia's water rights.

Surface Water and Groundwater

West Virginia follows the American rule of reasonable use in both surface and groundwater.

Most Significant Issue in West Virginia Water

Similar to Virginia, West Virginia, a water-rich state, is undergoing a statewide investigation into tap water and toxins found across a broad area of the state. The investigation is ongoing.[57]

Regulatory Agency Responsible for Water Rights

Department of Environmental Protection: Division of Water and Waste Management
601 57th Street SE
Charleston, WV 25304
(304) 926-0440
https://dep.wv.gov/water/Pages/default.aspx
Division of Natural Resources: Office of Land and Streams: http://www.wvdnr.gov

THE SOUTH AND SOUTHEAST

Alabama, North Carolina, South Carolina, Georgia, Florida, Mississippi, and Louisiana

Alabama

In Alabama, surface water and groundwater rights are determined by ownership of land appurtenant to or overlying a "water of the state." "Waters of the state" are defined as follows:

57. "A Look at One Community's Tap Water Journey on This West Virginia Morning," WV Public Broadcasting Corporation, June 7, 2022, https://wvpublic.org/a-look-at-one-communitys-tap-water-journey-on-this-west-virginia-morning.

1. (19) WATERS or WATERS OF THE STATE. A quantity of any spring, brook, creek, stream, river, pond, swamp, lake, reservoir, impoundment, sound, tidal estuary, bay, waterway, aquifer, or any other body or accumulation of water, surface water, or ground water, public or private, natural or artificial, that
   a. is contained within the borders of this state;
   b. flows through or to this state or any portion thereof; or
   c. borders upon this state or any portion thereof, including those portions of the Gulf of Mexico over which this state has jurisdiction.[58]

Notice the definition above includes groundwater.

According to Heather Elliott, professor of law at the University of Alabama, Alabama's water policy is based on nineteenth-century common law for both surface water and groundwater. Surface water in Alabama is governed following the riparian doctrine; the reasonable use doctrine applies to Alabama surface water riparian rights. The basic dispute in Alabama is similar to that in other states in that it is usually between riparian "upstreamers" and "downstreamers" and is often over whose use is "reasonable." As mentioned often in this book, of course, a landowner's use in his or her mind is always reasonable.

According to Professor Elliott, surface water is owned by the state of Alabama:

> Under the common law, the right to use water from a surface-water body is typically acquired by owning property riparian to that water body. A parcel is riparian if a body of water forms a boundary of the property, if a stream flows over the property, or if a lake or other static water body is present within the property. The riparian "has no property in the water itself, but a simple usufruct while it passes along."[59]

Groundwater in Alabama is governed following the American reasonable use rule. Groundwater export issues also often revolve around what harm is caused to other landowners, similar in concept to riparian determinations. According to Professor Elliott, "Alabama's common law of groundwater, like that of surface water, confers rights based on property ownership. Those who own land overlying an aquifer have the right to extract and use that groundwater on the overlying tract. To obtain groundwater rights, then, one must purchase an existing overlying tract or a new overlying tract created by

58. Alabama Code 9–10B-3. Definitions, (19).

59. Heather Elliott, "The Failings of Alabama Water Law," *Alabama Law Review*, https://www.law.ua.edu/lawreview/files/2011/07/The-Failings-of-Alabama-Water-Law.pdf, 765–66.

the subdivision of an existing tract. One Alabama case suggests in dicta that groundwater rights could also be acquired by prescription."[60]

Professor Elliott further opines on groundwater issues that the "American reasonable use doctrine [in Alabama groundwater] provides no rule to resolve competing uses among overlying landowners, leaving such owners to compete with their neighbors for who can dig the deepest well."[61]

Similar to Texas groundwater law, Alabama law ties legal use of groundwater to land ownership. Groundwater law in Alabama being based on the American reasonable use doctrine effectively results in a similar consequence to Texas's rule of capture: neighbors compete to capture the groundwater with deeper wells and more powerful pumps to extract the water before their neighbor.

No statute in Alabama sets up a regulatory regime over "groundwater withdrawals."[62] Registration and reporting are required by public water systems or individuals that "divert, withdraw, or consume" more than one hundred thousand gallons on "any day" from waters of the state and for persons who have the "capacity" to use one hundred thousand gallons on any day for purposes of irrigation.[63]

According to the Office of Water Resources (OWR) website,

> All public water systems and those other individuals and organizations who have a capacity to withdraw 100,000 gallons per day or more are required to register with OWR and obtain a Certificate of Use. The process begins with the submittal of an application form (called a "Declaration of Beneficial Use") and other required information. Once that information is reviewed and determined to be complete, OWR will issue what is called a Certificate of Use that lists the individual or organization's name and information concerning all registered surface and/or groundwater withdrawal points and their withdrawal information. Then annually the certificate owner submits water usage information back to OWR.[64]

The Alabama Water Resources Commission has authority to declare "capacity stress areas" as well.[65] The Water Resources Commission is "required to protect the availability of the waters of the state" as mentioned in Alabama Code 9–10B-21:

---

60. Ibid., 775.
61. Ibid., 760.
62. "Who Owns the Water," 16.
63. Ibid.
64. https://adeca.alabama.gov/Divisions/owr/watermanagement/Pages/WaterManagement.aspx.
65. Ibid.

> The commission shall review the critical use study submitted by the Office of Water Resources and determine if the implementation of water use restrictions in such area is necessary due to a finding by the commission that the aggregate existing or reasonably foreseeable uses of the waters of the state in such area exceed or will exceed the availability of such waters and is required to protect the availability of the waters of the state, and may initiate rule-making proceedings to have such area of the state designated as a capacity stress area; provided, however, that the commission shall not adopt or promulgate any rule or regulation with respect to any capacity stress area without the concurrence of 13 of the members of the commission.

But apparently, Alabama has yet to determine any area as a "capacity stress area"; hence, are they protecting the availability of the waters of the state? News reporter Ben Raines, in "Alabama's Rivers Are Crashing Thanks to Water Rules That Favor Industry," thinks that the protection is not occurring as yet:

> State officials say limiting water withdrawals here would be a time-consuming endeavor, requiring "either an individual court ruling" for each permit holder or the designation of a "capacity stress area." Under the state's current water use law, such a designation could be made if too many users were fighting over the water in a certain stretch of a river.
>
> But such a designation has never been issued in Alabama, and the rules for creating a stress area include multiple scientific studies and a majority vote by the Alabama Water Resources Commission, which is composed of politicians, factory owners, utility managers and other water users. Asked how long it would take to declare a capacity stress area, the Alabama Department of Economic and Community affairs (which supervises water use in the state) responded, "Since such a designation has never been made, there is no historical basis to make such an estimate."[66]

Water stress in Alabama is a reality and has been so at least for the last twenty years. Figure A.2 indicates the drought history of Alabama from 2000 to 2019. The levels of drought severity are shown as D0 to D4 with the percentage of the state impacted by the various levels.[67]

> The U.S. Drought Monitor started in 2000. Since 2000, the longest duration of drought (D1–D4) in Alabama lasted 137 weeks beginning on July 27, 2010 and

66. Ben Raines, "Alabama's Rivers Are Crashing Thanks to Water Rules That Favor Industry," AL.com, November 15, 2016, https://www.al.com/news/mobile/2016/11/alabamas_rivers_are_crashing_t.html.

67. https://www.drought.gov/drought/states/alabama.

ending on March 5, 2013. The most intense period of drought occurred the week of August 29, 2000 where D4 affected 77.9% of Alabama land.[68]

As periodic droughts will likely continue to occur with varying degrees of frequency and severity, whether or not the state of Alabama will use the statutory authority to create capacity stress areas is yet to be seen. The political will of the people eventually directs any and all governing bodies' willingness to use existing statutory regulatory tools to protect the waters of any state. Drought will be the catalyst to action.

Alabama, like most humid region states, is a riparian rights state limited by beneficial use. Water is managed by the Alabama Water Resources Act, which sets forth that:

> . . . waters of the state are a basic resource that should be conserved and managed for "full beneficial use . . . [and] not be restricted unless the existing or future water usage in an area exceeds the supply capacity." If restrictions are necessary, then human consumption is the priority.
>
> The Water Resource Commission and the Office of Water Resources in the Alabama Department of Economic and Community Affairs were created by the Water Resources Act to oversee and administer a water use reporting system.

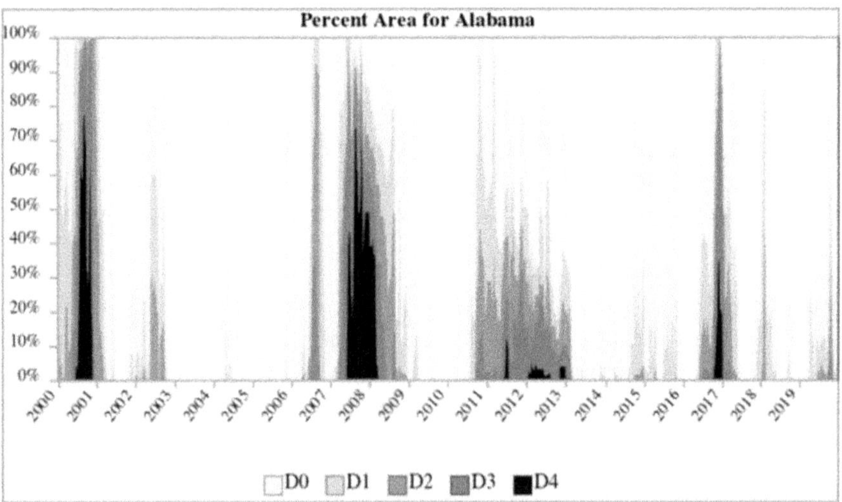

Figure A.2. Drought in Alabama from 2000 to 2019.
Source: U.S. Environmental Protection Agency

68. Ibid.

The Water Resources Commission has the specific authority to designate stress capacity areas, based on a study finding that the area will not have enough water supply capacity for current or future usage. But the Act specifically limits the Commission's authority to restrict water use otherwise. Further, this authority does not apply to any impoundment contained completely upon the property of a person if it is identified in a certificate of use. . . .

[Surface and ground]water use reporting is required for large users (100,000 gallons per day or more) under their certificate of use. . . . Certificates of use are generally issued for five to ten years and are renewable. If the terms of the certificate of use are not followed, or if a water user violates the Water Sources Act, the certificate of use can be modified or terminated.

Besides the goal of providing a comprehensive water resources framework for water usage, the Alabama Water Resources Act also provides a state-wide procedure to handle other aspects of water management including state response to emergencies such as floods and droughts, and a unified voice for the state when dealing with interstate water issues.

Water rights for small quantities are generally not quantified, and historically no public records were kept. The database of water usage now consists of the annual self-reported data from the large withdrawers. . . .

Groundwater is covered under the Alabama Water Resources Act, but historically Alabama courts have used a mixture of reasonable use, nuisance, and absolute ownership theories. At times, the Alabama Supreme Court has declared that one theory applies, while actually using the analysis and reasoning of another theory. In later cases, reasonable use theory seemed to emerge as the state courts' preferred methodology.[69]

Regulatory Agency Responsible for Water Rights

Department of Economic and Community Affairs: Office of Water Resources
401 Adams Avenue
Montgomery, AL 36104
https://adeca.alabama.gov/Divisions/owr/Pages/default.aspx
Department of Environmental Management: Water Division: http://www.adem.state.al.us/programs/water/default.cnt

North Carolina

North Carolina has not published a "waters of the state" definition.

69. Smoles, M.D., Mittelstet, Aaron, Harjo, Bekki. Biosystems and Agricultural Engineering Department, Oklahoma State University. "Whose Water is it Anyway," p. 11.

Surface and Groundwater

North Carolina follows the reasonable use concept and is a riparian state; anyone who owns land adjoining surface water has the right to make reasonable use of that water.

Regulatory Agency Responsible for Water Rights

Department of Environment and Natural Resources: Division of Water Resources
North Carolina Department of Environmental Quality
217 West Jones Street
Raleigh, NC 27603
(877) 623-6748
https://deq.nc.gov/about/divisions/water-resources

South Carolina

"Waters of the state" are all waters within the jurisdiction of this state, including all streams, lakes, ponds, impounding reservoirs, marshes, watercourses, waterways, wells, springs, irrigation systems, drainage systems, and all other bodies or accumulations of water, surface and underground, natural or artificial, public or private, situated wholly or partly within or bordering upon the state.[70]

Regulatory Agency Responsible for Water Rights

Department of Natural Resources: Water
1000 Assembly Street
Columbia, SC 29201
http://www.dnr.sc.gov

Link to an article about South Carolina water law, "South Carolina State Water Assessment, 2nd Edition, Chapter Two South Carolina Water Law"

https://www.tegacaysc.org/DocumentCenter/View/14474/SC-Water-Law-Ch2

70. http://legis.state.sd.us/statutes/DisplayStatute.aspx?Statute=34A-2–2&Type=Statute.

Georgia

"'Waters of this state' means any waters within the territorial limits of this state and the marginal sea adjacent to this state and the high seas when navigated as a part of a journey or ride to or from the shore of this state except ponds or lakes not open to the public, whether or not such ponds or lakes are within the lands of one title."[71]

According to the Georgia Department of Natural Resources, Environmental Protection Division, "Georgia is a riparian rights state, limited by beneficial use. Water is managed by the Georgia Environmental Protection Division of the Department of Natural Resources as mandated in the Georgia Water Pollution Control Act, which sets forth that: " . . . all waters of the state are basic resources that should be conserved and managed for maximum benefit of the people, and subject to reasonable usage. This beneficial use should not be restricted unless the existing or future water usage in an area exceeds the supply capacity or during an emergency water shortage. If restrictions are necessary, then human consumption would be the priority use, followed by agricultural and industrial usage as second priorities."

The Georgia Environmental Protection Division of the Georgia Department of Natural Resources issues permits for withdrawal, diversion, and impoundment of surface and ground waters for large users. No permit is required for the following:

- Diversion or withdrawal smaller than one hundred thousand gallons per day on a monthly average
- Diversion that does not reduce the flow of surface waters where it leaves the property by more than one hundred thousand gallons per day on a monthly average
- Diversion for construction for transportation purposes that does not reduce the flow of surface waters by more than 150,000 gallons per day on a monthly average
- Impoundment that does not reduce the flow of surface waters immediately downstream of the impoundment by more than one hundred thousand gallons per day on a monthly average
- Impoundment of water in a farm pond, constructed for the sole purpose of fish, wildlife, recreation, or other farm uses

No permit is required for the reduction of flow during construction or initial filling of an impoundment. Permits are generally issued for ten to twenty years, but can be extended up to fifty years for municipalities or other entities

---

71. http://law.justia.com/georgia/codes/27/27-1-2.html.

issuing bonds to construct facilities. Permit holders are required to report annually the average monthly and maximum daily use of water to the Georgia Environmental Protection Division.

Agricultural permits in Georgia are based on pumping capacity and fall under different requirements based on the date of application.

Regulatory Agency Responsible for Water Rights

Department of Natural Resources: Environmental Protection Division
2 Martin Luther King Jr. Drive SE
Suite 1456, East Tower
Atlanta, GA 30334
(404) 463-1511
https://epd.georgia.gov

An Article: "Georgia Water Law"

Water rights in Georgia vary according to the amount of water withdrawn from the water source, whether it is a surface water source (river, stream, reservoir) or a groundwater source (aquifer).

Georgia's water laws for surface and groundwater withdrawals greater than 100,000 gallons per day (herein "gpd") are regulated by a comprehensive permit system. However, for withdrawals from surface sources that are less than 100,000 gpd, Georgia's water laws closely follow the common law Riparian Rights doctrine, which is defined by decisions of the Georgia Courts. For withdrawals from groundwater sources that are less than 100,000 gpd, Georgia's water laws are somewhat unclear.

For those individuals who withdraw small amounts of surface water (less than 100,000 gpd on a monthly average), conflicts over existing sources of water are determined by application of the common law doctrine of Riparian Rights.

Georgia's Riparian Rights doctrine is codified in O.C.G.A. §§ 44-8-1 and 51-9-7. Section 44-8-1 provides:

Running water belongs to the owner of the land on which it runs, but the landowner has no right to divert it from the usual channel nor may he so use or adulterate it as to interfere with the enjoyment of it by the next owner.

Section 51-9-7 provides:

The owner of land through which non-navigable watercourses may flow is entitled to have the water in such streams come to his land in its natural and usual flow, subject only to such detention or diminution as may be caused by a reasonable use of it by other riparian proprietors; and the diverting of the stream, wholly or in part, from the same, or the obstruction thereof so as to impede its course or cause it to overflow or injure his land, or any right appurtenant thereto, or the pollution thereof so as to lessen its value to him, shall be a trespass upon his property.

The common law doctrine of Riparian Rights treats water as a common resource and the resolution of disputes is left to the courts. During the late 1970's it became apparent that there was a need for governmental legislation of large water users in order to prevent improper usage of surface waters and to allow coordination of such uses; thus, the Georgia Water Quality Control Act was amended to require the permitting of water diversions and withdrawals of more than 100,000 gpd on a monthly average. O.C.G.A. § 12-5-31.

As with surface water, individuals who withdraw small amounts of groundwater (less than 100,000 gpd on a daily basis) must resolve their disputes by application of case law developed in the 19th and early 20th centuries. Case law for groundwater withdrawal as developed in Georgia establishes a rule quite different from the common law doctrine of Riparian Rights and amounts to a modified absolute ownership rule based upon the principle that, in Georgia, the owner of realty has title downwards and upwards indefinitely. Stoner v. Patten, 132 Ga. 178 (1909).

In 1972, the General Assembly enacted the Ground-Water Use Act of 1972. O.C.G.A. § 12-5-90 et seq. Under this Act, groundwater is allocated by using the concept of "reasonable use." The Act provides that no person shall withdraw, obtain or utilize groundwater in excess of 100,000 gpd for any purpose unless that person obtains a permit from the Environmental Protection Division. O.C.G.A. § 12-5-96(a)(1).[72]

Florida

"'Waters' include, but are not limited to, rivers, lakes, streams, springs, impoundments, and all other waters or bodies of water, including fresh, brackish, saline, tidal, surface, or underground waters. Waters owned entirely by one person other than the state are included in regard to possible discharge on other property or water. Underground waters include, but are not limited to, all underground waters passing through pores of rock or soils or flowing through in channels, whether manmade or natural."[73]

Florida has a unique and complex two-tiered appropriation system to manage water use. Historically, Florida courts applied the doctrine of riparian rights to water rights cases, but all unexercised riparian rights were statutorily extinguished in 1974, two years after the passage of a comprehensive statutory permitting scheme in 1972. The Florida Department of Environmental Protection manages the water on a statewide level, but five regional water management districts implement the water use permits. Permit rules vary substantially from district to district, but there is very little difference in the rights of riparian versus nonriparian landowners.

---

72. "Georgia Water Law," HG.org Legal Resources. https://www.hg.org/legal-articles/georgia-water-law-32945.

73. http://www.dep.state.fl.us/legal/Rules/shared/62-520/62-520.pdf.

Regulatory Agency Responsible for Water Rights

Department of Environmental Protection: Water Resources Management
900 Commonwealth Boulevard
Tallahassee, FL 32399–3000
(850) 245-2118
https://floridadep.gov/water

Mississippi

"'Waters of the state' means all waters within the jurisdiction of this state, including all streams, lakes, ponds, impounding reservoirs, marshes, watercourses, waterways, wells, springs, irrigation systems, drainage systems and all other bodies or accumulations of water, surface and underground, natural or artificial, situated wholly or partly within or bordering upon the state, and such coastal waters as are within the jurisdiction of the state, except lakes, ponds, or other surface waters which are wholly landlocked and privately owned."[74]

Regulatory Agency Responsible for Water Rights

Department of Environmental Quality: Office of Land and Water Resources
P.O. Box 2261
Jackson, MS 39225
https://www.mdeq.ms.gov/water

Louisiana

"'Waters of the state' refers to both the surface and underground waters within the State of Louisiana including all rivers, streams, lakes, estuaries, groundwaters, and all other water courses and waters within the confines of the state, and all bordering waters and the Gulf of Mexico."[75]

Regulatory Agency Responsible for Water Rights

Department of Natural Resources
LaSalle Building
617 North Third Street
Baton Rouge, LA 70802
http://www.dnr.louisiana.gov/index.cfm/page/455

---

74. http://michie.com/mississippi/lpext.dll?f=templates&fn=mainh.htm&cp=.
75. http://www.deq.louisiana.gov/portal/Portals/0/planning/regs/title33/3 3v09-200809.pdf.

THE MIDWEST

Illinois, Ohio, Tennessee, Kentucky, Indiana, Iowa, Wisconsin, Michigan, Minnesota, and Missouri

Illinois

"'Waters' means all accumulations of water, surface and underground, natural, and artificial, public and private, or parts thereof, which are wholly or partially within, flow through, or border upon the State of Illinois, except that sewers and treatment works are not included except as specially mentioned; provided, that nothing herein contained shall authorize the use of natural or otherwise protected waters as sewers or treatment works except that in-stream aeration under agency permit is allowable."

Regulatory Agency Responsible for Water Rights

Office of Water Resources
One Natural Resources Way
Springfield, IL 62702
(217) 782-6302
https://dnr.illinois.gov

Ohio

"'Waters of the state' includes all streams, lakes, ponds, marshes, watercourses, waterways, wells, springs, irrigation systems, drainage systems, and other bodies or accumulations of water, surface and underground, natural or artificial, regardless of the depth of the strata in which underground water is located, that are situated wholly or partly within or border upon this state or are within its jurisdiction."[76]

Regulatory Agency Responsible for Water Rights

Department of Natural Resources: Division of Water
2045 Morse Road, Building B
Columbus, OH 43229
(614) 265-6620
https://ohiodnr.gov/discover-and-learn/safety-conservation/about-ODNR/water-resources

76. http://codes.ohio.gov/orc/1501.30.

Tennessee

According to the Tennessee Farm Bureau Federation,

> Tennessee is considered a riparian law state. The doctrine of riparian water rights means landowners who border a waterway have equal rights to use the water passing through or by their property. This doctrine mainly applies to surface waters, however groundwater rights are a type of riparian right with modifications. Riparian law in the U.S. is considered common law developed from English common law. Many states have adopted statutes to modify the riparian doctrine. These states, including Tennessee, are considered "regulated" riparian states.
>
> Through the Tennessee Water Quality Control Act, the state claims to "own" and exercise public trust over all surface and groundwater within the borders of Tennessee for the purpose of keeping waters unpolluted so the water may be used by all Tennesseans. However, there is very little statutory or court case law surrounding the withdrawal of water. Therefore, it is assumed common law governs water withdrawals in Tennessee. Even though water is considered a public resource, the riparian landowner has a specific right to the use of the water. Because of so little background cases in water rights it is very difficult to prepare for future water conflicts both within Tennessee and with bordering states. Conflicts between riparian users of surface water in Tennessee fall under the "reasonable use doctrine." The concept of reasonable use in riparian rights law is that each riparian landowner has a right to a reasonable use of the water adjoining his land if it does not affect water available to lower riparian landowners. The term "reasonable" is usually limited to uses on or for the benefit of the riparian land. There is very little guidance from Tennessee courts regarding the factors that determine "reasonable." There are general factors used nationwide such as economic benefits, time when each use began, amounts of water needed by competing users and adverse effects on other users.
>
> Groundwater conflicts are decided based on "correlative rights doctrine." This means that all landowners over an aquifer must limit their withdrawals to a reasonable amount and must consider the needs of other landowners. It is assumed Tennessee uses this same doctrine; however, again, there are virtually no court cases to reference. Conflicts over groundwater are very difficult to settle under this doctrine. Since groundwater cannot be seen and total amounts in an aquifer are difficult to estimate, there is not an amount of water or a specified pressure level given to any one landowner. There must be unreasonable harm to other landowners or unreasonable uses before a landowner is liable for affects to other landowners.
>
> Riparian water rights are a type of property right. Even though riparian landowners do not own the water, they have a right to use the water as long as it is a reasonable use from streams and from aquifers. Just as in adverse possession in property rights, a landowner can establish over time an amount of water used and defend their right to that amount of water. Many states require reporting of

water withdrawals within the state to build a database over time. This information is used to protect state citizens in the event an adjoining state files a federal court case to withdraw water from another state. However, this also applies in water conflicts between landowners. If a landowner can document an amount of water needed over a period of time then it would be a defense if there ever was a conflict with another landowner.[77]

Regulatory Agency Responsible for Water Rights

Department of Environment and Conservation: Division of Water Resources
312 Rosa L. Parks Avenue
Nashville, TN 37243
(888) 891-TDEC (8332)
https://www.tn.gov/environment/program-areas/wr-water-resources-home.html

Kentucky

"The word 'stream' or 'watercourse' shall mean any river, creek, or channel, having well defined banks, in which water flows for substantial periods of the year to drain a given area, or any lake or other body of water in the Commonwealth; The word 'diffused surface water' shall mean that water which comes from falling rain or melting snow or ice, and which is diffused over the surface of the ground, or which temporarily flows vagrantly upon or over the surface of the ground as the natural elevations and depressions of the surface of the earth may guide it, until such water reaches a stream or watercourse; The word 'groundwater' or 'subterranean water' shall mean all water which fills the natural openings under the earth's surface including all underground watercourses, artesian basins, reservoirs, lakes, and other bodies of water below the earth's surface."[78]

Regulatory Agency Responsible for Water Rights

Department for Environmental Protection, Division of Water
300 Sower Blvd
Frankfort, KY 40601
https://eec.ky.gov/Environmental-Protection/Water/Pages/default.aspx

77. Tennessee Farm Bureau Federation paper.
78. http://www.lrc.ky.gov/KRS/151-00/CHAPTER.HTM.

Indiana

"'Water of the state,' means a lake, reservoir, marsh, waterway, or other water: under public ownership, jurisdiction, or lease; or that has been used by the public with the acquiescence of any or all riparian owners."[79]

Regulatory Agency Responsible for Water Rights

Indiana Department of Environmental Management
Indiana Government Center North
100 North Senate Avenue
Indianapolis, IN 46204–2251
(317) 232-8603
https://www.in.gov/idem

Iowa

"'Waters of the state' means all of the waters under the jurisdiction of the state."[80]

Regulatory Agency Responsible for Water Rights

Iowa Department of Natural Resources
Headquarters Wallace State Office Building
502 East 9th Street, 4th Floor
Des Moines, IA 50319–0034
(515) 725-8200
https://www.iowadnr.gov

Wisconsin

"'Waters of the state' includes those portions of Lake Michigan and Lake Superior within the boundaries of this state, and all lakes, bays, rivers, streams, springs, ponds, wells, impounding reservoirs, marshes, watercourses, drainage systems, and other surface water or groundwater, natural or artificial, public or private, within this state or its jurisdiction."[81]

---

79. http://www.in.gov/legislative/ic/code/title14/ar8/ch2.html.
80. http://search.legis.state.ia.us/NXT/gateway.dll/2007codesupp/1/27810?f=templates&fn=default.htm.
81. http://nxt.legis.state.wi.us/nxt/gateway.dll/?f=templates&fn=default.htm.

Regulatory Agency Responsible for Water Rights

Wisconsin Department of Natural Resources
101 S. Webster Street
P.O. Box 7921
Madison, WI 53707–7921
(888) 936-7463
https://dnr.wisconsin.gov

Michigan

"'Waters of the state' means any of the following: groundwater; lakes, including the Great Lakes bordering the state; rivers; streams; all other water courses and bodies of water within the jurisdiction of the state, including wetlands as defined by part 303 of the act, wetlands protection, being SS324.30301 to 324.30323 of the Michigan Compiled Laws."[82]

Regulatory Agency Responsible for Water Rights

Water Resources Division
Constitution Hall
525 West Allegan Street
P.O. Box 30473
Lansing, MI 48909–7973
(517) 284-6700
https://www.michigan.gov/egle/about/organization/water-resources

Minnesota

"'Waters of the state' means surface or underground waters, except surface waters that are not confined but are spread and diffused over the land. Waters of the state includes boundary and inland waters."[83]

Regulatory Agency Responsible for Water Rights

Department of Natural Resources
Minnesota does not provide a physical address for the main office.
(651) 296-6157 or (888) 646-6367
https://www.dnr.state.mn.us

---

82. http://www.state.mi.us/orr/emi/admincode.asp?AdminCode=Departm ent&Dpt=EQ&Level_1 =Water+Bureau.

83. https://www.revisor.leg.state.mn.us/statutes/?id=103G.005.

Missouri

"'Waters of the state' refers to all rivers, streams, lakes, and other bodies of surface and subsurface water lying within or forming a part of the boundaries of the state which are not entirely confined and located completely upon lands owned, leased, or otherwise controlled by a single person or by two or more persons jointly or as tenants in common and includes waters of the United States lying within the state."[84]

Regulatory Agency Responsible for Water Rights

Department of Natural Resources
1101 Riverside Drive
PO Box 176
Jefferson City, MO 65102–0176
(573) 751-3443
https://dnr.mo.gov/water

THE SOUTHWEST

Texas, Oklahoma, and Arkansas

Texas

The surface waters of Texas are owned by the state and defined as follows:

a. The water of the ordinary flow, underflow, and tides of every flowing river, natural stream, and lake, and of every bay or arm of the Gulf of Mexico, and the storm water, floodwater, and rainwater of every river, natural stream, canyon, ravine, depression, and watershed in the state is the property of the state.
b. Water imported from any source outside the boundaries of the state for use in the state and which is transported through the beds and banks of any navigable stream within the state or by utilizing any facilities owned or operated by the state is the property of the state.[85]

Groundwater is owned by the landowner above it.[86]

84. http://www.moga.missouri.gov/statutes/C600-699/6440000016.HTM.
85. Water Code § 11.021: State Water.
86. SB 332, Texas Legislature, 2015.

I grew up in Texas during the drought of the 1950s and have witnessed countless droughts and dry spells my entire life. I tolerated the recurring times of little or no moisture and suffered both financially and spiritually through them. I, like most Texans, accept drought as a way of life, a demon that cannot be exorcised from "our parts." Water rights are the most fundamental "stick" in the "bundle of sticks" that determine all the "property rights" and represent much of the market value of any real property in Texas. I learned from personal experience, supported by historical research, that the market value of land is diminished by limited access to water. The consequences of lower real estate values are far reaching for all of us since much of the funding for the public services we hold dear (e.g., public school education) are based upon ad valorem taxation of real property.

The law and history of Texas are rooted in its Spanish heritage, which began in San Antonio in 1718. San Antonio was settled by the Spanish because of its prolific and breathtaking springs; when taken as a whole, the springs could have been the largest in the world at that time. The abundance of fresh water in San Antonio did not in itself ensure the establishment of a viable and lasting community; expertise in sharing and managing the water and the Spanish legal concept that water was to be used in common by all settlers were of equal importance. The Spanish created the fifty-mile acequia system in San Antonio not only for irrigation of crops but also to distribute the water for domestic use in the settlement; it was the first publicly owned and managed municipal water system built in North America. Spanish rules and management practices also made up the first water conservation program in North America. As San Antonio moved from Spanish control to Anglo control after 1836, the legal characteristics of water ownership changed from a common public resource to a privately owned commodity delivered to the consumer's doorstep and sold only to those who could afford it. Yet much of Spanish water law has survived in Texas water law. Spanish water law and practices of sharing and management indeed comprise the ultimate piers of the foundation of existing Texas water law.

The basic concept of water rights under English common law differs from the civil law of Spain and the Republic of Mexico. Water rights under English common law were generally riparian in nature, or based on land adjacent to water. Water rights under the Spanish and Mexican civil law were generally appropriative, or based on a grant or license from a sovereign. Since the early 1800s, some western state legislatures and courts have struggled with the conflict between the two legal systems over the rights to water of riparian lands. Texas struggled with this dual system until the Water Rights Adjudication Act of 1967.

The following are key terms important to understand as a prelude to a study of water right concepts in Texas:

- Acre-foot: volume of water needed to cover one acre to a depth of one foot. Each acre-foot = 325,851 gallons; each inch of rain per acre = 27,154 gallons.[87]
- Appropriative right: the right to impound, divert, store, take, or use a specific amount of state water acquired by law.
- Appropriator: person making beneficial lawful use under the statutes.
- Certificate of adjudication: evidence of surface water right pursuant to the Water Rights Adjudication Act of 1967.
- Conjunctive: joined together; combined (like all the geological containers of water).
- Correlative rights: rights that are coequal, relate to one another, so that one owner cannot take more than their share.
- Prior appropriation: the general concept of "first in time = first in right."
- Riparian: of or relating to or living or located on the bank of a watercourse (as a river or stream) or sometimes a lake; one that lives or has property on the bank of a river.
- Riparian rights: the right of one owning riparian land to have access to and use of the shore and water; rights to normal flow.

The riparian right in Texas is the right of a landowner appurtenant to a watercourse to access and use the shore and the normal flow of the water in the watercourse, or the "run of the river," as it is also known. This right is to *use* the water, not to own the water. This kind of right is known as a "usufruct," the right to use but not to own. Surface water rights in Texas are usufruct rights under Spanish law and Texas law. Riparian rights in Texas were partly eliminated by the Water Rights Adjudication Act of 1967; however, case law is reasonably clear that not all riparian rights were eliminated through the act. Domestic and livestock (D&L) riparian rights were excluded from the act, so those riparian rights still remain with protections from impairment—thus they have superior status in a river basin. The D&L right cannot be severed from the land and sold—it remains with the land. D&L riparian diversions are not limited to two hundred acre-feet per year; they are just limited to beneficial use for domestic and livestock purposes as those terms have been defined in the rules of the Texas Commission on Environmental Quality (TCEQ). In Texas, the TCEQ allows diversions or permit-exempted impoundments up to two hundred acre-feet per year.[88]

87. This applies to the entire earth.
88. See TCEQ rule 297.21.

Three Geological Containers and the Hydrologic Cycle

Ownership of Texas water is tied to three geological containers:

1. Natural surface water. Under the Texas Water Code, all natural surface water found in the watercourses is owned by the state and is held in trust for the people. Surface water is regulated by the Texas Commission on Environmental Quality. It includes the ordinary flow, underflow, and tides of every flowing natural watercourse (has a definite bed and banks) in the state. Storm water and floodwater found in natural lakes, rivers, and streams is also state water, as is water in springs that form the headwaters of natural streams. Surface water is allocated to the most senior rights during scarcity (i.e., if downstream irrigators with rights to use water have older rights than upstream users, then they have first use of the water and vice versa).

A "watercourse" is defined in Title 30 Texas Administrative Code (30 TAC) § 291.7(61) as "a definite channel of a stream in which water flows within a defined bed and banks, originating from a definite source or sources. (The water may flow continuously or intermittently, and if the latter, with some degree of regularity, depending on the characteristics of the sources)."

The courts have described watercourses as having

- a defined bed and banks,
- a current of water, and
- a permanent source of supply.

In Texas, the ordinary flow, underflow, and tides of every flowing river, natural stream, and lake, and of every bay or arm of the Gulf of Mexico, and the storm water, floodwater, and rainwater of every river, natural stream, canyon, ravine, depression, and watershed in the state is the property of the state. Before any diversion or impoundment, advise your client to hire an attorney and to contact the TCEQ before taking any action concerning natural surface water just to be sure the action is within the regulations.

2. Diffused surface water. Water that does not flow in a defined watercourse but flows across the surface of the land in a variant and without a pattern is termed diffused surface water. Generally, this is rain runoff, although water left in upland areas after a flood recedes may also be diffused surface water. Texas courts have ruled that diffused surface water belongs to the landowner until it enters a natural watercourse—then it becomes water owned by the state. Tanks and springs that do not create streams are owned by the landowner.

As the water molecule progresses along its 24/7/365 effort to reach sea level, in Texas, this molecule changes its ownership often from diffused surface water (rain runoff) that is owned by the landowner to surface water that is owned by the state to groundwater that is owned by the landowner. The geological containers impact one another often and many times as water seeks sea level. Diffused surface water feeds both surface water (watercourses) and groundwater, groundwater feeds surface water, and surface water feeds groundwater, conjunctively. A key challenge that Senator Charles Perry asked the Senate Natural Resources Committee to consider in 2016 in their interim work was how to modify our water policies to reflect the conjunctive relationship of the geological containers. No change in policy, as he requested, was offered by the committee or in the past legislative session.

3. Groundwater. This is the water that is beneath the land surface and fills the pore spaces of rock and soil material and that supplies wells and springs. This water is owned "in situ," or in place by the landowner. The preferred method of groundwater management according to the Texas Legislature is by groundwater conservation districts. There is a legal assumption in Texas law that all groundwater is considered to be percolating.

Further Details about Water Rights in Texas

Texas law recognizes three general classifications of water—surface water, groundwater, and diffused surface water. Because the hydrologic cycle ties all three resources together, the availability and use of one resource can have a measurable effect on the availability and use of another. The law, however, treats each as legally distinct resources with different governing principles. These distinctions are driven by the physical place where the resource is located. So recognizing where the water is found is a necessary first step to understanding what right a landowner has to the water—or if the landowner has any rights to the water at all.

Surface Water

Surface water is water that flows through, or is impounded in, a watercourse. Being located in a watercourse is an important consideration, because where the water is found determines whether the water is surface water or diffused surface water. The law has developed a broad definition of what constitutes a watercourse, but it can be best understood to be any draw, creek, stream, or river, including lakes and ponds that dam up flow in a watercourse. Even typically dry draws or wet weather streams that carry water only when it rains can be considered watercourses.

Because surface water is owned by the people of Texas and held in trust by the state, the state only authorizes rights to use surface water. Surface water rights do not convey ownership of the water itself.

Statutory Rights

Surface water rights fall into two general categories. Each has its own unique limits and obligations to other water right owners. One type of right is created by statute—a creature of the Texas Legislature. The other type of right is created by common law, which is law created by the courts. For well over one hundred years, Texas statutes have recognized some type of right to divert or impound, and beneficially use, surface water. Today, most of these statutory water rights exist as a certificate of adjudication or a water use permit. The Texas Commission on Environmental Quality issues, oversees, and enforces permitted water rights. Because permitted rights are reflected by tangible documents (most often certificates of adjudication or water use permits), these types of rights are sometimes referred to as "paper rights." They reflect the state's parameters of its permission to use state-owned water under specific conditions.

Permitted water rights identify the owner of the right, the river basin, and the specific watercourse where the diversion (pumping from the river) or impoundment is authorized, and the specific location within which the owner is authorized to use the diverted water. Additionally, these rights identify

Figure A.3. Horsehead Crossing is one of the most significant historical fords in Texas. The Pecos River is a transboundary river shared by Texas and New Mexico; there have been decades of off-and-on litigation over the shared water.

several conditions that the owner must follow, including the maximum volumes of water that can be diverted in a year, the specific diversion point, the maximum rate the water can be diverted at, the purpose the diverted water can be used for, and other limitations.

Importantly, the permitted right will include a priority date. This date reflects where the owner stands in line for water in the river system during times when the river cannot supply enough water to satisfy every paper right in the basin. The earlier in time the priority date, the further toward the front of the line the owner stands during times of limited flows. This concept is recognized as water right priority, and it's described in terms of water right seniority. A water right with a priority date of October 29, 1975, is senior to a water right with a priority date of October 29, 1985. But both water rights are junior to a right with a priority date of October 29, 1957. The older—or more senior—a water right is in priority, the better the chances are that the right can be fully satisfied during times of limited flows in the river basin.

Permit Exceptions and Exemptions

Unless otherwise expressly provided for by law, no person may impound or divert state water without first having obtained a permit from the Texas Commission on Environmental Quality. However, there are several important exemptions from surface water rights permitting requirements in Chapter 11 of the Texas Water Code—the chapter of the Water Code that governs the appropriation of surface water in Texas—and one important exception to Water Code regulation.

Impoundments for Domestic and Livestock Use Exemption

A landowner may construct a dam or reservoir on his or her own property without a paper right for domestic and livestock use. To qualify for this permitting exemption, the impoundment cannot store more than two hundred acre-feet. A landowner can still take advantage of this permitting exemption, even if his or her impoundment captures more than two hundred acre-feet of water at any given time, as long as the average volumes impounded in the reservoir over the course of a year do not exceed the two hundred acre-feet threshold. The impoundment must be located wholly within the landowner's own property and may be placed adjacent to a stream bed, on a contiguous piece of property through which the supplying stream runs, or on-channel.

The water use restriction imposed by the legislature for this exemption is equally as important as the reservoir size restriction. Water impounded by or diverted from the reservoir must be used exclusively for domestic and livestock purposes. The TCEQ defines "domestic use" to mean individual or household use to support domestic activity. Water for drinking, washing, or culinary purposes or for irrigation of lawns or a family garden or orchard all qualify as domestic uses. Similarly, water used to water domestic animals and for water recreation, including aquatic and wildlife enjoyment, qualify. Domestic use does not include water used to support activities that produce sold or bartered-for products. Livestock use is defined to mean the use of water for the open-range watering of livestock, exotic livestock, game animals, or fur-bearing animals.

The use of the reservoir for commercial operations could waive the exemption and require the landowner to apply to the TCEQ for a paper water right. The use of an exempt reservoir by free-ranging game and fur-bearing animals that are hunted or trapped by persons paying the landowner compensation for the ability to hunt or trap the animals is not considered a commercial operation. Nor is the use of the reservoir to support cow-calf grazing operations.

It is important to recognize that this exemption only applies to a dam constructed on a non-navigable stream. Streams are considered navigable when they maintain an average width of thirty feet or greater, measured from the mouth up. Measurements are calculated from the foot of the banks at the top of water in its ordinary state. Therefore, even if a stream bed is non-navigable as a matter of fact (e.g., without flow), it could still be a statutorily navigable stream.

Impoundments for Fish and Wildlife Management Exemption

Under the fish and wildlife management exemption, a landowner may construct a dam or impoundment on his or her property with a normal storage of no more than two hundred acre-feet of state water. Normal storage is the amount of water the reservoir may hold before water is released uncontrolled through a spillway or into a standpipe. The impounded water must be used only for wildlife management purposes or for fish management purposes. "Wildlife management" under this exemption is tied to the definition of the same term in the Texas Tax Code. Fish management includes fishing but does not include fish farming. The impoundment must be on qualified open-space land. In addition, a reservoir operating under this exemption cannot be used for industrial facilities, industrial parks, aquaculture facilities, fish farming facilities, or housing developments.

Riparian Water Rights Permitting Exception

Riparian rights are not paper rights; nor do they exist in laws passed by the legislature. They are rights that are incident to ownership of land that fronts a stream, creek, or river. A riparian right does not entitle the owner to a specific volume of water. Instead, riparian water rights owners may only divert a "reasonable" amount of water. Importantly, a riparian diverter may only divert water for domestic and livestock watering purposes, and the diversion must be made by pumping or gravity flow. Riparian rights do not entitle a landowner to impound water in a watercourse.

Not all landowners with river frontage have riparian rights. The state of Texas only recognizes riparian rights for lands patented on or before July 1, 1895. In other words, properties with patents granted after this date do not have riparian rights to water.

In addition, riparian rights entitle a landowner to divert only what is considered to be the "normal flow" of the watercourse. A river's normal flow is a difficult one to measure for most landowners. But the distinction is an important one with respect to reservoirs. With rare exceptions, lakeside property owners do not have riparian rights to water in the reservoir. Stored water is lawfully possessed by the owner of the reservoir water right. Accordingly, landowners should be aware that efforts to divert from a lake could subject the landowner to enforcement actions by the TCEQ or the reservoir owner.

Because riparian rights predated the state's statutory permitting system, riparian rights are superior to all other water rights in the basin. A riparian right owner therefore has a right to water in the watercourse that is superior to even the most senior permitted right in the basin.

Enforcing Water Right Priority

When flows in a river system are plentiful, there can sometimes be more than enough water in a river system to satisfy all rights—permitted and riparian—in the basin. Problems of water rights management become challenging during times of low flows, however. In most parts of the state, water right priority is managed by the honor system. Unless compelled by the state to cease or curb diversions, a water rights owner is left to his or her own devices to determine whether their diversions are negatively affecting the ability of a downstream senior or superior water right owner to lawfully access water. The TCEQ will become actively involved in water rights management when a water right owner initiates a formal priority enforcement process known as a "priority call." These calls are in essence requests by water rights owners to the TCEQ for the agency to force owners of rights with junior priority to stop diversions, allowing for more flows downstream.

In some parts of the state, however, water rights are overseen by a more structured management and enforcement system called watermasters. Each watermaster program is a division of the TCEQ. Instead of relying on the honor system to manage water right priority, however, a watermaster actively monitors diversion activities throughout their jurisdiction. Permitted water rights owners in a watermaster area must report their intent to divert to the watermaster before any diversions can be made. The watermaster then determines whether that particular water right owner can make all or part of the requested diversion without interfering with the planned or current diversions by any senior water rights owner.

Groundwater Rights

Surface water rights and groundwater rights in Texas are recognized and framed by two distinct areas of law. In 1904, the Supreme Court of Texas applied English common law to define the nature of groundwater rights in Texas. Since then, the nature, scope, and lawful ability to regulate groundwater production in Texas have been the subject of debate and controversy. With a recent clarification from the Supreme Court, the picture of groundwater rights has become less clouded—but it remains far from clear today.

Ownership

The rule of capture and the doctrine of absolute ownership together form the bedrock of groundwater rights in Texas. The rule of capture[89] is a rule of nonliability. Under the rule, a landowner can produce groundwater captured from beneath the surface of the producer's property without risking liability to his or her neighbor for drainage. There are a few exceptions to this liability protection. The doctrine of absolute ownership, on the other hand, is a doctrine of groundwater ownership. Under the doctrine of absolute ownership, a landowner owns not only the surface but everything above the surface of the property and everything below the surface of the property. The doctrine of absolute ownership therefore defines groundwater rights ownership. That is, a landowner owns the water found beneath his or her property. Courts have recognized that absolute ownership and the rule of capture work hand in hand. When both concepts are pieced together, a landowner owns the groundwater beneath his land, and when producing it to the surface, that landowner is protected from liability for draining the groundwater from below his neighbor's property. Be mindful that this structure works both ways. The neighbor owns the groundwater beneath his property under the doctrine of absolute ownership, and the rule of capture protects the neighbor from liability for water he drains from beneath the property of an adjoining landowner.

---

89. The rule of capture in Texas was established from the ruling in *Houston & Texas Central Railroad Company v. W. A. East*, 98 Texas Reports, 146 (June 13, 1904). I wrote an award-winning article about this significant case in Texas water policy. From the editor of the *East Texas Historical Journal*, "Charles—I am pleased to inform you that your article 'The History of W.A. East v. Houston and Texas Central Railway . . . ' has been chosen as the Association's 2013 Chamberlain Award winner, which honors the 'Best Article in the ETHJ' for the previous calendar year. I think that it is a very worthy choice and I congratulate you."

Regulatory Authority

In most parts of the state, groundwater production and use is regulated by groundwater conservation districts (GCDs). These are created by the Texas Legislature to preserve, conserve, and enhance groundwater resources within their boundaries while at the same time protecting groundwater rights. The boundaries of most GCDs track county lines. Some GCDs encompass multiple counties, while others are composed of just one county, or even just portions of property within counties. GCDs are composed of boards of directors who hire and oversee the actions of staff members—usually with a general manager and supporting staff.

GCD board selection takes a variety of different forms, depending on the structure of the specific district at issue. Some boards, as an example, are elected by the voters within their respective jurisdictions. In other instances, board members are chosen by county courts. Yet even other boards are composed of selections made by regulated entities and interest groups within the district. GCDs are typically funded through a property tax or through fees based on permitted or actual groundwater production. GCDs are political subdivisions of the state of Texas and are subject to the Texas Open Meetings Act and the Texas Public Information Act, as well as several other statutory requirements imposed on political subdivisions.

The Texas Constitution gives the legislature the ability to create and direct GCDs. Because GCDs exist as individual political units with their own rule-making power, they are authorized to—and typically do—create rules that are unique to rules of other GCDs. While most districts are required to adhere to general requirements imposed by the Texas Legislature, GCDs have some latitude in how they approach and craft their own rules. A requirement, or absence of a requirement, in one GCD is no guarantee that the same is true in another.

Common GCD-Regulated Issues

A landowner needs to be aware of a host of issues when producing groundwater, or even just owning a well, within a GCD. Always check the appropriate rules and seek legal counsel when unsure of any aspect of GCD oversight or regulation. This discussion is by no means a comprehensive discussion of all issues a landowner should be mindful of when considering groundwater ownership, production, and use. There are, however, several recurring practical issues that most landowners will face when producing and using groundwater within a GCD.

Registration

Many landowners confuse well registration with groundwater production permitting (discussed below). GCDs typically require that each groundwater well within their boundaries be registered with the district. Some districts require all groundwater wells be registered, whereas others require registration only of wells drilled or completed after the district was created. Others require registration of all wells except those that are exempted from permitting requirements (discussed below). The information required by a GCD can vary as well, but most require at least a well location, pump size, well depth, and completion date.

A well registration does not itself authorize or restrict groundwater production from a well (although production from unregistered wells in many GCDs is illegal under their rules). The registration puts the well on the district's "radar screen" for management and enforcement purposes.

Spacing

GCDs often develop and enforce well spacing requirements. These location restrictions are typically designed to protect groundwater quality, reduce interference between wells, and minimize the effect of drainage on adjoining landowners. Spacing requirements take a variety of forms. For example, some requirements are based simply on the distance between wellheads. Others are based on the productive capacity of the well. Others may be based on a combination of factors.

Where a GCD does not develop its own spacing requirements, the requirements imposed by the Texas Department of Licensing and Regulation (TDLR) usually apply. TDLR imposes minimum spacing requirements from property lines and from septic systems.

Permitting and Permitting Exemptions

Within most GCDs, groundwater production is subject to permitting requirements created by districts through their rulemaking efforts. Permitting approaches take a variety of forms across the state, depending on the individual geologic, political, and practical circumstances and conditions of each. However, most GCD permitting falls into one of a handful of basic approaches—permits based on historic use, permits based on water availability, and permits based on an acre-foot of water (or multiple) per surface acre.

Just as with surface water rights permitting, there are permitting exemptions for groundwater as well. Most GCDs are required to exempt domestic, livestock watering, and poultry watering wells from permitting requirements. To qualify, the wells must be located on a tract of land larger than ten acres and drilled, completed, and equipped to produce no more than twenty-five thousand gallons of groundwater per day. Districts have discretion on how they define domestic use, livestock watering, and poultry watering, so districts across the state use a variety of definitions. These requirements are the minimum requirements districts must recognize. However, many GCDs have created more generous permitting exemptions. The legislature has also created other permitting exemptions relating to surface mining and hydrocarbon exploration and production, which are beyond the scope of this discussion.

Metering and Reporting

Many GCDs impose well metering and production reporting requirements. These requirements are common in districts that assess fees for groundwater production. Exempt wells are typically exempt from metering requirements as well. Some districts offer alternatives to metering—for example, allowing a nonexempt well owner to calculate production based on electricity use records. Reporting requirements generally impose an obligation to take meter readings at some point or multiple points throughout the year—often monthly—and submit a report to the district reflecting groundwater production for the cycle based on those meter readings. GCDs sometimes dedicate staff to determining whether their metering requirements are being met and whether the readings are being reported accurately.

Agencies Responsible for Water Rights

Surface Water

Texas Commission on Environmental Quality
12100 Park 35 Circle
Austin, TX 78753
https://www.tceq.texas.gov

Groundwater

Texas Alliance of Groundwater Districts
www.texasgroundwater.org

The Texas Alliance of Groundwater Districts is the trade association of GCDs, although not all of Texas has elected to be included in groundwater regulation. The local GCD can also be found on the TCEQ website.

Arkansas

"'Waters of the state' means all streams, lakes, marshes, ponds, watercourses, waterways, wells, springs, irrigation systems, drainage systems, and all other bodies or accumulations of water, surface and underground, natural or artificial, public or private, which are contained within, flow through, or border upon this state or any portion of the state."[90]

Agency Responsible for Water Rights

Arkansas Department of Agriculture: Department of Natural Resources
10421 W. Markham Street
Little Rock, AR 72205
(501) 682-1611
https://www.agriculture.arkansas.gov/natural-resources

State of Arkansas Energy and Environment, Environmental Quality: https://www.adeq.state.ar.us

Oklahoma

"'Waters of the state' means all streams, lakes, ponds, marshes, watercourses, waterways, wells, springs, irrigation systems, drainage systems, storm sewers, and all other bodies or accumulations of water, surface and underground, natural or artificial, public or private, which are contained within, flow through, or border upon this state or any portion thereof, and shall include under all circumstances the waters of the United States which are contained within the boundaries of, flow through or border upon this state or any portion thereof. Provided, waste treatment systems, including treatment ponds or lagoons designed to meet federal and state requirements other than cooling ponds as defined in the Clean Water Act or rules promulgated thereto and prior converted cropland are not waters of the state."[91]

Agency Responsible for Water Rights

Oklahoma Water Resources Board[92]
3800 North Classen Boulevard
Oklahoma City, OK 73118

---

90. http://www.arkleg.state.ar.us/NXT/gateway.dll?f=templates&fn=defa ult.htm&vid=blr:code.
91. https://oksenate.gov/sites/default/files/2019-12/os82.pdf.
92. "Waters of the state" from Oklahoma Environmental Quality Code, Title 27A, Oklahoma Statutes, Section 1-1-201 (20).

(405) 530-8800
https://www.owrb.ok.gov

THE WEST

California, Montana, Colorado, Kansas, Arizona, Nebraska, Nevada, North Dakota, South Dakota, New Mexico, Utah, Alaska, Hawaii, and Wyoming

A Brief Introduction to the West

"The story of the West in water rights is the story of surface water diversion and groundwater development. Without irrigation created by diversion dams and canals, this region of the United States would not enjoy agribusiness as a key industry. Without diversion dams, this region would be all but unlivable for human beings most of the year. Even for non-irrigation use, the region generally lives on two sources of water, surface water held in reservoirs and groundwater."[93]

As most of this region was originally claimed as a part of the Spanish colonial empire in North America, much of the West's water rights and laws, at one time, stemmed from Spanish water law concepts. In lieu of riparian rights to surface water, the West's water policies are mostly based on appropriative rights to surface water allocated according to "first in time is first in right," or what is known as the prior appropriative system. In some western states, groundwater is owned by the surface landowner and regulated loosely if at all. The ownership and use of diffused surface water differ from state to state in the West. A background discussion of the West's water rights must begin with a brief history of irrigation.

Since some of the states in the West officially recognized their mixed Spanish/Anglo heritage, the confusion and frustration over irrigation water and riparian rights to use it was a prolific issue in water rights disputes. In England and on the East Coast of the United States, home to naturally well-watered lands with ample rainfall, riparian rights are rarely controversial; there is generally plenty of water for everyone. This is not true in the arid West; riparian rights of irrigation create serious water shortages during the recurring and, at times, lengthy periods of drought. When water is ample, few disputes arise, but when it becomes scarce due to drought or excessive use by one party over another, conflict explodes.

93. Charles R. Porter Jr., *The World of the American West* (Milton Park, UK: Routledge, Taylor & Francis, 2011), chap. 11.

The western states adopted English common law in which "riparians," or those who owned land adjacent to water, had the right to take the water from flowing streams for irrigation based solely upon their adjacency to it. Under Spanish and Republic of Mexico law, however, water could not be taken from a river or stream for irrigation without an explicit grant from the sovereign; adjacency to the stream or being riparian in the Spanish West did not guarantee a water right for irrigation. The Spanish and Mexican system was an appropriative system, and many of the courts in the West have also relied upon the customary practices and application of Spanish laws to support their rulings and set legal precedents from time to time on water issues.

The most heated and challenging disputes have always been over irrigation use, whether from surface water or groundwater. Why? Irrigation of land requires huge amounts of water; its use is considered artificial. Domestic use for households and watering livestock is considered natural. Until the late nineteenth century, most irrigation water came from rivers and streams. By the end of the first decade of the twentieth century, claims to surface water exceeded the amount of water that flowed in most of the rivers of the western United States. With late-nineteenth-century technology, which made deep drilling and large pumping equipment available across the West, irrigation using groundwater became increasingly popular. For example, irrigation today accounts for almost two-thirds of all groundwater use in Texas; other states similarly use high quantities of groundwater for irrigation purposes. Groundwater irrigation puts pressure on aquifers and can dry up springs and the streams flowing from them all around the West during times of drought.

Irrigation is critical to the success of agriculture, which is especially true in the western United States. Known collectively as "the West," the area is composed of the states of Arizona, California, Colorado, Idaho, Kansas, Montana, Nebraska, Nevada, New Mexico, North Dakota, Oklahoma, South Dakota, Texas, Utah, Washington, and Wyoming. Most of the West is arid, short of reliable rainfall, and prone to drought at times. Settlers from the generally moist East were confronted with a very different climate upon crossing the ninety-eighth meridian. Not all areas of the West suffer from a lack of rainfall; this varies from state to state, and in some areas of some states it can be plentiful. However, for most of the West, agriculture, industry, and communities exist on water drawn from the diversion of streams and rivers through irrigation canals, from water wells, or from rainfall and flood waters stored in reservoirs.

Agriculture is successful not only when rainfall is plentiful but when the soil moisture is adequate to support the particular crop being grown. The total amount of rainfall is not always a reliable indicator of the success of any growing season. Ask most professional farmers about the weather in their area, and typically the reference will be to levels of "moisture" instead of inches of “rain.” “Moisture” factors into the needs of the specific crops and grasses they depend on in their area. For example, all farmers know that too much rain at the wrong time can be as destructive to agriculture as too little rain. When their response to questions about the weather is “we have had good moisture this year,” they really mean they have had adequate rainfall to make their crops and grasses grow to an economically successful harvest. In the West, many years go by when moisture is simply not available or reliable for successful farming. Irrigation is essential to the survival of agribusiness in the West.

The history of irrigation in the western United States can be divided into three distinct periods, the era prior to Spanish contact or generally prior to 1540; the era under the claim of Spain and Mexico from 1540 to 1848; and the period after Texas independence and the Treaty of Guadalupe-Hidalgo of 1848. The Spanish system of water rights, laws, and irrigation dominated the West for three centuries, twice as long as the current “Anglo” system. The Spanish system continues to influence the region’s laws, especially those pertaining to water.

The problem facing the settlers of the West was to apply a limited quantity of available water to an unlimited quantity of available lands in the hands of a constantly increasing number of people to get the maximum of benefit and good to the maximum of people, the community as a whole.

Gold was discovered in California in 1848, drawing thousands of new immigrants virtually overnight. Gold and silver were also discovered in the mountains of Colorado, which led to the new city of Denver exploding into existence in the same manner. Silver was discovered in Arizona. The large influx of the miners mostly came from the East Coast of the United States, where they understood water rights to be of a riparian nature. Water was desperately needed for these early mining ventures, and riparian concepts were inappropriate for their work. According to Hildebrand,

> Water was necessary to mining and was taken from streams on public lands, often at great expense and over long distances. It became the custom to recognize that he who first diverted the water from a stream was first in right as to so much water as he put to beneficial use. The federal government was the only riparian owner, and its silence was regarded by the settlers as acquiescence to the custom.

The activity of miners was considered to be beneficial use, and early on their rights were given priority across the West. The early California miners, called “Forty-Niners,” are given credit for introducing the concept of prior appropriation to the West; miners in the states of Colorado and Wyoming may also have a claim to being the first to introduce the doctrine of prior appropriation in the West. The early Mormons in Utah also were practitioners of an appropriative doctrine.

Congress officially passed into law the doctrine of prior appropriation of water on federal land in the Mining Act of 1866, which read in part, "By priority of possession, rights to use of water for mining, agricultural, manufacturing, or other purposes, have vested and accrued." On July 9, 1870, Congress strengthened prior appropriation on federal lands with "all patents granted, or pre-emption or homesteads allowed, shall be subject to any vested and accrued water-rights, or rights to ditches and reservoirs used in connection with such water-rights, as may have been acquired under or recognized by the preceding section."

Water law scholar Donald J. Pisani opined about prior appropriation, "The greatest legal innovation in the history of the arid west was the doctrine of prior appropriation, which made water as much of a commodity as land, minerals, trees, crops and livestock. . . . The California mining industry, and specifically its enormous need for capital, transformed water into a species of private property." Miners needed water and lots of it. By the late 1880s the use of surface water had significantly declined, but the concept of prior appropriation stayed across the West as the dominant legal idea in water rights.

Mining brought innovative water laws, but mining activities had unintended consequences. According to western legal scholar Gordon Morris Bakken,

> Water and gold mining were joined when the first pan filled with pay dirt and water left a trace of color in the pan. Water was flumed to gravel and processed more dirt until 1853 when the invention of the penstock concentrated water at high pressure. From there American invention abounded until rivers of water were run through hoses, nozzled at even higher pressure into mountains of gravel, and sluiced away downstream leaving more gold. . . . Downstream riparians saw something else. Polluted water, dead cattle, destroyed pastures, and buried private property caught their eye. Lawsuits resulted, and mining engineers went to work gathering evidence.

Large portions of hills and mountains were simply washed away, leaving death and destruction behind. Edward E. Mattison is given credit for inventing "modern" hydraulic mining in 1853. Describing the effectiveness of the technique, Pisani comments, "The toughest clay dissolves like wax, this disintegrating much fine gold, a greater part of which has hitherto been lost. . . . The reduction of manual labor at least two-thirds."

The typical cycle of business efficiencies in America was in place in early hydraulic mining ventures in the West. Capital investment demanded profits, which resulted in increasing returns on investment. Profit and returns only increase when more revenue flows into a business at less cost. "Modern" hydraulic mining, while the ultimate in destructiveness to the environment, nonetheless was the inevitable step in early-stage mining in the West. As capital investments increased, the providers of the capital required protection for their most important raw material used to pull the gold from the dirt: water. The doctrine of prior appropriation was the logical way for the investment community to best guarantee their efforts could continue at the cheapest cost and give their existing operations an edge over the competition. Competitors were of little consequence if they were unable to obtain access to water for their hoses.

> The prior appropriation doctrine had overall advantages according to Pisani:
>
> First, no value judgments had to be made about how or where the water was used. As long as the water was claimed for a "beneficial use," no one could overturn the original right—even if a subsequent claimant needed the water more or promised greater wealth with it. Prior appropriation offered equal access to wealth, if not equal opportunity; it was consistent with American ideas about political liberty. . . . It did not require an expensive bureaucracy to administer or maintain, a bureaucracy whose cost would have been prohibitive in frontier California. . . . Finally, it was consistent with the cherished American ideal that individuals, not society, should control their destiny. The welfare of the community became the product of a multitude of discrete decisions made in the marketplace, with no sense of planning and little of collective responsibility.

Prior appropriation has been followed on public and private lands in Texas, Arizona, Colorado, Utah, Idaho, Nevada, New Mexico, and Wyoming. According to Hildebrand, in its most basic form, "[Prior appropriation] rests upon the general proposition that he who is first in time is first in right." Pisani summed up the importance of prior appropriation in the West: "Without prior appropriation, the capital needed to transform the West into a region of dams, and canals could not have been raised, and it is easy to forget that private capital reclaimed most of the West's irrigated land."

However, over the years some legal scholars have opined that the freedom of the appropriator has decreased, and the control of state authorities who issue licenses for diversion of water from the stream or river has increased to the point that the doctrine of prior appropriation has been all but effectively abandoned. According to A. A. White and Will Wilson, "The tendency toward public supervision is manifest in the other arid States, and it seems only a question of time when the doctrine of appropriation will give way to complete public supervision." Their 1955 comments have proven to be correct.

Other states in the West regulate groundwater in the same manner in which they regulate surface water and closely manage it. For example, in 1931, New Mexico enacted its Ground Water Code. The state engineer was given jurisdiction over groundwater in the ground water basins, which were declared at varying dates throughout the state. The code requires a permit for any appropriation of groundwater in the declared basins.

One of the weaknesses that must be addressed in the West is development of a coordinated groundwater policy not only between the states but also with Mexico. The Eighth Report of the Good Neighbor Environmental Board reported, "Knowledge about groundwater resources in the border region lags far behind what is known about surface waters. And yet, in the meantime, there are sizable areas throughout the arid southwest where groundwater is being withdrawn at rates which some consider alarming." The most pressing future issue of irrigation will revolve around groundwater, especially from aquifers that travel under several states and nations.

How the States and Territories Addressed Water Issues

As the western states came into the Union, they convened constitutional conventions. Water rights, rules about allocation, and resulting management practices were in the forefront of their fundamental policy statements. The key water policy chosen by most of the state constitutional conventions in the West was to reward those who put water to "beneficial use."

For example, New Mexico's constitution was drafted in 1910. Article XVI, paragraph 1 reads in part, "All existing rights to the use of any waters in the state for any useful or beneficial purpose are hereby recognized and confirmed." Note the use of the words "any waters," which include all waters, surface and groundwater. According to Charles T. Dumars, "The New Mexico Constitution makes no mention of groundwater. While at first this appears to be an oversight, in fact the drafters may have had more wisdom than we understood. Water is water. . . . Groundwater is a reserve source of surface water encased in soils and protected from air and wind-born contaminants."

Article XVI, paragraph 2 of the New Mexico Constitution states that water rights available to the public are "subject to [prior] appropriation for beneficial use, in accordance with the laws of the state. Priority of appropriation shall give the better right. . . . [B]eneficial use shall be the basis, the measure, and the limit of the right to use the water."

In 1932 the New Mexico Supreme Court made clear the public ownership of water in their state with this statement: "We already had a policy, also time-honored, as to waters. We had nationalized them. Not as a source of public revenue, as minerals are retained for royalties; but as an elemental necessity, like air, which must not be allowed to fall under private control."

Nevada has similar water laws to New Mexico. Nevada is the driest state in the nation with average precipitation of only nine inches; some parts of the state receive four inches or even less. According to Sylvia Harrison, "The scarcity of Nevada's water is the defining circumstance of its water laws."

Nevada's water laws are based upon the principle of prior appropriation. The second decision of the Nevada Supreme Court found in part that "where the right to the use of running water is based upon appropriation and not upon ownership of the soil, the first appropriator has the superior right as against subsequent appropriators." In 1913, Nevada passed the Water Law, which made clear that all water "within the boundaries of the state, whether above or beneath the surface of the ground, belongs to the public." Section 2 provided, "Subject to existing rights, all water may be appropriated for beneficial use as provided in this chapter and not otherwise." Nevada and New Mexico are quite similar, as are the laws of the other western states, except the usual outlier, Texas.

Territorial and state courts gradually assumed the brunt of resolving water right disputes, not their legislatures. As states entered the union, the rules and laws were applied based upon the English common law of the United States. Yet in states such as Texas, which adopted common law but honored Spanish and Mexican water rights, dual systems of riparian rights and appropriative rights were supported by many of the courts, resulting in confusion and frustration. Determining jurisdiction between courts in the individual states started an expensive nightmare for many litigants.

No matter where the disputes occurred, water by its nature, coupled with the prior appropriative doctrine, created hard-to-solve procedural problems in the courts. For example, does a junior appropriator who has a claim of injury against a senior appropriator need to bring in other senior appropriators as defendants? Who is the actual damaging party to the junior appropriator? In what county does the venue lie? Does a single county judge have jurisdiction to adjudicate water rights of parties in the many counties through which the water runs? Often the private litigant could find no justice simply because he or she could not afford the process and fees. Those with money could at times better control the disputes from the first filing due their influence in the procedural processes. These procedural problems have not been fully resolved even in today's state court systems. Assuring these basic problems will continue, the state legislatures still prefer that the courts address water issues. Partly because of their ignorance of the complicated laws pertaining to water and partly because they simply do not have the political will and courage to address long-term solutions, the legislatures are as much to blame for water rights disputes as are the litigants.

The most successful efforts to expand irrigation systems came from the creation of irrigation districts with the power to issue bonds. In 1887, California's Wright Act led the way for sixteen other states to follow this practice. The bonds were secured by the taxes imposed on all agricultural land in the county of the district, a use of the credit of the entire county to develop irrigation systems for all farmers. When state supervision became the rule after 1897, the irrigation districts thrived. Millions of acres are under irrigation in all seventeen western states today due to irrigation districts. According to Bertsen, "Established as public institutions, irrigation districts were formed to benefit specific groups of private landowners. This fact gave irrigation districts a chameleon-like quality through their ability to 'affect public colors when advantageous, but resort to private camouflage when needed.'" Using public credit to finance private enterprise is most noticeable today in local construction of our professional sports arenas.

A major advantage given to irrigation districts by Congress in 1922 and 1926 ensured their continued success. The 1922 act authorized the Bureau of Reclamation to contract with irrigation districts for federal funds to repay project costs, and the 1926 act made the irrigation districts the sole and exclusive irrigation organization that could contract for federal funds to repay costs.

Irrigation districts' ability to issue bonds and tax via assessments made them viable. They were political subdivisions of the states and exempt from federal income taxes. Most states certified the bonds while not directly guaranteeing them. The strongest advantage of certification was that the states declared "the bonds eligible as investment vehicles for private trust funds and the funds of insurance companies, banks, and public institutions." The district owned the appropriative rights to water, and the combination of these rights with the strong vehicles of bonds and taxing authority, irrigation districts became the most viable institutions to build irrigation systems.

The Wright Act has had far-reaching impact across the West. The Turlock Irrigation District, the first district established in California under the Wright Act, along with the Modesto Irrigation District, provides irrigation for over two hundred thousand acres today. These two districts alone equal 2.5 percent of the total irrigated acreage in California.

The states of the West chose prior appropriation when the federal government chose to allow them to make up their own rules about water allocation in their state. In 1978, in two separate cases, *California v. the United States* and *United States v. New Mexico*, the Supreme Court of the United States confirmed its historical attitude of deference to state law on water issues in comments written by Associate Justice William Rehnquist about the history of federal and state relations over irrigation: "[*California v. United States*] is both long and involved, but through it runs the consistent thread of purposeful and continued deference to state water law by Congress. [In *United States v. Mexico*] [w]here Congress has expressly addressed the question of whether federal entities must abide by state water law, it has almost invariably deferred to state law."

From state to state, water laws and management practices vary but little from a general theme of prior appropriation overseen by local watermasters or state agencies, or in most cases a combination of both. Wyoming's Board of Control adjudicated water rights starting in Wyoming's first year of statehood, 1890, prompted to accomplish adjudication at the recommendation of the state's territorial engineer, young Elwood Mead. As mentioned before, Texas "fully" adjudicated its surface water rights in the mid-1960s, which eliminated one of its major sources of litigation. States that do not have fully adjudicated surface water rights are either in the process of doing so or will do so soon.

Watermasters are the field managers and regulators of irrigation systems in the West and have similar jobs across the West. For example, in Texas watermaster duties include measurement of reservoirs and Doppler measurements on diverters' water pipes, with the option of setting stream-flow markets to help water right holders comply with guidelines. They also keep databases on the amounts of water authorized and used and update and maintain water right ownerships and assessments on each water right account.

The South Texas Watermaster Program is responsible for an area that encompasses fifty counties in South-Central Texas. Five field deputies patrol these counties from offices located near their jurisdictional areas. Water right management is based on "run of the river rights." That means the deputies oversee a constantly changing, dynamic surface water system of rivers and tributaries that allow diversions as water is available and as it passes individual diversion points.

In New Mexico, the job responsibilities of the Middle Rio Grande Watermaster include

- evaluation of water rights;
- determination of those who lose water rights due to abandonment, the relinquishment of the right by the owner with the intention to forsake and desert it, or forfeiture, the involuntary or forced loss of a water right, caused by the failure of the appropriator or owner to put the water to beneficial use;
- distribution of surface waters within the Middle Rio Grande River;
- maintenance of a water rights inventory; and
- management of a geodatabase that maps all water declarations, all transfers of pre-1907 surface water rights to ground water, and all irrigation wells. The geodatabase is an important tool for the watermaster's administration of water rights in the basin.

Watermasters have similar but varying duties across the water basins and irrigation systems of the West. They have far-reaching power and influence on the irrigation systems of the West, and their authority will continue to be expanded in the upcoming years.

Most western states now have or are in the process of developing complex licensing systems to allow diversion of waters from their rivers or streams for irrigation. The surface waters of most states are likely over-appropriated in dry years. In Texas, it is all but impossible today to obtain a permit to divert water for irrigation purposes from any river or stream from the ruling agency, the Texas Commission on Environmental Quality, except in all but the rarest of temporary circumstances. Today, across the West there are many highly vocal supporters of government ownership and total control of all water-related resources, whether surface or groundwater. The proponents of total government control strongly criticize the prior appropriation doctrine, especially when it interferes with environmental issues such as endangered species protection.

Future Challenges for Irrigation and Water in the West

There seems to be no end to the growth of the West. With this growth there will be increasing pressure on its scarce water resources. As water resources become more and more limited per individual user, especially in times of drought, the importance of water laws and water rights may become the most critical natural resource issue of our time. The state legislatures, the United States Congress, and state and federal agencies will find themselves in a highly sensitive and challenging national debate.

Surface water laws, rights, and management practices have been addressed and are in the process of final adjudication across many areas of the West. Groundwater is yet another matter. The ways in which groundwater interfaces with surface water, the flows of groundwater in aquifers that cross under several state lines and the interrelationship of rights to this groundwater from state to state, and the needs of the individual rural groundwater user versus the needs of the ever-expanding urban sprawl cannot be ignored. A uniform and fair state and national policy must be addressed. The outcome of the myriad of groundwater issues cannot be predicted and will be determined by decades of political debate and thousands of lawsuits in the local, state, and federal courts.

Kansas draws 97.25 percent of its irrigation water from groundwater sources, Nebraska, 89.05 percent, and Texas, 87.38 percent. Texas has the rule of capture, which means irrigation from groundwater is all but unregulated in the state. These three states share the Ogallala Aquifer, which is under tremendous pressure these days during dry years, and with the growth of population, especially in Texas, the pressure will surely increase. Groundwater management remains a key issue for these states.

The cities of the United States have sovereignty and are in the process of exercising their power to obtain water for their needs, creating a crisis across the West for those who claim individual water rights. The cities have the financial resources to challenge both corporate and individual water rights and are doing so aggressively. The city of Del Rio, Texas, purchased a small tract from a landowner on the outskirts of the city with the water rights retained by the seller. The city immediately proceeded to drill three water wells for municipal use nonetheless. Even though the city of Del Rio stipulated in the subsequent lawsuit with the seller that the seller explicitly did not transfer any water rights to them in the purchase contract and deed, they claimed the right to the water anyway since the landowner had not "captured" it as yet. This suit is an example of the determination of cities to increase their water resources and their willingness to challenge even the most obvious water rights concepts. The entire West will likely see hundreds of battles between cities and individuals—especially individuals and companies whose agricultural activities depend upon irrigation from groundwater—over water in the next century. The outcome of these conflicts will shape the future of irrigation.

In 1996, the National Research Council Committee on the Future of Irrigation in the Face of Competing Demands summed up the three major "forces of change" facing irrigators and the agricultural community. These are "competition over water supplies, changing economic conditions, and environmental concerns. . . . The underlying premise of this study is that given the increasing competition for water supplies, changes in how water is managed, allocated, and valued are inevitable." Perhaps these issues have faced irrigation from its beginning in the West. Irrigation transformed the landscape, shaped the culture, and built the society and economy of the West. It will surely continue to do so.

New Mexico

"All natural waters flowing in streams and watercourses, whether perennial or torrential, within the limits of the state of New Mexico, belong to the public and are subject to appropriation for beneficial use. A watercourse is hereby defined to be any river, creek, arroyo, canyon, draw, or wash, or any other channel having definite banks and bed with visible evidence of the occasional flow of water."[94]

Agency Responsible for Water Rights

New Mexico Environment Department
Harold L. Runnels Building

94. http://www.conwaygreene.com/nmsu/lpext.dll?f=templates&fn=main -h.htm&2.0.

1190 St. Francis Drive, Suite N4050
Santa Fe, NM 87505
(800) 219-6157
https://www.env.nm.gov/water

Arizona

"Public Nature of Waters of the State: The waters of all sources, flowing in streams, canyons, ravines or other natural channels, or in definite underground channels, whether perennial or intermittent, flood, waste, or surplus water, and of lakes, ponds, and springs on the surface, belong to the public and are subject to appropriation and beneficial use as provided in this chapter. Any person, the State of Arizona, or a political subdivision thereof may appropriate unappropriated water for domestic, municipal, irrigation, stock watering, water power, recreation, wildlife, including fish, nonrecoverable water storage pursuant to section 45–833.01 or mining uses, for his personal use or for delivery to consumers. A water source that is located on land owned by the United States and that has been or may be appropriated under state law may be beneficially used on any land whether or not owned by the United States."[95]

Agency Responsible for Water Rights

Arizona Department of Water Resources
1110 W. Washington Street, Suite 310
Phoenix, AZ 85007
https://new.azwater.gov

California

"California has a unique system of surface water rights that combines a traditional riparian system with the appropriative system found elsewhere in the West. The result is a confused approach to water rights that often leads to more questions than certainty."[96]

---

95. http://www.azleg.state.az.us/ArizonaRevisedStatutes.asp?Title=45.
96. Gary Sawyers, "A Primer on California Water Rights," University of California Agricultural Issues Center, https://aic.ucdavis.edu/events/outlook05/Sawyer_primer.pdf. Sawyers's article is one of the very best sources for an initial understanding of California water rights. We should all thank him for his work.

"'Waters of the state' means any surface water or groundwater, including saline waters, within the boundaries of the state."[97] Water rights law in California is very complicated in many ways due to the mix of Spanish colonial, state of California, and United States rights. California requires a water right if anyone takes water from a stream or from underground. In California, water rights are regulated by the State Water Resources Control Board, also known generally as the "State Water Board." The California Water Boards website offers this explanation: "If you take water from a lake, river, stream, or creek, or from underground supplies for a beneficial use, the California Water Code (Division 2) requires that you have a water right. Because California water right law is complicated, you may have a water right (such as a riparian or pre-1914 appropriative) even if you do not have a water right permit or other type of water right issued by the state."[98]

How can one discover if they have a water right in California? The Water Board offers this explanation:

> The Division of Water Rights issues water right permits and licenses. You can check to see if you have a water right permit by using the eWRIMS Database System. See our eWRIMS introductory web page. Other entities issue permits or other types of approvals that may allow you to build a dam, or engage in another kind of construction activity. These permits are not water rights and do not allow you to use water. We index our water rights by the name of the last known owner. However, we are not informed by the county recorder, county tax assessor, or title company when property is transferred. Instead, water right owners are required to notify the Division of Water Rights when they transfer their rights. This frequently does not occur. If a previous owner has not notified us that he or she sold the property, there is a chance that the water right will still be shown under the name of the old owner. You can also find whether a water right exists for a piece of property if you know the location of your point of diversion. You can visually inspect maps available on our GIS system at https://waterrightsmaps.waterboards.ca.gov using your Internet Browser. We are in the process of developing our GIS system so that we can also show where water used under permits and licenses can be used. That information will be added to the system as our resources allow.[99]

Keep in mind that government website addresses change often, but a researcher can always use a search engine as a guide. For example, enter "California State Water Resources Control Board" into the search engine.

97. http://www.leginfo.ca.gov/cgibin/waisgate?WAISdocID=797811557+5+0+0&WAISaction=retrieve.
98. https://www.waterboards.ca.gov/waterrights/board_info/faqs.html#_top.
99. Ibid.

This method, if you discover the website addresses mentioned above are not active, will bring you to the new address.

According to the California Constitution, the state of California owns *all* the water in the state. The California State Water Resources Control Board is charged with the administration and allocation of water rights. As in other states, riparian rights are available to owners of property in California that are appurtenant to a watercourse; the right is a usufruct, or a right to use the water only, not to own it. Riparian rights to use surface water are subject to "reasonable and beneficial use" parameters, opening the discussion of what uses are reasonable and beneficial. Riparian rights are senior to appropriators and correlative as to other riparians. Riparian rights cannot be lost to nonuse. According to the Pacific Legal Foundation, "California's first settlers brought with them the theory of riparian rights, under which the owner of property next to a river owns the right to use water from that river. During the Gold Rush, miners adopted a system of appropriative rights which gave ownership to the first person to claim the water, regardless of who owned the land next to it. Today, California's dual system recognizes both types of water rights, but at the root of this complex system is one very simple concept: water rights are property rights."[100]

California follows the *source of title rule* in riparian rights. For example, once a tract that had riparian rights is split, then the smallest parcel remaining appurtenant to the watercourse that has been continuously held under single ownership maintains the riparian right. The severed tract that no longer is appurtenant to the watercourse loses its riparian rights.[101] According to Gary Sawyers, "It is possible to reserve riparian rights to a severed parcel if the reservation is explicit in the deed creating the division, but this infrequently occurs."[102]

Appropriative rights are based on actual use and follow prior appropriative theory, or "first-in-time, first-in-right," creating senior right holders and junior right holders. The State Water Resources Control Board may issue permits to those who apply. Their approval is based on availability of the water and reasonable and beneficial use. The right to use the water can be lost by nonuse.[103]

California has what is known as the *public trust doctrine*, which holds that certain resources are above private ownership and are held in trust by the government for the benefit of the people. Surface water in Spanish colonial times

---

100. Erin Wilcox, "Water, Property Rights and the Public Trust Doctrine," Pacific Legal Foundation, February 4, 2019, https://pacificlegal.org/water-property-rights-and-the-public-trust-doctrine (first published in the *Daily Journal* on January 30, 2018).

101. Sawyers, "A Primer on California Water Rights."

102. Ibid.

103. California Water Code 1450.

in California was also held in trust by the king for the benefit of the people. The Environmental Law Foundation described the public trust doctrine as "an ancient legal doctrine under which some waters, tidelands and wildlife resources of the State are held in trust for all of the people, and the State acts as the Trustee to protect these resources for present and future generations. In California, this Doctrine has been recognized to extend to the protection of navigable surface waters, to non-navigable tributaries of those waters, to aquatic resources, and to birds and other wildlife."[104]

According to Gary Sawyers, "In its role as trustee for all the people of California, the state must manage its resources in a manner in which the resources generate the 'highest public interest'[105] or 'derive the maximum benefit for its citizenry.'"[106] The trustee may determine that one use of water would better serve the public than a current use of water. The state then has both the "power and the obligation to reallocate that water in accordance with the public's interest." In Sawyers's opinion, no water rights in California are "vested in the traditional sense of property rights."[107]

California water law includes *prescriptive claims* of water rights. A prescriptive claim is similar to adverse possession in real property law. For example, if a junior water right holder "openly and notoriously" uses water adverse to a senior water right holder then after some period of time, the junior holder could gain an equal priority with the at-one-time senior holder. The key cases involving prescriptive claims have been among municipalities.[108] Further explanation of the California concept of prescriptive water rights is offered by the State Water Board: "A prescriptive right is a right that is acquired through adverse possession of someone else's water right. It is similar to a 'squatter's right' to land. Prescriptive rights are difficult to obtain and can only be granted by a court. Most people in California do not have and cannot acquire a prescriptive right. The courts have clarified that since 1914, the only way to acquire a new water right is to apply for and receive a water right permit from the State Water Board."[109]

Groundwater rights in California also are tied to land ownership. A landowner has the right to use the groundwater beneath their land, but these rights are correlative with respect to other landowners' overlying groundwater.[110]

---

104. "California's Public Trust Doctrine," Environmental Law Foundation, https://www.envirolaw.org/documents/ScottFAQ.pdf. Published by the Environmental Law Foundation, Pacific Coast Federation of Fishermen's Associations, and Institute for Fisheries Resources in a Scott River case against the California State Water Resources Control Board.

105. http://waterscape.org/pubs/factsheet_waterrights/FS_CaliforniaWaterRights.htm.

106. Sawyers, "A Primer on California Water Rights."

107. Ibid.

108. Ibid.

109. https://www.waterboards.ca.gov/waterrights/board_info/faqs.html#_top.

110. Sawyers, "A Primer on California Water Rights."

Sawyers opined that "the use of water for overlying landowners prevails over non-overlying lands."[111] According to the State Water Board,

> If you already have a water right, you do not need to apply for a permit. California law distinguishes between surface water and groundwater. To get a right to groundwater, you simply extract the water and use it for a beneficial purpose. There is one exception, which applies to "subterranean streams flowing in known and definite channels." If you use groundwater on land that is over the groundwater basin from which you took the water, you have an "overlying groundwater right." If you use the water somewhere else, you have an "appropriative groundwater right." Overlying groundwater rights have a higher priority than appropriative groundwater rights. The State Water Board does not have authority to issue permits for groundwater diversions, except for diversions from subterranean streams. However, the state does have the authority to take action to stop wasteful or unreasonable uses of groundwater or to stop groundwater diversions that harm state resources, such as fisheries. If you live in certain areas and pump groundwater, you may be subject to regulation by a local entity, like the county or a groundwater management district, even if you do not need a water right permit. Check with local authorities before pumping.[112]

California passed the California Sustainable Groundwater Management Act in 2014, effective January 1, 2015. The act requires formation of local groundwater sustainability agencies (GSAs) that are obligated to assess conditions in their basins and adopt locally based management plans.[113] According to the Water Systems Council, "Under the Act, GSAs are given 20 years to implement plans and achieve long-term groundwater sustainability. California Water Code 10720.5(b) purports to protect existing surface water and groundwater rights, and the Act claims to not impact current drought response measures. However, much uncertainty exists at this time with respect to the impact that the Act may have on water rights in California."[114]

According to the frequently asked questions publication of the California Department of Water Resources Sustainable Groundwater Management Office, "The 2014 Sustainable Groundwater Management Act (SGMA) required the formation of groundwater sustainability agencies (GSAs) in the State's high- and medium-priority groundwater basins and subbasins (basins) by the statutory deadline of June 30, 2017. Over 260 GSAs in over 140 basins were formed by that initial planning milestone. However, as the priorities of some basins have changed and numerous requests for basin boundary modifications have been approved, new GSAs will continue to be formed

---

111. Ibid.
112. Ibid.
113. "Who Owns the Water," 20.
114. Ibid.

and existing GSAs may adopt changes that must be reflected in DWR's SGMA Portal."[115]

Farm Progress Magazine, on August 29, 2017, reported, "Nearly all of California's groundwater basins deemed medium and high priorities by the state met their June [2017] deadline to form groundwater sustainability agencies." California Department of Water Resources director Grant Davis said, "It's encouraging to see such a strong commitment from land owners and communities to manage this critical water source now and for future generations." The reported 99 percent participation in this first step of the formation of locally managed sustainability agencies avoids having their groundwater regulated by the state.

There are a few unmanaged areas. "An unmanaged area is a portion of a high- or medium-priority groundwater basin that is not within the management area of a groundwater sustainability agency (GSA), an adjudication, or an alternative sustainability plan. The deadline to establish a GSA was June 30, 2017. Anyone that extracts groundwater from an unmanaged area, with the exception of small domestic well users, must file a groundwater extraction report with the State Water Resources Control Board (State Water Board) each year."[116]

Californians, like Texans, apparently prefer their groundwater to be managed by local agencies rather than at the state level. It is interesting to note that Texas passed legislation that created their equivalent of California's GSAs, groundwater conservation districts (GCDs), in 1949. For over seventy years GCDs have often been the center of local controversies in Texas. California may experience similar situations. It is encouraging that California has already formed 260 GSAs since the 2014 legislation.

After years of severe drought and ever-changing water use restrictions, especially in 2021,[117] the recent 2023 "atmospheric rivers"[118] (see Figure A.3)

---

115. "Frequently Asked Questions," California Department of Water Resources Sustainable Groundwater Management Office.

116. https://waterboards.maps.arcgis.com/apps/MapJournal/index.html?appid=3ca8bf4bbd6e40aaa561b7ed06821f72.

117. An example of one area's water use restrictions was posted on *Maven's Notebook*, a fine source for up-to-date information on California water policies. On August 20, 2021, in the midst of the severe drought conditions in the delta watershed, Maven offered this article, "State Water Board Issues Notice Containing Important Information about the Curtailment Status of Water Rights and Claims of Right within Delta Watershed," *Maven's Notebook*, August 20, 2021, https://mavensnotebook.com/2021/08/20/this-just-in-state-water-boards-initial-order-imposing-curtailments-and-reporting-requirements-in-the-delta-watershed. Thanks go to Robin Deshayes, attorney-at-law of Miltonian Capital in Santa Barbara, for pointing me to Maven's fine water rights notebook.

118. According to the National Oceanic and Atmospheric Administration, "Atmospheric rivers are relatively long, narrow regions in the atmosphere—like rivers in the sky—that transport most of the water vapor outside of the tropics. These columns of vapor move with the weather, carrying an amount of water vapor roughly equivalent to the average flow of water at the mouth of the Mississippi River. When the atmospheric rivers make landfall, they often release this water vapor in the form of

of rain that California has enjoyed, or been a victim of in some flooded areas, have broken the drought.

Is the long-term severe drought over? It was too early to tell as of March 23, 2023, but in the last few days after the most recent "atmospheric river," many sources appear to be convinced this current multiyear drought has come to an end. According to the *San Bernardino Sun* on March 22, 2023, "It's been less than six months, but California's drought conditions have all but disappeared." The Drought Index Map in Figure A.4 seems to indicate that in most areas of California the severe drought has ended.

The March 22, 2022, drought map in Figure A.5 indicated that all of California was in either severe or extreme drought. At least for now, the drought appears to have ended. Drastic water restrictions are gradually being lifted across many areas of the state.

Some offer the opinion that even with the atmospheric river conditions California experienced over the past few months, the drought is not over. According to *Vox*'s Umair Irfan, a correspondent writing about climate change,

> Another atmospheric river is pouring over California this weekend, triggering flash floods and evacuations. Yet, despite the state being wedged between deluge and drought, most of the recent rain is washing away, doing little to alleviate the West's stunning dry spell. The Western United States remains parched in the worst drought in more than 1,200 years. The torrential downpours over California this year have quenched some of that thirst, but on its own, this epic precipitation can't undo decades of hot, dry weather. Experts say, though, that more of that water could be saved up for a sunny day.[119]

California state agencies are beginning to consider new reservoirs. My experience with reservoir building in Texas is that it takes decades to move from idea to reservoir building due to resistance from the people in the area of the proposed reservoir, eminent domain issues, and conflicts between storing runoff water and environmental flow regulations both at the state and federal levels.

Agency Responsible for Water Rights

State Water Resources Control Board
1001 I Street
Sacramento, CA 95814
https://www.waterboards.ca.gov

---

rain or snow." "What Are Atmospheric Rivers?," NOAA, March 14, 2023, https://cleantechnica.com/2023/03/14/what-are-atmospheric-rivers.

119. https://www.vox.com/science-and-health/23553924/california-rain-atmospheric-river-drought-aquifer-reservoir.

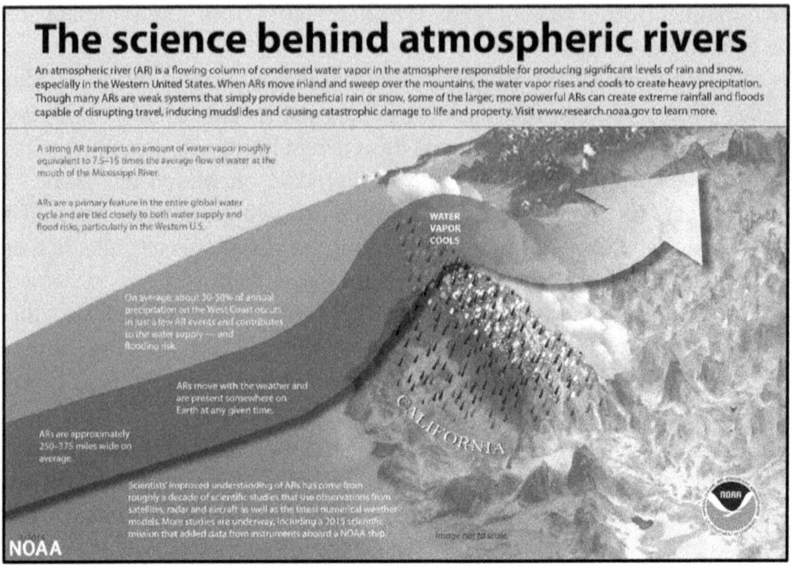

Figure A.3

Source: National Oceanic and Atmospheric Administration

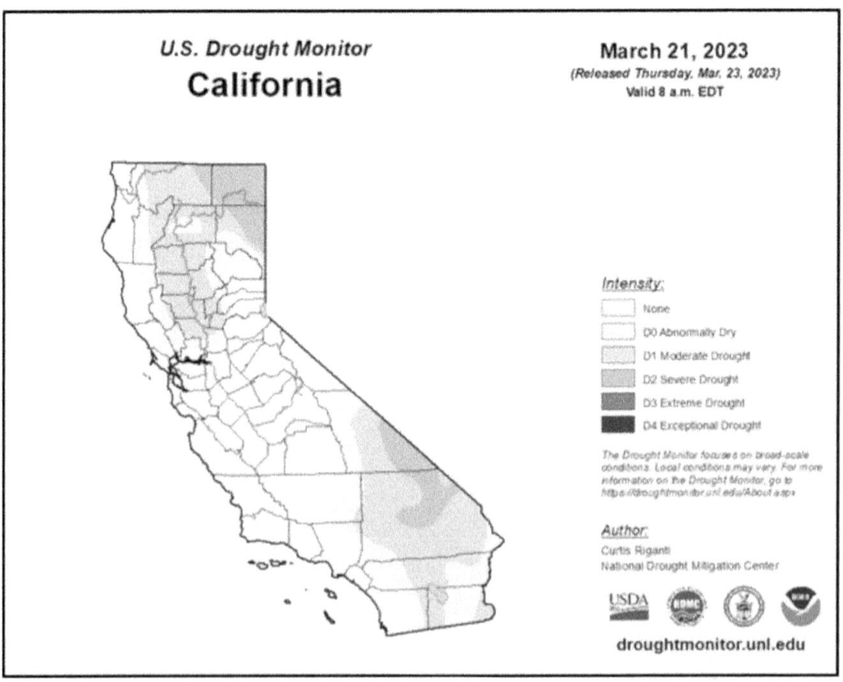

Figure A.4

Source: National Drought Migration Center

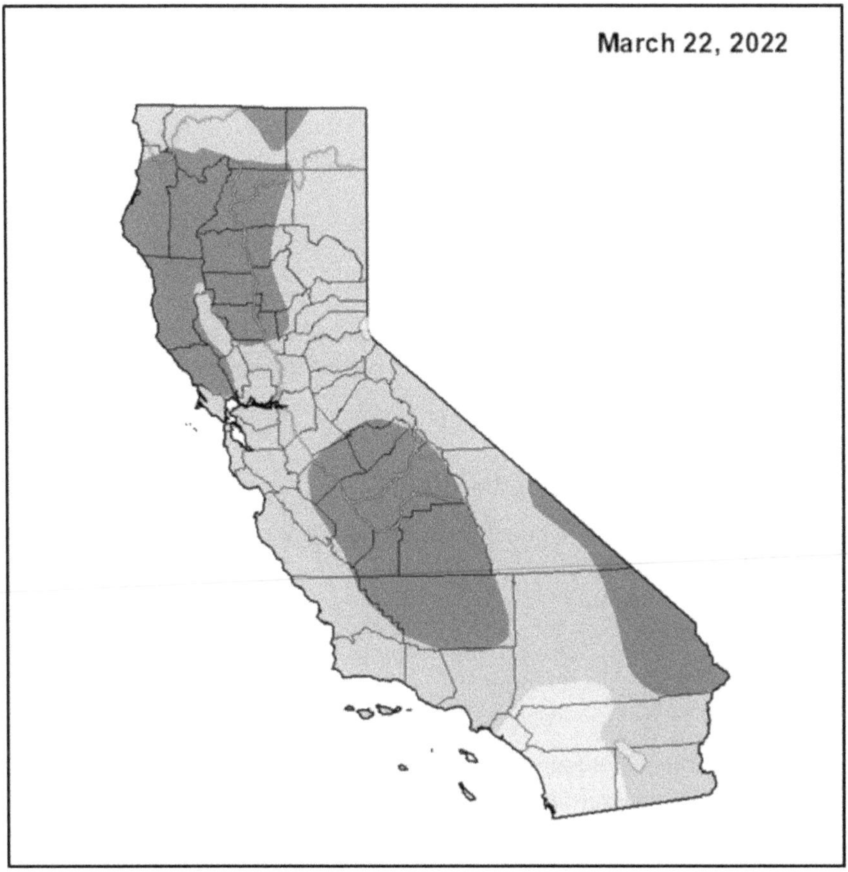

Figure A.5
Source: National Oceanic and Atmospheric Administration archives

Colorado

"'State waters' means any and all surface and subsurface waters which are contained in or flow in or through this state, but does not include waters in sewage systems, waters in treatment works of disposal systems, waters in potable water distribution systems, and all water withdrawn for use until use and treatment have been completed."[120]

120. http://www.michie.com/colorado/lpext.dll?f=templates&fn=mainh.htm&cp=.

Agency Responsible for Water Rights

Colorado Division of Water Resources
1313 Sherman Street, Suite 821
Denver, CO 80203
(303) 866-3581
https://dwr.colorado.gov

Kansas

"'Waters of the state' means all surface and subsurface waters occurring within the border of the state, or forming part of the border between Kansas and one of the adjoining states."[121]

Agency Responsible for Water Rights

Kansas Department of Agriculture: Division of Water Resources
1320 Research Park Drive
Manhattan, KS 66502
(785) 564-6700

Montana

"'State waters' means a body of water, irrigation system, or drainage system, either surface or underground."[122]

Agency Responsible for Water Rights

Montana Water Rights Bureau
DNRC Headquarters
1539 Eleventh Avenue
Helena, MT 59601
https://dnrc.mt.gov/Water-Resources

Nebraska

"The water of every natural stream not heretofore appropriated within the State of Nebraska, including the Missouri River, is hereby declared to be the property of the public and is dedicated to the use of the people of the state,

121. http://www.kdheks.gov/pdf/regs/28-16-58.pdf.
122. http://data.opi.mt.gov/bills/mca_toc/75_6_1.htm.

subject to appropriation. Waters of this state shall mean any waters within the territorial limits of Nebraska."[123]

Agency Responsible for Water Rights

Nebraska Department of Natural Resources
245 Fallbrook, Suite 201
Lincoln, NE 68521–6729
(402) 471-2363
https://dnr.nebraska.gov

Nevada

"'Waters of the state' means all waters situated wholly or partly within or bordering upon the state, including but not limited to: 1. All streams, lakes, ponds, impounding reservoirs, marshes, water courses, waterways, wells, springs, irrigation systems, and drainage systems; and 2. All bodies or accumulations of water, surface and underground, natural or artificial. (Added to NRS by 1973, 1709) (Substituted in revision for NRS 445.191)"[124]

Agency Responsible for Water Rights

State of Nevada Division of Water Resources
901 S. Stewart Street, Suite 2002
Carson City, NV 89701
(775) 684-2800
http://water.nv.gov

North Dakota

"Waters of the state—Public Waters. All waters within the limits of the state from the following sources of water supply belong to the public and are subject to appropriation for beneficial use and the right to the use of these waters for such use must be acquired pursuant to chapter 61–04: waters on the surface of the earth excluding diffused surface waters but including surface waters whether flowing in well-defined channels or flowing through lakes, ponds, or marshes which constitute integral parts of a stream system, or waters in lakes; waters under the surface of the earth whether such waters flow in defined subterranean channels or are diffused percolating underground water; all residual

123. http://uniweb.legislature.ne.gov/LegalDocs/view.php?page=s371200 6000.
124. http://water.nv.gov/home/PDFs/realtor%20Presentation.pdf.

waters resulting from beneficial use, and all waters artificially drained; and all waters, excluding privately own waters, in areas determined by the state engineer to be noncontributing drainage areas. A noncontributing drainage area is any area that does not contribute natural flowing surface water to a natural stream or watercourse at an average frequency more often than once in three years over the latest 30-year period."[125]

Agency Responsible for Water Rights

Division of Water Resources
1200 Memorial Highway
(Bank of North Dakota Building)
Bismarck, ND 58504
(701) 328-2750
https://www.swc.nd.gov

South Dakota

"Waters of the State—According to South Dakota Codified Law (SDCL) 46-1-3, all water within the state is the property of the people of the state but the right to the use of water may be acquired by appropriation as provided by law."

Agency Responsible for Water Rights

South Dakota Department of Agriculture and Natural Resources
523 E. Capitol Avenue
Pierre, SD 57501–3182
(605) 773-5559
https://danr.sd.gov

Utah

"'Waters of the state' means all streams, lakes, ponds, marshes, watercourses, waterways, wells, springs, irrigation systems, drainage systems, and all other bodies or accumulations of water, surface and underground, natural or artificial, public or private, which are contained within, flow through, or border upon this state or any portion of the state; and does not include bodies of water confined to and retained within the limits of private property, and

125. https://www.swc.nd.gov/thedwr/water_appropriation.html#:~:text=The%20Water%20Appropriation%20Division%20is,the%20Doctrine%20of%20Prior%20Appropriation.

which do not develop into or constitute a nuisance, a public health hazard, or a menace to fish or wildlife."

Agency Responsible for Water Rights

Division of Water Rights
1594 West North Temple, Suite 220
P.O. Box 146300
Salt Lake City, UT 84114–6300
(801) 538-7240

Wyoming

"'Waters of the state' means all surface and groundwater, including waters associated with wetlands, within Wyoming. http://deq.state.wy.us/out/spills .htm (Section 21-13-101) 'Waters of this state' means any waters within the jurisdiction of Wyoming. All water within the State of Wyoming is the property of the State of Wyoming. Water rights granted by the State of Wyoming allow use of certain portions of the waters of the state to be used for specific purposes and are administered by their priority dates."[126]

Agency Responsible for Water Rights

Wyoming State Engineer's Office
122 West 25th Street
Herschler Building
2nd Floor West
Cheyenne, WY 82002
https://seo.wyo.gov

Alaska

"'Waters' include lakes, bays, sounds, ponds, impounding reservoirs, springs, wells, rivers, streams, creeks, estuaries, marshes, inlets, straits, passages, canals, the Pacific Ocean, Gulf of Alaska, Bering Sea, and Arctic Ocean, in the territorial limits of the state, and all other bodies of surface or underground water, natural or artificial, public or private, inland or coastal, fresh or salt, which are wholly or partially in or bordering the state or under the jurisdiction of the state."[127]

---

126. http://legisweb.state.wy.us/statutes/statutes.aspx?file=titles/Title41/T 41CH13.htm.
127. http://touchngo.com/lglcntr/akstats/Statutes/Title46/Chapter03/Sectio n900.htm.

Agency Responsible for Water Rights

State of Alaska Department of Natural Resources
550 W. 7th Avenue, Suite 1360
Anchorage, AK 99501–3557
(907) 269-8400
http://dnr.alaska.gov

https://pubs.iseralaska.org/media/6ef6045d-493b-485c-8e1e-4389e71b6c4c/2017_02-UnderstandingWaterRights.pdf

Hawaii

"'Water' or 'waters of the state' means any and all water on or beneath the surface of the ground, including natural or artificial watercourses, lakes, ponds, or diffused surface water and water percolating, standing, or flowing beneath the surface of the ground."[128]

Agency Responsible for Water Rights

Commission on Water Resource Management
Kalanimoku Building
1151 Punchbowl Street, Room 227
Honolulu, HI 96813
(808) 587-0214
https://dlnr.hawaii.gov/cwrm

THE NORTHWEST

Washington, Oregon, and Idaho

Washington

"'Waters of the state' includes lakes, rivers, ponds, streams, inland waters, underground water, salt waters, estuaries, tidal flats, beaches and lands adjoining the seacoast of the state, sewers, and all other surface waters and watercourses within the jurisdiction of the State of Washington."[129]

---

128. http://www.state.hi.us/dlnr/cwrm/regulations/Code174C.pdf.
129. http://search.leg.wa.gov/pub/textsearch/ViewRoot.asp?Action=Html &Item=1&X=1006080048&p=1.

Agency Responsible for Water Rights

State Department of Ecology[130]
300 Desmond Drive SE
Lacey, WA 98503
P.O. Box 47600
Olympia, WA 98504–7600
(360) 407-6000

Oregon

"'Water' or 'the waters of the state' include lakes, bays, ponds, impounding reservoirs, springs, wells, rivers, streams, creeks, estuaries, marshes, inlets, canals, the Pacific Ocean within the territorial limits of the State of Oregon, and all other bodies of surface or underground waters, natural or artificial, inland or coastal, fresh or salt, public or private (except those private waters which do not combine or effect a junction with natural surface or underground waters), which are wholly or partially within or bordering the state or within its jurisdiction."[131]

Agency Responsible for Water Rights

Water Resources Department
725 Summer Street NE, Suite A
Salem, OR 97301
https://www.oregon.gov/owrd

Idaho

"'Waters' means all accumulations of water, surface and underground, natural and artificial, public and private or parts thereof, which are wholly or partially within, flow through, or border upon this state except for private waters as defined in section 42–212, Idaho Code."[132]

---

130. https://mrsc.org/Home/Explore-Topics/Environment/Water-Topics/Water-Rights.aspx#:~:text=The%20State%20Department%20of%20Ecology,for%20surface%20and%20ground%20water.
131. http://www.leg.state.or.us/ors/468b.html.
132. http://www.legislature.idaho.gov/idstat/Title39/T39CH1SECT39–103.htm.

Agency Responsible for Water Rights

Idaho Department of Water Resources
322 E. Front Street
Boise, ID 83702
https://idwr.idaho.gov

Appendix B

A Partial List of Significant State-versus-State Court Disputes in Water

1902–1907 *Kansas v. Colorado*

Kansas sues to prevent Colorado from diverting water from the Arkansas River for irrigation.

1914–1922 *Wyoming v. Colorado*

Wyoming sues to curb Colorado's diversions from the Laramie River for irrigation.

1931 *New Jersey v. New York*

New Jersey sues to prevent New York from diverting water from the Delaware River for New York City's water supply.

1943 *Colorado v. Kansas*

Colorado and Kansas feud again over the Arkansas River. The court recommends the states sign a compact, laying out how to share the river.

1945 *Nebraska v. Wyoming*

Nebraska sues Wyoming, in part to hold the western state accountable for impairing the flow of the North Platte River.

1954–1963 *Arizona v. California*

Arizona sues California during a decades-long fight over the Colorado River, which was allocated among multiple states in a 1920s compact.

1974–1987 *Texas v. New Mexico*

Texas sues to enforce the Pecos River Compact, claiming New Mexico is pumping too much groundwater, depleting the river.

1978–1984 *Colorado v. New Mexico*

Colorado seeks equitable apportionment of the Vermejo River. The court allocates the entire river to New Mexico.

1985–2009 *Kansas v. Colorado*

Kansas sues Colorado (again) for violating their compact by overpumping groundwater and depleting flows across state lines.

1991 *Oklahoma and Texas v. New Mexico*

Oklahoma and Texas sue, alleging New Mexico is storing and diverting more water than allowed by the Canadian River Compact.

1998–2003 *Kansas v. Nebraska*

Kansas sues to enforce the Republican River Compact, claiming Nebraska's groundwater pumping is reducing flows to Kansas.

2007–2010 *South Carolina v. North Carolina*

South Carolina seeks equitable apportionment of the Catawba River. The states settle the case.

2008–2018 *Montana v. Wyoming*

Montana sues to enforce the Yellowstone River Compact and protect itself from expansions in Wyoming's water usage.

2010–2015 *Kansas v. Nebraska*

Kansas sues Nebraska (again) after the northern state pumps more groundwater than it's allotted, reducing river flows. Kansas wins damages.

2014 *Texas v. New Mexico*

Texas sues to enforce the Rio Grande Compact and limit New Mexico's groundwater pumping.

2014 *Florida v. Georgia*

Florida seeks equitable apportionment of a shared river basin following intensive groundwater pumping in Georgia during a drought.

2015 *Mississippi v. Tennessee*

Mississippi claims Tennessee's groundwater pumping of an interstate aquifer amounts to trespass and the taking of Mississippi property.

Appendix C

Waters of the United States (WOTUS) "Fact Sheets"

From the U.S. Environmental Protection Agency (EPA) and the Department of the Army:

Final Rule:
Revised Definition of "Waters of the United States"
Fact Sheet
December 2022

Overview

On Dec. 30, 2022, the U.S. Environmental Protection Agency (EPA) and Department of the Army (the agencies) announced a final rule founded upon the pre-2015 definition of "waters of the United States," updated to reflect consideration of Supreme Court decisions, the science, and the agencies' technical expertise.

The agencies chose the familiar, pre-2015 definition as a foundation because it has supported decades of clean water progress and has been implemented by every administration in the last 45 years. Changing regulatory definitions due to court decisions and final rules issued by the agencies in 2015, 2019, and 2020 have caused uncertainty that harmed communities and our nation's waters. The rule restores fundamental protections so that the nation will be closer to achieving Congress' direction in the Clean Water Act that our waters be fishable and swimmable. It will also ensure that our waters support recreation and wildlife.

This action provides clear rules of the road that will help advance infrastructure projects, economic investments, and agricultural activities—all while protecting water quality. EPA and Army are prioritizing and enhancing practical, on-the-ground implementation by providing tools and resources to support timely and consistent jurisdictional determinations under this definition of "waters of the United States."

Categories of "Waters of the United States"[1]

The agencies' definition of "waters of the United States" provides jurisdiction over waterbodies that Congress intended to protect under the Clean Water Act, including traditional navigable waters (e.g., certain large rivers and lakes), territorial seas, and interstate waters. For upstream waters that may significantly affect the integrity of downstream waters that Congress intended to protect, the rule provides a reasonable approach that recognizes regional and geographic differences. The rule accounts for regional differences in waters because regionally tailored implementation tools as well as local and regional conditions help determine whether waters are covered under this rule.

[1] This table is provided for informational purposes; the rule establishes the requirements defining "waters of the United States."

Page 1 of 4

Types of Waters	Features	Examples of Waters Likely to Be Jurisdictional Under the Final Rule	Regulatory Text Paragraph
Traditional Navigable Waters	Large rivers and lakes that could be used in interstate or foreign commerce, as well as waterbodies affected by tides.	Mississippi River, Erie Canal, Great Lakes	(a)(1)
Territorial Seas	Territorial seas that extend three miles out to sea from the coast.	Atlantic Ocean, Pacific Ocean	(a)(1)
Interstate Waters	Includes waters like streams, lakes, or wetlands that cross or form part of state boundaries.	Lake Tahoe, portions of the Columbia River, portions of Savannah River	(a)(1)
Impoundments	Impounded bodies of water created in or from "waters of the United States," like reservoirs and beaver ponds.	Bear Gulch Reservoir in California	(a)(2)
Tributaries	Branches of creeks, streams, rivers, lakes, ponds, ditches, and impoundments that ultimately flow into traditional navigable waters, the territorial seas, interstate waters, or impoundments of jurisdictional waters. Tributaries are jurisdictional if they meet either the relatively permanent standard or significant nexus standard.	Wolftrap Run in Virginia, Puppy Creek in Arkansas	(a)(3)
Adjacent Wetlands	These wetlands can be next to, abutting, or near other jurisdictional waters or behind certain natural or constructed features. They are most often within a few hundred feet of jurisdictional waters. Adjacent wetlands are jurisdictional if they meet either the relatively permanent standard or the significant nexus standard, or where the wetland is adjacent to a traditional navigable water, the territorial seas, or an interstate water.	Parts of the Florida Everglades, Horicon Marsh in Wisconsin	(a)(4)
Additional Waters	These lakes, ponds, streams, or wetlands do not fit into the above categories. They are jurisdictional if they meet either the relatively permanent standard or the significant nexus standard.	Certain local lakes, streams, wetlands, etc.	(a)(5)

Page **2** of **4**

Standards for Determining Jurisdiction

To determine jurisdiction for tributaries, adjacent wetlands, and additional waters, the final rule relies on the longstanding approach of applying two standards. Certain types of waters are jurisdictional under the final rule if they meet either the relatively permanent standard or significant nexus standard.

- **Relatively Permanent is a test that** provides important efficiencies and clarity for regulators and the public by readily identifying a subset of waters that will virtually always significantly affect paragraph (a)(1) waters. To meet the relatively permanent standard, the waterbodies must be relatively permanent, standing, or continuously flowing waters connected to paragraph (a)(1) waters or waters with a continuous surface connection to such relatively permanent waters or to paragraph (a)(1) waters.
- **Significant Nexus is a test that** clarifies if certain waterbodies, such as tributaries and wetlands, are subject to the Clean Water Act based on their connection to and effect on larger downstream waters that Congress fundamentally sought to protect. A significant nexus exists if the waterbody (alone or in combination) significantly affects the chemical, physical, or biological integrity of traditional navigable waters, the territorial seas, or interstate waters.

Exclusions from "Waters of the United States"

The agencies' definition of "waters of the United States" does not affect the longstanding activity-based permitting exemptions provided to the agricultural community by the Clean Water Act. Additionally, the final rule codifies eight exclusions from the definition of "waters of the United States" in the regulatory text to provide clarity, consistency, and certainty to a broad range of stakeholders. **The exclusions are:**

- **Prior converted cropland**, adopting USDA's definition and generally excluding wetlands that were converted to cropland prior to December 23, 1985.
- **Waste treatment systems,** including treatment ponds or lagoons that are designed to meet the requirements of the Clean Water Act.
- **Ditches** (including roadside ditches), excavated wholly in and draining only dry land, and that do not carry a relatively permanent flow of water.
- **Artificially irrigated areas,** that would revert to dry land if the irrigation ceased.
- **Artificial lakes or ponds,** created by excavating or diking dry land that are used exclusively for such purposes as stock watering, irrigation, settling basins, or rice growing.
- **Artificial reflecting pools or swimming pools,** and other small ornamental bodies of water created by excavating or diking dry land.
- **Waterfilled depressions,** created in dry land incidental to construction activity and pits excavated in dry land for the purpose of obtaining fill, sand, or gravel unless and until the construction operation is abandoned and the resulting body of water meets the definition of "waters of the United States."
- **Swales and erosional features** (*e.g.*, gullies, small washes), that are characterized by low volume, infrequent, or short duration flow.

Page **3** of **4**

Public Input on this Action

The final rule is based on extensive outreach and engagement that began before the rule was proposed and continued through the public comment period of the proposed rule. The agencies received and considered over 114,000 written public comments in developing the final rule.

For More Information

Additional information, along with the final rule and supporting analyses, are available on EPA's website at https://www.epa.gov/wotus.

Final Rule:
Revised Definition of "Waters of the United States"
Fact Sheet for the Agricultural Community
December 2022

Overview

On Dec. 30, 2022, the U.S. Environmental Protection Agency (EPA) and Department of the Army (the agencies) announced a final rule founded upon the pre-2015 definition of "waters of the United States," updated to reflect consideration of Supreme Court decisions, the science, and the agencies' technical expertise.

The agencies chose the familiar, pre-2015 definition as a foundation because it has supported decades of clean water progress and has been implemented by every administration in the last 45 years. This action establishes a durable and reasonable definition of "waters of the United States."

The approach provides clear rules of the road to advance agricultural activities, infrastructure projects, and economic investments while protecting water quality. EPA and Army are prioritizing practical, on the ground implementation by providing tools and resources to support timely and consistent jurisdictional determinations under this definition of "waters of the United States."

Exemptions in the Clean Water Act

The agencies' definition of "waters of the United States" does not affect the longstanding activity-based permitting exemptions provided to the agricultural community by the Clean Water Act.

Agricultural activities that are exempt from section 404 permitting include:

- Normal farming, silviculture, and ranching activities such as plowing, seeding, cultivating, minor drainage, harvesting for the production of food, fiber, and forest products, or upland soil and water conservation practices;
- Maintenance of dikes, levees, groins, riprap, and transportation structures;
- Construction of farm or stock ponds or irrigation ditches, or the maintenance of drainage ditches, and
- Construction or maintenance of farm roads, in accordance with best management practices.

Page **1** of **3**

Exclusions in the Final Rule

The final rule codifies exclusions from the definition of "waters of the United States" in regulatory text—delivering clarity to the agricultural community. The final rule includes two longstanding exclusions from the definition of "waters of the United States."

- **Prior converted cropland**. The final rule defines prior converted cropland consistent with the U.S. Department of Agriculture's (USDA) definition. Prior converted cropland remains excluded from the definition of "waters of the United States" as long as it is available for agricultural commodity production. The agencies interpret availability for agricultural commodity production to include uses such as crop production, haying, grazing, agroforestry, or idling land for conservation uses.
- **Waste treatment systems.** Features excluded under this category include treatment ponds or lagoons that are designed to meet the requirements of the Clean Water Act.

The final rule includes six additional exclusions from the definition of "waters of the United States" to further increase regulatory certainty.

- **Ditches** (including roadside ditches) excavated wholly in and draining only dry land, and that do not carry a relatively permanent flow of water.
- **Artificially irrigated areas** that would revert to dry land if the irrigation ceased.
- **Artificial lakes or ponds** created by excavating or diking dry land that are used exclusively for such purposes as stock watering, irrigation, settling basins, or rice growing.
- **Artificial reflecting pools or swimming pools** and other small ornamental bodies of water created by excavating or diking dry land.
- **Waterfilled depressions** created in dry land incidental to construction activity and pits excavated in dry land for the purpose of obtaining fill, sand, or gravel unless and until the construction operation is abandoned and the resulting body of water meets the definition of "waters of the United States."
- **Swales and erosional features** (*e.g.*, gullies, small washes) that are characterized by low volume, infrequent, or short duration flow.

Jurisdictional Waters in the Final Rule

The agencies' definition of "waters of the United States" provides jurisdiction over waterbodies that Congress clearly intended to protect under the Clean Water Act, such as traditional navigable waters (e.g., certain large rivers and lakes), territorial seas, and interstate waters. For upstream waters that may significantly affect the integrity of the downstream waters that Congress clearly intended to protect, the rule provides a reasonable approach that recognizes geographic differences in waters. The rule accounts for regional differences in waters because regionally tailored implementation tools as well as local and regional conditions help determine whether waters are covered under this rule.

The final rule includes the longstanding categories for: (1) traditional navigable waters, the territorial seas, and interstate waters; (2) jurisdictional impoundments of "waters of the United States"; (3) jurisdictional tributaries; (4) jurisdictional adjacent wetlands; and (5) intrastate lakes and ponds, streams, or wetlands not identified in categories (1) through (4) that meet the rule's jurisdictional criteria.

Outreach on the Final Rule

The final rule is based on extensive outreach and engagement that began before the rule was proposed and continued through the public comment period of the proposed rule. The agencies received input from farmers and ranchers through pre-proposal public meetings, pre-proposal written recommendations, public hearings, public comments, and meetings specifically for small entities.

For More Information

Additional information, along with copies of the final rule and supporting analyses, are available on EPA's website at https://www.epa.gov/wotus.

Final Rule:
Revised Definition of "Waters of the United States"
A Guide for Landowners

December 2022

On Dec. 30, 2022, the U.S. Environmental Protection Agency (EPA) and Department of the Army (the agencies) announced a final rule defining "waters of the United States." The final rule establishes a durable and implementable approach to determining which waters are jurisdictional under the Clean Water Act, and which are not. The following brief guide is intended to assist landowners in determining whether activities on their land require a Clean Water Act permit.

Step 1:
Is the activity I want to carry out on my property exempt from needing a Clean Water Act permit?

The following activities are exempt from the Clean Water Act's dredged and fill permit requirements,[1] even if they take place in "waters of the United States:"

- Established (ongoing) farming, ranching, and silviculture activities such as plowing, seeding, cultivating, minor drainage, harvesting for the production of food, fiber, and forest products, or upland soil and water conservation practices;
- Maintenance (but not construction) of drainage ditches;
- Construction and maintenance of irrigation ditches;
- Construction and maintenance of farm or stock ponds;
- Construction and maintenance of farm and forest roads, in accordance with best management practices, and
- Maintenance of structures such as dams, dikes, and levees.

Additionally, many discharges of pollutants other than dredged or fill material do not require permits:[2]

- Pollutants from nonpoint-source agricultural and silvicultural activities, including storm water runoff from orchards, cultivated crops, pastures, range lands, and forest lands;
- Return flows from irrigated agriculture, and
- Discharges from a water transfer.

[1] Note, however, that Clean Water Act section 404(f) establishes circumstances (based on certain effects on "waters of the United States") under which an activity listed as exempt is no longer exempt. For more detail, see section 404(f) and the regulations on "discharges not requiring a permit" at 33 CFR 323.4.
[2] See 40 CFR 122.3 for the regulatory provisions.

Step 2:
Is the water on my property covered by this rule?

The Clean Water Act does not cover every geographic feature with water in it, nor does it subject all activities in waters meeting the definition of "waters of the United States" to regulation (as discussed in Step 1). Puddles are not "waters of the United States." The rule also has a well-established, very specific definition of wetlands. That definition requires the presence of particular wetland hydrology, soils, and vegetation. If a landowner's property does *not* contain the types of waters, including wetlands, covered by this rule, it is not jurisdictional.

Step 3:
Is the water on my property excluded from the definition of "waters of the United States"?

1) What are the exclusions in the final rule?

The rule excludes certain features that commonly contain water but are not "waters of the United States":

- Prior converted cropland;
- Ditches (including roadside ditches) excavated wholly in and draining only dry land and that do not carry a relatively permanent flow of water;
- Artificially irrigated areas that would revert to dry land if the irrigation ceased;
- Artificial lakes or ponds created by excavating or diking dry land to collect and retain water and which are used exclusively for such purposes as stock watering, irrigation, settling basins, or rice growing;
- Waterfilled depressions created in dry land incidental to construction activity and pits excavated in dry land for the purpose of obtaining fill, sand, or gravel unless and until the construction or excavation operation is abandoned and the resulting body of water meets the definition of "waters of the United States;"
- Swales and erosional features (*e.g.*, gullies, small washes) characterized by low volume, infrequent, or short duration flow, and
- Waste treatment systems, including treatment ponds or lagoons, designed to meet the requirements of the Clean Water Act.

Where a feature located on a landowner's property satisfies the terms of an exclusion, it is not jurisdictional under the Clean Water Act, and does not require a federal permit, even where the feature would otherwise be jurisdictional. However, certain types of waters—traditional navigable waters, the territorial seas, and interstate waters—are always jurisdictional, even if they satisfy the terms of an exclusion.

2) How do I know if areas on my property satisfy the prior converted cropland exclusion?

Page **2** of **5**

Prior converted cropland under the Clean Water Act encompasses all areas designated by the United States Department of Agriculture (USDA) as prior converted cropland under the Food Security Act.[3] Areas USDA has not so designated are **not** eligible for this Clean Water Act exclusion. The Clean Water Act exclusion for prior converted cropland only covers wetlands and does not exclude other types of aquatic resources (*e.g.*, tributaries, ponds, ditches) that are located within the prior converted cropland area.

The prior converted cropland exclusion would no longer apply if the land use changes so that it is no longer available to produce agricultural commodities. This would include a proposed or planned modification of prior converted cropland for filling and development, so that the area would no longer be available for commodity crop production after development. For example, if prior converted cropland is left idle for several years and reverts to wetland, and the property is then sold for conversion to a residential development, the exclusion no longer applies and the discharge of dredged or fill material from development would require prior authorization under Clean Water Act section 404.

Changes in use do not include idling land for conservation uses (*e.g.*, habitat; pollinator and wildlife management; and water storage, supply, and flood management); irrigation tailwater storage; crawfish farming; cranberry bogs; nutrient retention; idling land for soil recovery following natural disasters like hurricanes and drought; crop production, haying, and grazing, so long as the area remains available for the production of agricultural commodities. An area has not experienced a change in use if, for example, it transitions into a long-term rotation to agroforestry or perennial crops, such as vineyards or orchards. Generally speaking, idle land retains its availability to produce an agricultural commodity. Areas used in any of these ways can retain their availability for commodity crop production and therefore their prior converted cropland designation.

Additionally, if the agencies determine that a land area does not meet the prior converted cropland exclusion because of a planned or proposed "change in use," this does not necessarily mean the area contains "waters of the United States." Any area that has not reverted to a wetland that meets this rule's jurisdictional requirements will not be regulated as a "water of the United States."

Step 4:
If the activity I want to carry out on my property is not exempt from permitting requirements, and the feature on my property is likely a water for purposes of the rule (and is not excluded), what do I do next?

If a landowner's property is not covered by one of the exclusions and an activity is not covered by one of the exemptions, the next step is to determine if the water is a "water of the United States" under one of the longstanding categories in the rule: (1) traditional navigable waters, the territorial seas, and

[3] USDA interprets prior converted cropland to be a "converted wetland where the conversion occurred prior to December 23, 1985, an agricultural commodity had been produced at least once before December 23, 1985, and as of December 23, 1985, the converted wetland did not support woody vegetation and did not meet the hydrologic criteria for farmed wetland." 7 CFR 12.2.

interstate waters; (2) jurisdictional impoundments of "waters of the United States"; (3) jurisdictional tributaries; (4) jurisdictional adjacent wetlands; and (5) intrastate lakes and ponds, streams, or wetlands not identified in categories (1) through (4) that meet either the relatively permanent standard or the significant nexus standard.

1) *What is the relatively permanent standard?*

Waterbodies that meet this standard are relatively permanent, standing, or continuously flowing waters connected to traditional navigable waters, the territorial seas, and interstate waters. Waters that meet this standard also include waters with a continuous surface connection to such relatively permanent waters or traditional navigable waters, the territorial seas, and interstate waters.

2) *What is the significant nexus standard?*

Certain waterbodies, such as tributaries and wetlands, can have the required connection to and affect larger downstream waters that Congress fundamentally sought to protect. The significant nexus exists if the waterbody (alone or in combination) significantly affects the chemical, physical, or biological integrity of traditional navigable waters, the territorial seas, or interstate waters.

If the water feature fits one of the categories of "waters of the United States" and the activity is not covered by one of the exemptions, the landowner will need to seek a permit to carry out the activity.

Step 5:
Are there resources or help from the agencies to aid me in this process?

1) *Publicly available tools and resources*

Publicly available tools and resources can assist landowners in understanding the jurisdictional status of waters, including tributaries and wetlands, that may be present on their lands. For example, EPA's EnviroAtlas (available on EPA's website) is a map viewer that facilitates surface water assessments using data such as land cover, stream hydrography, soils, and topography. Users can quickly and easily input a location (*e.g.*, a city and state, or latitude and longitude) and select relevant map layers.

2) *Jurisdictional determinations*

There are circumstances under which it may be difficult for landowners to determine on their own whether a water on their land is jurisdictional. If landowners want certainty as to whether areas on their property meet the definition of "waters of the United States," they may request an approved jurisdictional determination from their local Corps district regulatory office at any time. The Corps has long provided jurisdictional determinations as a public service and does not charge a fee for this service. A landowner who would like to know whether areas on their property meet the definition of "waters of the United States" may contact their local Corps district regulatory office at any time. The list of local district regulatory offices and their contact information is available on the Corps' website.

3) ***Are there general permits under section 404 of the Clean Water Act for individual landowners? How do I obtain coverage under a nationwide permit?***

Even if landowners wish to pursue activities that are or may be subject to the permit requirements of the Clean Water Act and that will impact "waters of the United States" on their property, they may be able to obtain coverage under a general permit. General permits are issued on a nationwide, regional, or statewide basis for specific categories of activities that have minimal individual or cumulative adverse environmental effects. The general permit process allows certain activities to proceed with little or no delay if the conditions of the general permit are met. For example, nationwide permit (NWP) 18 authorizes minor discharges of less than 25 cubic yards that result in the loss of no more than 1/10-acre of "waters of the United States." Corps personnel in the local district office can help explain the requirements of each NWP. Information on NWPs is also available on the Corps' website.

4) ***If I need an individual section 404 permit, how do I obtain coverage?***

The vast majority of activities subject to Clean Water Act section 404 permits are authorized under general permits; however, some activities do require authorization under an individual permit (generally because of a high level of impact on "waters of the United States" or because the applicant cannot comply with all conditions of a general permit). Landowners may reach out to their local Corps district regulatory office, who will help them determine how to request an individual permit.

Bibliography

PRIMARY SOURCES

Arricivita, Juan Domingo. Tr. Hammond, George P., and Rey, Agapito. *Cronica serfica y apostolica del colegio de propaganda fide de la Santa Cruz de Querétaro* (Apolistic Chronicle of Juan Domingo Arricivita: The Franciscan Mission Frontier in the Eighteenth Century in Arizona, Texas, and the Californias). Berkeley, CA: Academy of American Franciscan History, 1992 and 1996 (original: Mexico: Don Felipe de Zuniga y Ontiveros, 1792).

Bexar Archives Translations at the Center for American History. University of Texas, Austin.

Bexar County Appraisal District. San Antonio, Texas.

Bexar County District Clerk Archives. Court Journals, Indices, and Archived Pleadings. San Antonio, Texas.

Bexar County Real Property Records and Archived Records. County Clerk. San Antonio, Texas.

Black, Henry Campbell. *Black's Law Dictionary Sixth Edition.* Saint Paul, MN: West Publishing Company, 1990.

Brackenridge (John Thomas) Papers. State of Texas Archives. Austin, Texas.

Brackenridge (John Thomas and George W.) Papers. Center for American History. University of Texas, Austin.

Brackenridge Book Collection. University of the Incarnate Word Library Special Collections. San Antonio, Texas.

Chamber of Commerce. San Antonio, Texas.

City Map of San Antonio. Southwell Map Company, 1946.

City of San Antonio, Archives of City Council Minutes, City Clerk, Leticia M. Vacek. San Antonio, Texas.

Corner, William, ed. *San Antonio de Baxar*. San Antonio, TX: Bainbridge & Corner, 1890.

Cortina Letters, ed. Tr. Thompson, Jerry D. *Juan Cortina and the Texas-Mexico Frontier, 1859–1877*. El Paso: Texas Western Press, 1994.

Cutter, Donald C., ed. Tr. O'Conor, Hugo. *Informe sobre los Presidios del Norte de Nueva Espana dado alVcry Marques de Croix 1777* (named by translator Hugo

O'Conor's Report to Teodoro de Croix, July 22, 1777). Dallas: Southern Methodist University Press, 1994.

Davis, Chester B. *Report upon a Valuation of the Plant of the Water Works Company of San Antonio, Texas*. San Antonio, TX: Private Press, June 1902.

Edrey, Yuval. Israeli. Live interview, June 7, 2016. Austin Club, Austin, Texas.

Erwin, Frank C., Jr. Letter to the Members of the Board of Regents, July 10, 1973. From the Board of Regents, University of Texas, Austin.

Espinosa, Fray Felix de Espinosa, OFM. *Cronica de los Colegios de Propaganda Fide de la Nueva Espana*. Mexico, 1746.

European Union. "Commission Refers Spain to Court over Illegal Landfills." Press release. Brussels. July 16, 2015. http://ec.europa.eu. Accessed August 22, 2015.

———. "Environment: Commission Takes Spain to Court over Urban Waste Water and River Basin Plans." Press release. Brussels. June 16, 2015. http://ec.europa.eu. Accessed August 22, 2015.

———. "Environment: Commission Urges Spain to Adopt River Basin Management Plans." Brussels. 2011. http://ec.europa.eu. Accessed August 22, 2015.

———. "Infringements: Frequently Asked Questions." Strasbourg. January 17, 2012. http://ec.europa.eu. Accessed August 22, 2015.

———. Official Journal of the European Communities. "Council Directive of 21 May 1991 Concerning Urban Waste Water Treatment (91/27/EEC)."

———. Official Journal of the European Union. "Directive 2008/98/EC of the European Parliament and of the Council of 19 November 2008 on Waste and Repealing Certain Directives." November 22, 2008. L 312/3.

———. "Spain: Commission Pursues Legal Action over Breaches in Environmental Law." Brussels. 2008. http://ec.europa.eu. Accessed August 22, 2015.

Glazer, Yael. Israeli. Live interview, June 7, 2016. Austin Club, Austin, Texas.

Guadalupe County District Clerk Archives. Court Journals, Indices, and Archived Pleadings. Seguin, Texas.

Herff, Peter Ferdinand, MD. *The Doctors Herff: A Three Generation Memoir*, ed. Laura L. Barber. San Antonio, TX: Trinity University Press, 1973.

Institute for Texan Culture Vertical Files and Library. University of Texas, San Antonio.

Inventory of the Mission San Antonio de Valero: 1772. Austin: Texas Historical Commission, 1977.

Journal of a Texas Missionary: The Diario Historico of Fr. Cosme Lozano Narvais, pen name Fr. Mariano Antonio de Vasconcelos. Transcript of the Spanish original.

Lacoste Papers. Center for American History. University of Texas, Austin.

LaPrelle-Brackenridge Papers. Austin History Center. Austin, Texas.

Leutenegger, Fr. Benedict, tr. *Instruccion para el Ministro de la Mision de la Purissima Concepcion de la Provincia de Texas, 1787* (Instruction for the Minister of the Mission Purissima Concepcion of the Province of Texas, 1787). San Antonio, TX: Our Lady of the Lake University, 1994.

———. *The Zacatecan Missionaries in Texas, 1716–1834*. Texas Historical Survey Committee, Office of the State Archeologist Reports, Number 23. Austin: Office of the State Archeologist, 1973.

Matson, Daniel S., and Fontana, Bernard L., ed. Tr. Father Bringas. *Reports to the King, Methods of Indoctrination on the Frontier of New Spain, 1796–97*. Tucson: University of Arizona Press, 1977.

McLean, Bert J. *The Romance of San Antonio's Water Supply and Distribution*. San Antonio, TX: For the Water Company Shareholders, 1924.

Montoya, Juan de. Tr. Hammond, George P., and Rey, Agapito. *New Mexico in 1602*. Albuquerque: Quivera Society, 1938.

Morrison, Andrew. *San Antonio: Her Prosperity and Prospects*. San Antonio, TX: Private, 1897.

Mousa, Amani. Palestinian. Live interview, November 8, 2015. Austin, Texas.

Nixon, Pat Ireland, MD. *A Century of Medicine in San Antonio*. San Antonio, TX: Private, 1936.

Olmsted, Frederick Law. *A Journey through Texas*. Lincoln: University of Nebraska Press, 2004.

Period Post Card and Map Collection of the Author. Austin: Private.

Rodriquez, Jose Maria. Memoirs of Early Texas. http://www.tamu.edu/ccbn/dewitt/rodmemoirs.htm accessed 6/21/2007.

San Antonio National Bank. *San Antonio and Your First National Bank through the Years*. San Antonio, TX: Claude Aniol & Associates, 1953.

San Jose Papers. Translated from original documents with unknown publisher, unbound, copied from the Institute of Texan Cultures, loose files. University of Texas, San Antonio.

Sanborn Maps, July 1885 and 1892, San Antonio, Texas. New York: Sanborn Map and Publishing Co., 1885 and 1892.

Siete Partidas (Seven-Part Code), Partida 3, Titulo 28, Ley 1 (part 3, title 28, law 1).

State of Texas, Chapter 36, Texas Water Code.

State of Texas, Laws of the State of Texas. Austin: State of Texas, 1862.

Stillman, Chauncey Devereux. *Charles Stillman*. New York: Private, 1956.

Terrell (A.W.) Papers. Center for American History. University of Texas, Austin.

Travis Central Appraisal District. Austin, Texas.

United States Geographical Survey Maps.

Newspapers

Chicago Tribune, 2006–2016.

Dallas Morning News, 2006–2016.

Fredericksburg Standard-Radio Post, 1986.

New York Times, 2006–2016.

Recorder-Times, 1983.

San Antonio Daily Express, 1872–1896.

San Antonio Evening Paper, 1850–1890.

San Antonio Express, 1890–2007.

San Antonio Herald, 1872–1890.

Semi-Weekly News, 1862–1880.

Texas Democrat, 1849.

Wall Street Journal, 2006–2016.
Washington Post, 2006–2016.

Special Research Sources

Bhattacharya, Suryatapa. "Why Is Delhi's Water Supply So Vulnerable?" *Wall Street Journal*. February 22, 2016.
Recent Reports on the Jat v. Delhi (City) Water Riots:
http://www.bbc.com/news/world/asia/india.
http://www.hindustantimes.com/india/traffic-restored-on-nh-1-khattar-says-action-against-rioters-who-set-fire-to-shops/story-xoOMOlhubgE08gMMK53byI.html.
http://www.indiaonlinepages.com/population/delhi-population.html.
https://news.vice.com/contributor/vice-news-and-reuters.
https://www.kent.co.in/pdf/news/Annexure-1.pdf.
http://www.cnn.com/2016/02/22/asia/india-unrest-water-crisis.

Court Cases

Adjudication of Water Rights of the Lower Guadalupe River Segment, 730 S.W.2d 64, 67 (Tex. App.—Corpus Christi 1987, writ ref'd n.r.e.).
City of Del Rio, Petitioner, vs. Clayton Sam Colt Hamilton Trust, by and through its Trustee, J. R. Hamilton, Respondent, 08–755.
Chronological Documents in the Texas Supreme Court Case File:
Petition for Review—Filed: October 30, 2008 [119 KB].
Response to Petition [1.14 MB] | Appendix [8.11 MB]—Filed: February 5, 2009.
Amicus Brief—San Antonio Water System—Received: February 19, 2009 [625 KB].
Amicus Brief—Mesa Water—Received: February 27, 2009 [910 KB].
Amended Reply to Response to Petition—Filed: March 25, 2009 [111 KB].
Amicus Brief—Texas Farm Bureau—Received: March 25, 2009 [87 KB].
Petitioner's Brief on the Merits—Filed: May 27, 2009 [2.28 MB].
Respondent's Brief on the Merits [213 KB] | Appendix [9.17 MB]—Filed: June 30, 2009.
Amicus Brief—CRMWA—Received: June 30, 2009 [1.10 MB].
Amicus Brief—City of Amarillo—Received: June 30, 2009 [397 KB].
Reply Brief—Filed: July 20, 2009 [1.48 MB].
Amicus Brief—Stewart Title Guaranty Company—Received: August 5, 2009 [105 KB].
Petitioner's Response to Post-Briefing Article and Amicus Brief—Filed: August 11, 2009 [479 KB].
Amicus Brief—San Antonio Water System—Received: August 12, 2009 [561 KB].
Petitioner's Response to Amicus Brief—Filed: August 20, 2009.
Court of Justice, European Commission. Curia documents, statistics, pleadings, judgments. http://curia.europa.eu/juris. Accessed daily/weekly from January 2, 2015, to June 9, 2016.

———. "Notes for the Guidance of Counsel." Notes for the guidance of counsel in written and oral proceedings before the Court of Justice of the European Communities, February 2008. http://www.curia.europa.eu.

Edwards Aquifer Authority and the State of Texas Petitioners, v. Burrell Day and Joel McDaniel, Respondents, 08–0964. (For the February 24, 2010, ruling in full, visit www.supreme.courts.state.tx.us/historical/2012/feb/080964.pdf.)

Chronological Documents in the Texas Supreme Court Case File:

Day—Petition for Review January 30, 2009.

State—Petition for Review—February 2, 2009.

EAA—Petition for Review—February 2, 2009.

Amicus Brief—Medina County Irrigators Alliance—March 3, 2009.

EAA—Response to Petition—March 4, 2009.

Amicus Brief—Angela Garcia—March 6, 2009.

Amicus Brief—City of Victoria—March 30, 2009.

Amended Amicus Brief—Medina County Irrigators Alliance—April 8, 2009.

Amicus Brief—Texas Farm Bureau—Received: April 29, 2009 [0.99 MB].

Amicus Brief—HGSD—Received: May 1, 2009 [941 KB].

Day—Response to State's Petition—Filed: May 5, 2009 [875 KB].

Day—Response to EAA's Petition—Filed: May 5, 2009 [931 KB].

Amicus Brief—Texas and Southwestern Cattle Raisers Association—Received: May 5, 2009 [494 KB].

State—Response to Petition—Filed: May 6, 2009 [441 KB].

State—Reply in Support of Petition—Filed: May 20, 2009 [298 KB].

EAA—Reply to Response to Petition—Filed: May 20, 2009 [1.76 MB].

Amicus Brief—The Alliance of EAA Permit Holders—Filed: June 8, 2009 [221 KB].

Supplement to Amicus Brief—The Alliance of EAA Permit Holders—Received: June 9, 2009 [121 KB].

Supplement to Amicus Brief—The Alliance of EAA Permit Holders—Received: June 18, 2009 [76.9 KB].

EAA—Petitioner's Brief on the Merits—Filed: September 18, 2009 [2.53 MB].

State—Petitioner's Brief on the Merits—Filed: September 18, 2009 [1.47 MB].

Day—Petitioners' Brief on the Merits—Filed: September 18, 2009 [5.35 MB].

Amicus Brief—Canadian River Municipal Water Authority—Received: October 27, 2009 [2.52 MB].

Day—Respondent's Brief to State's Brief—Filed: October 30, 2009 [931 KB].

Day—Respondent's Brief to EAA's Brief—Filed: October 30, 2009 [1.73 MB].

EAA—Respondent's Brief on the Merits—Filed: November 2, 2009 [6.34 MB].

Joint Amicus Brief—Texas Farm Bureau and Texas Cattle Feeders Association—Received: November 2, 2009 [1.14 MB].

State—Respondent's Brief on the Merits—Filed: November 2, 2009 [920 KB].

Amicus Letter—Texas Comptroller of Public Accounts—Received: December 15, 2009 [1.72 MB].

EAA—Reply Brief—Filed: December 17, 2009 [1.10 MB].

State—Reply Brief—Filed: December 17, 2009 [1.53 MB].

Day—Reply Brief to State's Response Brief—Filed: December 17, 2009 [705 KB].

Day—Reply Brief to EAA's Response Brief—Filed: December 17, 2009 [3.32 MB].

Amicus Brief—Texas Wildlife Association—Received: January 12, 2010 [173 KB].

Amicus Brief—Angela Garcia—Received: January 26, 2010 [1.23 MB].

Amicus Brief—Harris-Galveston Subsidence District—Received: February 1, 2010 [213 KB].

Amicus Brief—Mesa Water—Received: February 10, 2010 [127 KB].

Amicus Brief—Texas Landowners Council—Received: February 12, 2010 [211 KB].

Amicus Brief—Pacific Legal Foundation—Received: February 12, 2010 [135 KB].

Amicus Brief—Bragg—Received: February 16, 2010 [7.54 MB].

Amicus Letter Brief—City of Amarillo—Received: February 16, 2010 [393 KB].

Amicus Letter Brief—City of El Paso—Received: February 16, 2010 [3.84 MB].

EAA—Petition for Writ of Mandamus—Filed: March 5, 2010 [176 KB].

Day—Response to Post-submission Letter Brief—Filed: March 18, 2010 [18 KB].

Amicus Post-submission Letter—Bragg—Received: May 10, 2010 [21 KB].

Amicus Letter Brief—Bragg—Received: May 25, 2010 [30 KB].

Post-submission Amicus Brief—Texas Alliance of Groundwater Districts—Received: May 28, 2010 [142 KB].

Amicus Letter—Duncan—Received: June 3, 2010 [74 KB].

State—Post-submission Brief—Filed: June 10, 2010 [78 KB].

Day—Response to Amicus Brief—Filed: June 10, 2010 [233 KB].

Day—Response to Post-submission Brief—Filed: June 28, 2010 [432 KB].

Amicus Letter—Texas Farm Bureau—Received: July 9, 2010.

Edwards Aquifer Authority—Response to Amicus Letter, August 30, 2010.

Amicus Curiae Brief—The Texas Farm Bureau, Texas Wildlife Association and Texas and Southwestern Cattle Raisers Association, July 11, 2011.

Amicus Curiae Brief of the City of San Antonio by and through the San Antonio Water System in Support of Petitioner San Antonio Water System, November 3, 2011.

Day/McDaniel Response to the Amicus Curiae Brief of the City of San Antonio by and through the San Antonio Water System in Support of the Edwards Aquifer Authority, November 14, 2011.

Edwards Aquifer Authority and the State of Texas Petitioners, v. Burrell Day and Joel McDaniel, Respondents Amended Day/McDaniel Response to the Amicus Curiae Brief of the City of San Antonio by and through the San Antonio Water System in Support of the Edwards Aquifer Authority, December 20, 2011.

Glenn and Jo Lynn Bragg, Petitioners v. Edwards Aquifer Authority and Gregory Ellis, General Manager of the Edwards Aquifer Authority, Respondents, 01–0436.

Edwards Aquifer Authority v. Chemical Lime, Ltd., 06–0911.

Petition for Review—Filed: January 29, 2006 [663 KB].

Petitioners' Brief on the Merits—Filed: July 6, 2007 [2.22 MB].

Petitioners' Reply Brief—Filed: October 5, 2007 [1 MB].

Amicus Brief—State of Texas—Received: December 27, 2006 [132 KB].

Amicus Brief on the Merits—State of Texas—Received: August 8, 2007.

Respondent's Brief on the Merits—Filed: August 24, 2007 [2 MB].

The Adjudication of Water Rights in the Medina River Watershed of the San Antonio River Basin v. Alamo National Bank Independent Executor, 645 S.W.2d 596; 1982 Tex App. LEXIS 5610 (1982).

Barshop et al. v. Medina County Underground Water Conservation District et al., 95–0881.

Bart Sipriano v. Great Spring Waters of America, No. 98–0247, Supreme Court of Texas (1998–1999).

Charles C. Motl et al. v. R. W. Boyd et al. 116 Tex. 82; 286 S.W. 458; 1926 Tex. LEXIS 96, Supreme Court of Texas (1926).

City of Aspermont v. Rolling Plains Groundwater Conservation District, 2008 Tex. App. LEXIS 3274, Court of Appeals of Texas, Eleventh District, Eastland (2008).

City of Del Rio v. Clayton Sam Colt Hamilton Trust, Supreme Court of Texas Court Case. LEXIS 723 (2009).

Court of Justice of the European Union. December 2010 edition. http://curia.europa.eu/jcms/upload/docs/application/pdf/2012-05/cjue_en.pdf.

Court of Justice. Luxembourg, January 1, 2015. "COURT OF JUSTICE OF THE EUROPEAN UNION ANNUAL REPORT 2014 Synopsis of the Work of the Court of Justice, the General Court and the Civil Service Tribunal." Luxembourg, 2015. www.curia.europa.eu.

Edwards Aquifer Authority v. Burrel Day and Joel McDaniel. Court of Appeals of Texas, Fourth District, San Antonio. LEXIS 9777 (2008).

Friendswood Development Company et al. v. Smith-Southwest Industries, 576 S.W.2d 21; 1978 Tex. LEXIS 404; 22 Tex. Sup. J. 107; 5 A.L.R.4th 591; 62 Oil & Gas Rep. 218; 9 ELR 20452, Supreme Court of Texas (1978).

Guitar Holding Company, LP, Hudspeth County Underground Water Conservation District No. 1 v. CL Machinery Company and Cimarron Agricultural, LTD. Court of Appeals of Texas, Eighth District, El Paso. LEXIS 7869 (2006).

Heofs v. Short, 273 S.W. 785 (Tex. 1925).

Hugh Coates et al. v. Charles Hall, 2007 U.S. Dist. LEXIS 26294, United States District Court for the Western District of Texas, San Antonio Division (2007).

In re the Contests of the City of Laredo et al., To the Adjudication of Water Rights in the Middle Rio Grande Basin and Contributing Texas Tributaries, 675 S.W.2d 257; 1984 Tex. App. LEXIS 5687, Court of Appeals of Texas, Third District, Austin (1984).

InfoCuria—Case Law of the Court of Justice. List of results. http://curia.europa.eu/juris/documents.

Lee, Thomas F. "Re: Glenn and JoLynn Bragg v. Edwards Aquifer Authority; Cause No. 06–11–18170-CV in the 38th District Court of Medina County, Texas" (May 2010).

Lupe Alonzo, Jim Alonzo, Joe Alonzo, and Valentino Alonzo v. United States of America, 249 F.2d 189, United States Court of Appeals Tenth Circuit (1957).

Oscar C. Gordon v. San Antonio Water System, 2007 Tex. App. LEXIS 1932, Court of Appeals of Texas, Fourth District, San Antonio (2007).

Pecos County Water Control and Improvement District No. 1 v. Clayton W. Williams et al. Court of Civil Appeals of Texas, El Paso, LEXIS 2113 (1954).

San Antonio River Authority, Petitioner v. G. Garrett Lewis et al., Respondents, No.!-8304, Supreme Court of Texas, 363 S.W. 2d 444. Austin: Supreme Court of Texas, 1962.

San Antonio River Authority v. G. Garrett Lewis, 363 S.W.2d 444; 1962 Tex. LEXIS 699; 6 Tex. Sup. J. 137, Supreme Court of Texas (1962).

South Plains Lamesa Railroad, Ltd., and Kitten Family Living Trust v. High Plains Underground Water Conservation District No. 1, 52 S.W.3d 770; 2001 Tex. App. LEXIS 2497, Court of Appeals of Texas, Seventh District, Amarillo (2001).

State et al. v. Heard et al., 146 Tex 139, 204 SW 2d 344, Court of Civil Appeals of Texas, Austin (1946).

State of New Mexico ex rel. Eluid L. Martinez, State Engineer v. City of Las Vegas, 118 N.M. 257, 880 P.2d 868, Court of Appeals of New Mexico (1994).

State of Texas et al., Appellants, v. Valmont Plantations et al., Appellees, No. 13583, Civil Court of Appeals of Texas, San Antonio, 346 S.W.2d 853; 1961 Tex. App. San Antonio, TX: Civil Court of Appeals, 1961.

State of Texas v. Valmont Plantations, 346 S.W.2d 853; 1961 Tex App. LEXIS 2336 (1961).

The Texas Company v. Joe Burkett. Supreme Court of Texas. LEXIS 138 (1927).

Texas Commission on Environmental Quality. "Rights to Surface Water in Texas." GI-228 (Rev. 3/09). http://www.tceq.state.tx.us/publications/gi/gi-228.html/at_download/file.

United States of America in Behalf of the Pueblo of San Ildefonso v. Harley Brewer and Mrs. Harley Brewer, 184 F.Supp. 377, United States District Court D. New Mexico (1960).

United States of America v. Jose I. Abeyta, 632 F.Supp. 1301, United States District Court, D. New Mexico (1986).

United States v. Candelaria et al. 271 U.S. 432, 46 S.Ct. 561, Unites States Circuit Court of Appeals for the Eighth Circuit (1925–1926).

United States Army Corps of Engineers, Petitioner, v. Hawkes Co., Inc. et al. Respondents. ———— On Writ of Certiorari to the United States Court of Appeals for the Eighth Circuit ———— Brief for California Farm Bureau Federation, California Cattlemen's Association, California Building Industry Association, Building Industry Legal Defense Foundation, & California Business Properties Association as Amici Curiae in Support of Respondents ———— Peter Prows Counsel of Record Briscoe Ivester & Bazel LLP, 155 Sansome Street, Seventh Floor, San Francisco, CA 94104 (415) 402-2700 pprows@briscoelaw.net. March 2016.

Books and Journal Articles

The Alcalde. Austin: University of Texas, 1912–1922.

Almaráz, Felix D., Jr. "San Antonio's Franciscan Missions." *The Americas* 44 (July 1987).

Amos, Adell L., David Getches, and Sandra Beth Zellmer. *Water Law in a Nutshell.* 5th ed. St. Paul, MN: West Academic, 2015.

Anonymous, ed. Muir, Andrew Forest. Austin: University of Texas Press, 1958.
Armstrong, Ellis L., ed. *History of Public Works in the United States, 1776–1976*. Chicago: American Public Works Association, 1976.
Arneson, Edward P. "Early Irrigation in Texas." *Southwestern Historical Quarterly* 25, no. 2. http://www.tsha.utexas.edu/publications/journals/shq/online/v025/n2/contrib_DIVL1538_print.html.
Austin, Mattie Alice. "The Municipal Government of San Fernando de Bexar, 1730–1800." *Southwestern Historical Quarterly* 8, no. 4: 277–352 http://www.tsha.utexas.edu/publications/journals/shq/online/v008/n4/article_1_print.html.
Bannon, John Francis. *The Spanish Borderlands Frontier, 1513–1821*. Albuquerque: University of New Mexico Press, 1970.
Baxter, John O. *Spanish Irrigation in the Taos Valley*. Santa Fe: New Mexico State Engineer Office, 1990 (gift from the New Mexico state engineer).
Benoist, Dr. Howard, and Flores, Sr. Maria Carolina, CP. *The Spanish Missionary Heritage of the United States*. San Antonio, TX: United States Department of the Interior/National Park Service and Los Compadres de San Antonio Missions National Historical Park, 1990.
Blake, Nelson M. *Water for the Cities*. Syracuse, NY: Syracuse University Press, 1956.
Bolton, Herbert E. "The Mission as a Frontier Institution in the Spanish-American Colonies." *American Historical Review* 23, no. 1 (October 1917): 42–61.
———. *Texas in the Middle Eighteenth Century*. Austin: University of Texas Press, 1970.
Breeden, James O., ed. *A Long Ride in Texas: The Explorations of John Leonard Riddell*. College Station: Texas A&M Press, 1994.
Brookings Institution. "Water in the Israel-Palestinian Peace Process: Sharing Resources to Share the Future." Washington, DC: Brookings Institution, 2013.
Brooks, David B., and Trottier, Julie. "An Agreement to Share Water between Israelis and Palestinians: The FoEME Proposal." Czech Republic Development Cooperation with Support of the European Union. Amman: Friends of the Middle East, 2012.
Brueggeman, William B., and Fisher, Jeffrey D. *Real Estate Finance and Investments*. 14th ed. New York: McGraw-Hill Irwin, 2011.
Burkholder, Mary V. *Down the Acequia Madre*. San Antonio, TX: Private, 1976.
———. *The King William Area: A History and Guide to the Houses*. San Antonio, TX: Private, 1973.
Burns, Robert Ignatius. "Irrigation Taxes in Early Mudjar Valencia: The Problem of the Alfarda." *Speculum* 44, no. 4 (October 1969).
Cabré, Alexander. "Human Right to Environment and Its Effective Protection in Catalonia, Spain and Europe." *International Journal of Legal Information* 42, no. 1 (spring 2014): 121–34.
Casado-Perez, Vanesa. "Missing Water Markets: A Cautionary Tale of Governmental Failure." *New York University Environmental Law Journal* 23 (2015): 157–241.
Castañeda, Carlos E. *Our Catholic Heritage in Texas, 1519–1936*. Vols. 1–7. Austin, TX: Von Boeckmann-Jones Co., 1938.
Chabot, Frederick C. *With the Makers of San Antonio*. San Antonio, TX: Private, 1937.

Chipman, Donald E. *Spanish Texas, 1519–1821*. Austin: University of Texas Press, 1992.

Clopper, J. C. "J. C. Clopper's Journal and Book of Memoranda for 1828. 1 Province of Texas." *Southwestern Historical Quarterly* 13, no. 1: 44–80. http://www.tsha.utexas.edu/publications/journals/shq/online/v013.n1/article_4_print.html.

Coplin, William D., and O'Leary, Michael K. *Public Policy Skills*. Croton-on-Hudson, NY: Public Policy Associates, 1988.

Coppini, Pompeo. *From Dawn to Sunset*. San Antonio, TX: Naylor Company, 1949.

"Corn." Agriculture Irrigation Water Management. University of California Agriculture and Natural Resources. http://ucmanagedrought.ucdavis.edu/Agriculture/Crop_Irrigation_Strategies/Corn (adjusted for acre-feet by the author).

Cox, I. J. "The Early Settlers of San Fernando." *Southwestern Historical Quarterly* 5, no. 2 (1901). http://www.tsha.utexas.edu/publications/journals/shq/online/v005/n2/article_6_print.html.

Cox, I. Waynne. *The Spanish Acequias of San Antonio*. San Antonio, TX: Maverick Publishing, 2005.

Cresswell, John W. *Research Design: Qualitative, Quantitative, and Mixed Methods Approaches*. Los Angeles, CA: Sage Publications, 2014.

Cronon, William. *Nature's Metropolis: Chicago and the Great West*. New York: W. W. Norton, 1991.

Cuevas, P., and Mariano, S. J. *Historia de la Iglesia en Mexico*. Vol. 4: *1700–1800*. El Paso, TX: Editorial "Revista Catolica," 1928.

Cutter, Charles R. "Community and the Law in Northern New Spain." *The Americas* 50, no. 4 (April 1994): 467–80.

De la Teja, Jesús F., ed. *Preparing the Way*. Preliminary Studies of the Texas Catholic Historical Society 1. Austin: Texas Catholic Historical Society, 1997.

———. *San Antonio de Bexar: A Community on New Spain's Northern Frontier*. Albuquerque: University of New Mexico Press, 1995.

De Leon, Arnoldo. *The Tejano Community, 1836–1900*. Dallas, TX: SMU Press, 1982.

De Stefano, Lucia, and Llamas, M. Ramón, eds. *Water, Agriculture and the Environment in Spain: Can We Square the Circle?* London: Taylor & Francis Group, 2013.

Dellepenna, Joseph, ed., *The Appropriative Rights Model Water Code*. Report of the Committee on Laws and Institutions. Reston, VA: American Society of Civil Engineers, 2007.

———. "Developing a Suitable Water Allocation Law for Pennsylvania." *Villanova Environmental Law Journal* 17, no. 1 (2006).

———. "The Evolution of Riparianism in the United States." *Marquette Law Review* 95: 53–90.

Department of the Interior. *Water Supply and Irrigation Papers of the United States Geological Survey No. 13*. Washington, DC: US Government Printing Office, 1896.

Dobbins, Betty Eakle. *The Spanish Element in Texas Water Law*. Austin: University of Texas Press, 1959.

Doolittle, William E. "Agriculture in North America on the Eve of Contact: A Reassessment." *Annals of the Association of American Geographers* 82, no. 3 (September 1992): 386–401.

Elliott, Heather. "The Failings of Alabama Water Law." *Alabama Law Review*. https://www.law.ua.edu/lawreview/files/2011/07/The-Failings-of-Alabama-Water-Law.pdf, 765–66.

Elliott, Mark. "If European Union Law Is Supreme, Can Parliament Be Sovereign?" *Public Law for Everyone* (blog). February 21, 2016. http://publiclawforeveryone.com/2016/02/21/1000-words-if-european-union-is-supreme-can-parliament-be-sovereign (accessed April 3, 2016).

Escrig-Olmedo, Elena; Muñoz-Torres, María Jesús; and Fernández-Izquierdo, María Ángeles. "Sustainable Development and the Financial System: Society's Perceptions about Socially Responsible Investing." *Business Strategy and the Environment* 22 (2013): 410–28.

Everett, Donald E. *San Antonio: The Flavor of Its Past, 1845–1898*. San Antonio, TX: Trinity University Press, 1959.

Fernandez, Gilad. "Economics Aspects in Water Management in Israel." Jerusalem: Water Authority, State of Israel, 2000.

Fireman, Janet R. *The Spanish Royal Corps of Engineers in the Western Borderlands*. Glendale, CA: Arthur H. Clark Company, 1977.

Fisher, Lewis F. *Crown Jewel of Texas: The Story of San Antonio's River*. San Antonio, TX: Maverick Publishing Company, 1997.

Fornés, Juan Maria; de la Hera, África; Llinas, Ramón; and Martínez-Santos, Pedro. "Legal Aspects of Groundwater Ownership in Spain." *International Water Resources Association* 32, no. 4 (December 2007).

Foster, William C. *Spanish Expeditions into Texas, 1689–1768*. Austin: University of Texas Press, 1995.

Foundation for Middle East Peace (FMEP). "The Socio-economic Impact of Settlements on Land, Water, and the Palestinian Economy." Washington, DC: FMEP, 1998.

Friends of the Earth Middle East (FoEME) Priority Initiatives Team. "Cross Border 'Priority Initiatives' of the Good Water Neighbors Project." Amman: FoEME, 2013.

Gesick, E. John, Jr. *Under the Live Oak Tree: A History of Seguin*. Seguin, TX: Seguin Bank & Trust Company, 1988.

Glick, Thomas F. *Islamic and Christian Spain in the Early Middle Ages*. Princeton, NJ: Princeton University Press, 1979.

Goldshore, Lewis P. *New Jersey Riparian Rights Handbook*. State of New Jersey County and Municipal Government Study Commission, 1979.

Gómez-Limón, J. A., and Riesgo, L. "Water Pricing: Analysis of Differential Impacts on Heterogeneous Farmers." *Water Resources* 40, no. 7 (2004). Doi:10.1029/2003WR002205.

Graham, Don. *Kings of Texas*. Hoboken, NJ: John Wiley & Sons, 2003.

Grant, Sue, and Vidler, Chris. *Economics in Context*. Oxford, UK: Heinemann Educational Providers, 2000.

Green, Christine. "The Tribunal de las Aquas"

Greenhill, Joe R., and Gee, Thomas Gibbs. "Ownership of Ground Water in Texas: The East Case Reconsidered." *Texas Law Review* 33 (1955).

Griggs, Blake W. "Beyond Drought: Water Rights in the Age of Permanent Depletion." *Kansas Law Review* 62 (2014).

Habig, Marion A. *The Alamo Chain of Missions*. Chicago: Franciscan Herald Press, 1968.

———. *San Antonio's Mission San Jose*. Chicago: Franciscan Herald Press, 1968.

Hall, Molly Elizabeth. "Environmental Law in the European Union: A New Approach to Enforcement." *Tulane Environmental Law Journal* 20 (summer 2007): 278.

Handy, Mary Olivia. *History of Fort Sam Houston*. San Antonio, TX: Naylor Press, 1951.

Henslin, James M. *Social Problems: A Down-to-Earth Approach.* Boston: Pearson, 2011.

Highsmith, Richard M., Jr. "Irrigated Lands of the World." *Geographical Review* 55, no. 3 (July 1965): 382–89.

Hildebrand, Ira P. "The Rights of Riparian Owners at Common Law in Texas." *Texas Law Review* 6 (1927–1928).

House, Boyce. *San Antonio City of Flaming Adventure*. San Antonio, TX: Naylor Company, 1949.

Hundley, Norris, Jr. *The Great Thirst: Californians and Water—a History*. Rev. ed. Berkeley: University of California Press, 2001.

Hunt, Robert C., and Hunt, Eva. "Canal Irrigation and Local Social Organization." *Current Anthropology* 17, no. 3 (September 1976): 389–411.

Hutchins, Wells A. "The Community Acequia: Its Origin and Development." *Southwestern Historical Quarterly* 31, no. 3 (1928): 261–84. http://www.tsha.utexas.edu/publications/journals/shq/online/v031/n3/article_5_print.html

———. *The Texas Law of Water Rights*. Austin: Texas Legislature and Texas Board of Water Engineers, 1961.

Hutchins, Wells, and Harry Steele. "Basic Water Rights Doctrines and Their Implications for River Basin Development." *Law and Contemporary Problems* 22, no. 2 (1957): 284.

Isaac, Jad. "Core Issues of the Palestinian-Israeli Water Dispute." Jerusalem: Applied Research Institute, 1994.

Jackson, Jack. *Los Mesteños*. College Station: Texas AM Press, 1986.

Jackson, Robert H. *Missions and the Frontiers of Spanish America*. Scottsdale, AZ: Pentacle Press, 2005.

Jackson, Robert H., and Castillo, Eduardo. *Indians, Franciscans, and Spanish Colonization*. Albuquerque: University of New Mexico Press, 1995.

Keinan, Tamar. "Water Justice: Water as a Human Right in Israel." Amman: Friends of the Middle East, 2005.

Kelly, William W. "Concepts in the Anthropological Study of Irrigation." *American Anthropologist, New Series* 85, no. 4 (December 1983): 880–86.

Kent, James. *Commentaries on American Law* (1826–1830).

Kent, Paul G., and Dudiak, Tamara A. *Wisconsin Water Law: A Guide to Water Rights and Regulations*. University of Wisconsin, Stevens Point. 2001. https://

www3.uwsp.edu/cnr-ap/UWEXLakes/Documents/resources/bookstore/Wisconsin %20Water%20Law-Edition2-G3622.pdf.

Koek, Elizabeth. "Water for One People Only: Discriminatory Access and 'Water Apartheid' in the OPT." Ramallah: Al-Haq, 2013.

Kwasniak, Arlene J. "Inflating and Deflating: Courts and State/Crown Ownership and Management of Water." *Public Land & Resources Law Review* 33 (2012): 95.

Lauer, T. E. "The Common Law Background of the Riparian Doctrine." *Missouri Law Review* 28 (winter 1963).

Lea, Tom. *The King Ranch, I and II*. Boston: Little, Brown & Co., 1957.

Leal, John Odgen, Bexar County Archivist. *After the Secularization of the Mission San Antonio de Valero, Known as the Alamo, 1792*. San Antonio, TX: Bexar County, 1991.

Leutenegger, Benedict, tr., with intro. And notes by Habig, Marion A., OFM, and Diekemper, Barnabas, OFM. "Memorial of Father Benito Fernández Concerning the Canary Islanders, 1741." *Southwestern Historical Quarterly* 82, no. 3 (January 1979): 265–96.

Lin, Albert C. "Fracking and Federalism: A Comparative Approach to Reconciling National and Subnational Interests in the United States and Spain." *Environmental Law* 44, no. 4 (fall 2014): 1039–78.

Louka, Elli. *Water Law and Policy.* New York: Oxford University Press, 2008.

Lusch, David P. "An Overview of Existing Water Law in Michigan Related to Irrigation Water Use and Riparian Considerations." Michigan State University. February 2011. https://www.canr.msu.edu/uploads/235/67987/lyndon/Michigan _Water_Law.pdf.

Maas, Arthur, and Anderson, Raymond L. *And the Desert Shall Rejoice: Conflict, Growth, and Justice in Arid Environments*. Cambridge, MA: MIT Press, 1978.

Mahoney, James. "Revisiting General Theory in Historical Sociology." *Social Forces* 83, no. 2 (2004): 459–89.

Mandelker, Daniel R. "Investment-Backed Expectations: Is There a Taking?" *Washington University Journal of Urban and Contemporary Law* 31 (January 1987): 3–43.

Margat, Jean, and van der Gun, Jac. *Groundwater around the World*. London: Taylor & Francis–CRC Press, 2013.

Marks, Paula Mitchell. *Turn Your Eyes to Texas*. College Station: Texas A&M Press, 1989.

Matovina, Timothy M. *Guadalupe and Her Faithful*. Baltimore: Johns Hopkins University Press, 2005.

———. *Tejano Religion and Ethnicity San Antonio, 1821–1860*. Austin: University of Texas Press, 1995.

Matson, Daniel S., and Fontana, Bernard L., ed. Tr. Father Bringas. *Reports to the King, Methods of Indoctrination on the Frontier of New Spain, 1796–97*. Tucson: University of Arizona Press, 1977.

Mauldin, Raymond P. *Exploring Drought in the San Antonio Area between 1700 and 1979*. San Antonio: University of Texas, San Antonio Center for Archaeological Research, 2003.

Mesa-Jurado, M. A., Berbel, J., and Orgaz, F. "Estimating Marginal Value of Water for Irrigated Olive Grove with the Production Function Method." *Spanish Journal of Agricultural Research* 8, Suppl. 2 (2010): S197–S206.

Meyer, Michael C. *Water in the Hispanic Southwest*. Tucson: University of Arizona Press, 1984.

Miller, Char, ed. *On the Border: An Environmental History of San Antonio*. San Antonio, TX: Trinity University Press, 2005.

Montejano, David. *Anglos and Mexicans in the Making of Texas, 1836–1986*. Austin: University of Texas Press, 1987.

Moore, Steven A. *Alternate Routes to the Sustainable City: Austin, Curitiba, and Frankfurt*. Lanham, MD: Lexington Books, 2007.

Morales, Francisco, OFM. "Mexican Society and the Franciscan Order." *The Americas* 54 (January 1998).

Morfi, Fray Father Juan Agustin. Ed. Castañeda, Carlos. *The History of Texas, 1673–1779*. Albuquerque: Quivera Society, 1935 (manuscript written in 1782–1783).

Newcomb, W.W. *The Indians of Texas*. Austin: University of Texas Press, 1961.

O'Rourke, Thomas P. *The Franciscan Missions in Texas (1690–1793)*. N.p., 1927.

Ostrom, Elinor, and Gardner, Roy. "Coping with Asymmetries in the Commons: Self-Governing Irrigation Systems Can Work." *Journal of Economics Perspectives* 7, no. 4 (autumn 1993): 93–112.

Parsons, James J. "The Migration of Canary Islanders to the Americas: An Unbroken Current since Columbus." *The Americas* 39 (April 1983): 447–69.

Patton, Michael Quinn. *Qualitative Evaluation and Research Methods*. 2nd ed. Newbury Park, CA: Sage Publications, 1990.

Perko, Anthony. "Case Note: Watershed Management: A Comparison between Efforts in the United States and the European Union." *University of Denver Law Review* 16 (fall 2012): 166.

Phelan, Richard. *Texas Wild*. New York: E. P. Dutton & Co., Inc., 1976.

Porter, Charles R., Jr. "Farm and Ranch for Texas Agents." Austin: Texas Real Estate Commission, 2008 (accredited continuing education course).

———. "Financing Groundwater Conservation Districts in Texas: Results of a Preliminary Study." *Texas Water Journal* 4, no. 1 (2013).

———. "The History of W. A. East v. Houston and Texas Central Railway Company, 1904: Establishment of the Rule of Capture in Texas Water Law or 'He Who Has the Biggest Pump Gets the Water.'" *East Texas Historical Journal* 50, no. 2 (fall 2012): 107–19.

———. "The Hydraulic West: The History of Irrigation." Chapter 11 in *The World of the American West*, ed. Bakken, Gordon Morris, 308–35. New York: Routledge, 2011.

———. *Maker of Modern Texas, George W. Brackenridge*. Austin, TX: Publisher pending, 2013.

———. "'Of Urgent Concern': What Prompted House Bill 162, the Groundwater Conservation Act of 1949." Papers of the Texas Water Law Conference, Austin, Texas, 2015.

———. *Public Water Policies: The Ultimate Weapons of Social Control*. Lanham, MD: Bernan Press, 2018.
———. "Querétaro in Focus: The Franciscan Missionary Colleges and the Texas Missions." *Catholic Southwest: A Journal of History and Culture* 19 (2008).
———. *Sharing the Common Pool: Water Rights in the Everyday Lives of Texans*. San Marcos, TX: River Books, 2014.
———. *Spanish Water/Anglo Water*. College Station: Texas A&M University Press, 2009.
———. "Texas Out of Water?" *Houston Chronicle*. October 23, 2011.
———. "Water Rights for Texas Agents." Austin: Texas Real Estate Commission, 2008 (accredited continuing education course).
Poyo, Gerald E., and Hinojosa, Gilberto. *Tejano Origins in Eighteenth-Century San Antonio*. Austin: University of Texas Press, 1991.
Queen, Stuart A. "What Is a Community?" *Journal of Social Forces* 1, no. 4 (May 1972): 375–82.
Rae, Stephen R., and Minor, Joseph E. "Early Engineering in the American Southwest." *American Society of Civil Engineers Proceedings* 99, no. 2 (April 1973): 142–57.
Ramsdell, Charles W. *San Antonio: A Historical and Pictorial Guide*. Austin: University of Texas Press, 1959.
Raup, H. F. "Transformation of Southern California to a Cultivated Land." *Annals of the Association of American Geographers* 49, no. 3 (September 1959): 58–78.
Rawson, Michael. "The Nature of Water: Reform and the Antebellum Crusade for Municipal Water in Boston." *Environmental History* 9, no. 3 (2004): 411–35.
Reisner, Marc. *Cadillac Desert*. New York: Viking, 1986.
Ricard, Robert. *The Spiritual Conquest of Mexico*. Berkeley: University of California Press, 1966 (original title: *Conquete spirituelle du Mexique*. Paris: University of Paris, 1933).
Rivera, Jose A. *Acequia Culture*. Albuquerque: University of New Mexico Press, 1988.
Rodriquez, Sylvia. *Acequia: Water Sharing, Sanctity, and Place*. Santa Fe: School for Advanced Research Press, 2006.
Roemer, Dr. Ferdinand. Tr. Mueller, Oswald. *Roemer's Texas, 1845–1847*. San Antonio, TX: Standard Printing Company, 1935.
Sanchez, Jose Maria. "A Trip to Texas in 1828." *Southwestern Historical Quarterly* 29, no. 4 (April 1926): 249–88. http://www.tsha.utexas.edu/publications/journals/shq/v029/n4/article_3_print.html.
Schuetz, Mardith. "Professional Artisans in the Hispanic Southwest." *The Americas* 40 (July 1983).
"A Short Course in Water Rights." *Environment Hawaii* 1, no. 2 (August 1990). https://www.environment-hawaii.org/?p=4008.
Shuttleworth, Kate. "How Israel's War Has Left Gaza Dry." *The National*. April 25, 2015. https://www.thenationalnews.com/world/how-israel-s-war-has-left-gaza-dry-1.27396.
Sibley, Marilyn McAdams. *George W. Brackenridge, Maverick Philanthropist*. Austin: University of Texas Press, 1973.

Siegel, Seth M. *Israel's Solution for a Water-Starved World: Let There Be Water*. New York: St. Martin's Press, 2015.

Skocpol, Theda, ed. *Vision and Method in Historical Sociology*. London: Cambridge University Press, 1984.

Sneddon, Chris; Harris, Usa Leila; Dimitrov, Radoslav; and Ozesmi, Uygar. "Contested Waters: Conflict, Scale, and Sustainability in Aquatic Socioecological Systems." *Society and Natural Resources* 15, no. 66 (2002): 663–75.

Stratfor Worldview. "Industrial Expansion Will Strain Mexico's Water Resources." 8th Occasional Water Scarcity Issues Report. Austin, Texas, 2015.

———. "The Sea Is a Relief for Spain." 10th Occasional Water Scarcity Issues Report. Austin, Texas, 2015.

Swearingen, William Scott, Jr. *Environmental City: People, Place, Politics, and the Meaning of Modern Austin*. Austin: University of Texas Press, 2010.

Taleb, Yana Abu; Alexander, Michael; Robillard, Catherine-Emeline; Al Khateeb, Nader; Bromberg, Gidon; and Mehyar, Munqeth. "Why Cooperate over Water: Shared Waters of Palestine, Israel and Jordan: Cross-Border Crises and the Need for Trans-national Solutions." Amman: Friends of the Middle East, 2010.

Tal-Spiro, Ori. "Israeli-Palestinian Cooperation on Water Issues." Jerusalem: Center for Research and Information, 2011.

Taylor, Virginia H. *The Spanish Archives of the General Land Office of Texas*. Austin, TX: Lone Star Press, 1955.

Taylor, William B. *Magistrates of the Sacred*. Stanford, CA: Stanford University Press, 1996.

Terán, Manual de, ed. Tr. Jackson, Jack, and Wheat, John. *Texas by Terán: The Diary Kept by General Manual de Terán on His 1828 Inspection of Texas*. Austin: University of Texas, 2000.

Texas Comptroller of Public Accounts (TCPA). *Forces of Change: Shaping the Future of Texas*. Austin: TCPA, November 1993, Vol. 2, Pt. 1.

Texas Water Development Board. "A Texan's Guide to Water and Water Rights Marketing." Austin: Texas Water Development Board, 2003.

Tijerina, Andrés. *Tejanos and Texas under the Mexican Flag, 1821–1836*. College Station: Texas A&M University Press, 1994.

Torres, Luis. *Voices from the San Antonio Missions*. Lubbock: Texas Tech University Press, 1997.

Turlock, Anthony Dan, and Jason Anthony Robison. *Law of Water Rights and Resources*. Environmental Law Series. Eagan, MN: Thomson Reuters, 2018, 190.

Turton, Anthony, and Henwood, Roland, eds. *Hydropolitics in the Development World: A South African Perspective*. Pretoria: University of Pretoria, 2002.

Valenzuela-Bock, Catherina. "Court of Justice of the European Union Orders Greece to Pay Fine for Delay in Implementing Waste Water Directive (October 15, 2015)." American Society of International Law. https://www.asil.org/blogs/court-justice-european-union-orders-greece-pay-fine-delay-implementing-waste-water-directive.

Water Authority, State of Israel. "The Water Issue between Israel and the Palestinians." PowerPoint presentation, 2012.

Water Resources Center at Texas Tech University. *The Acequias of San Antonio, Historic American Engineering Record TX-1*. Washington, DC: National Parks Service, 1973.

Weber, David J. *Barbaros: Spaniards and Their Savages in the Age of Enlightenment*. New Haven, CT: Yale University Press, 2005.

———. *The Mexican Frontier, 1821–1846: The American Southwest under Mexico*. Albuquerque: University of New Mexico Press, 1982.

———, ed. *New Spain's Far Northern Frontier*. Dallas, TX: Southern Methodist University Press, 1979.

———. *The Spanish Frontier in North America*. New Haven, CT: Yale University Press, 1992.

Weber, David J., and Arnoldo De León, eds. *Foreigners in Their Native Land: Historical Roots of the Mexican Americans*. Albuquerque: University of New Mexico Press, 1982.

Website of the Edwards Aquifer. www.edwardsaquifer.net.

Website of the San Antonio Water System (SAWS). www.saws.org.

Weddle, Robert S. *San Juan Bautista—Gateway to Spanish Texas*. Austin: University of Texas Press, 1968.

Wegener, Elaine Hoffman, ed. *George C. Vaughan, Early Entrepreneur*. San Antonio, TX: Watercress Press, 1984 (gift from the Vaughan family and Tom Monroe).

Weniger, Del. *The Explorers' Texas: The Land and Waters*. Austin, TX: Eakin Press, 1984.

Wheeler, Kenneth W. *To Wear a City's Crown: The Beginnings of Urban Growth in Texas, 1836–1865*. Cambridge, MA: Harvard University Press, 1968.

White, A. A., and Wilson, Will. "The Flow and Underflow of Motl v. Boyd: The Problem." *Southwestern Law Journal* 9, no. 1 (1955).

Wood, Alexander. "Watering Down Federal Court Jurisdiction: What Role Do Federal Courts Play in Deciding Water Rights?" *Journal of Environmental Law and Litigation* 23, no. 1 (2008): 241–74.

Worster, Donald. *Rivers of Empire: Water, Aridity, and the Growth of the American West*. New York: Pantheon Books, 1985.

Xie, Oliver Hong. "Water: The Real Perpetrator of the Israeli-Palestinian Conflict?" Conference paper, 2007.

Zeitoun, Mark. *Power and Water in the Middle East: The Hidden Politics of the Palestinian-Israel Water Conflict*. London: I. B. Tauris, 2012.

Monographs

Almaráz, Felix D. *Crossroad of Empire: The Church and State on the Rio Grande Frontier of Coahuila and Texas, 1700–1821*. Report No. 1. San Antonio: University of Texas, San Antonio, Center for Archaeological Research, 1979.

Cox, I. Waynne. *Archaeological Monitoring at Espada Road Acequia Crossing*. Report No. 221. San Antonio: University of Texas, San Antonio, Center for Archaeological Research, 1993.

———. "10th Street Substation Excavation of the Acequia Madre (41 BX 8), San Antonio, Bexar County, Texas." Archaeological Survey Report No. 153. San Antonio: University of Texas, San Antonio, Center for Archaeological Research, 1985.

———. "Excavations of Portions of the San Pedro Acequia (41 BX 337) and a Search for the Arocha Acequia." Archaeological Survey Report No. 161. San Antonio: University of Texas, San Antonio, Center for Archaeological Research, 1986.

Cox, I. Waynne, and Houk, Brett A. "Archaeological Monitoring of the HEB-GSA Parking Lot: Impacts to the San Pedro Acequia." Archaeological Survey Report No. 279. San Antonio: University of Texas, San Antonio, Center for Archaeological Research, 1998.

Cox, Patrick. "Our Water and the Threat to the Heart of Our Existence." *Policy: Water, Government, and the People*. February 3, 2015. https://texaswaterpolicy.org/2015/02.

Frkuska, Augustine. "Archaeological Investigations at the San Pedro Acequia." Archaeological Survey Report No. 103. San Antonio: University of Texas, San Antonio, Center for Archaeological Research, 1981.

Glick, Thomas F. *The Old World Background of the Irrigation System of San Antonio Texas*. Southwestern Studies Series No. 35 El Paso: Texas Western Press, 1972.

Ivey, Jake. *Mission Land Use in the San Antonio River Valley*. N.p: n.p., 1991. Acquired from the Center for Archaeological Research at the University of Texas, San Antonio, Library.

Nickels, David L., Cox, I. Waynne, and Gibson, Connie. "Excavation of the San Pedro Acequia on the Grounds of the San Antonio Housing Authority." Archaeological Survey Report No. 243. San Antonio: University of Texas, San Antonio, Center for Archaeological Research, 1996.

OTHER SOURCES

Aiken, Rob, and Lamm, Freddie. "Managing Deficit Sprinkler Irrigation of Sunflower." *The Sunflower*. February 1, 2011.

Ankrum, Nora. "Water Fall: Between Austin Water's Conservation Goals and its Execution . . . Lies a Shadow." *Austin Chronicle*. June 17, 2011.

Baade, Hans W. "The Historical Background of Texas Water Law: A Tribute to Jack Pope." *St. Mary's Law Journal* 18, no. 1 (1986).

Benson, Reed D. "Deflating the Deference Myth: National Interests vs. State Authority under Federal Laws Affecting Water Use." *Utah Law Review* 241 (2006).

Bhatia R., and Falkenmark, M. "Over Exploitation of Groundwater and its Adverse Effects." International Conference on Water and the Environment, Dublin, Ireland, January 26–31, 1992.

Bishop, Pamela. "A Short Review of Pennsylvania Water Law."

Blankenship, Grant. "Drought Spreads Pain from Florida to Arizona." *New York Times*, July 11, 2011.

Bogener, Stephen. *Ditches across the Desert: Irrigation in the Lower Pecos Valley*. Lubbock: Texas Tech University Press, 2003.

Booth, F. R. "Adjudication on Water." Paper presented to North Texas Bar Association, 1967.

Brody, Jane E. "Water Holds Pleasures, and Menaces That Lurk." *New York Times*. July 11, 2011.

Brown, Timothy L., and Jason T. Hill. "Surface and Groundwater in Texas." *The Water Report*. October 15, 2019.

Bullock, Bob, and Hubert, Martin. "Senate Bill 1, the First Big and Bold Step toward Meeting Texas's Future Water Needs." *Texas Tech Law Review* 30 (1999): 53.

"California's Public Trust Doctrine." Environmental Law Foundation. https://www.envirolaw.org/documents/ScottFAQ.pdf.

Callahan, Charles C. "Principles of Water Rights Law in Ohio." School of Environment and Natural Resources, Ohio State University. 1979. https://senr.osu.edu/sites/senr/files/imce/files/course_materials/5451ReadingMaterials/Principles_of_Water.pdf.

Campbell, Augustus L. "Texas Watermasters: A Legal History and Analysis of Surface Water Rights Enforcement." *Texas Tech Administrative Law Journal* 143 (spring 2006).

Campoy, Ana, and Gold, Russell. "Oil's Growing Thirst for Water." *Wall Street Journal*. December 2011.

Canseco, Susana Elena. "Landowner's Rights in Texas Groundwater: How and Why Texas Courts Should Determine Landowners Do Not Own Groundwater in Place." *Baylor Law Review* 60, no. 2 (spring 2008): 492–525.

Caroom, Doug, and Elliot, Paul. "Water Rights Adjudication-Texas Style." *Texas Bar Journal* 44 (November 1981): 1183–90.

Caroom, Douglas G., and Maxwell, Susan M. "Overview of Texas Water Rights and Water Development." Continuing education paper, University of Texas School of Law, 2008.

Caughey, John. "The Pueblo Water Right of Laredo." Library of Sherry L. Peel Attorney at Law, Austin, Texas, July 1979.

Caughey, John, and Mares, Jose Fuentes. "Adjudication of the Water Rights in the Middle Rio Grande River and Its Contributing Tributaries." Library of Sherry L. Peel Attorney at Law, Austin, Texas, 1979.

Chahin, Dinniah M. "Is the Once Mighty River Not So Mighty? How the Distribution of Water Rights and Water Planning along the Texas Portion of the Rio Grande River Affects Future Texans." *Texas Tech Journal of Texas Administrative Law* 6 (spring 2005): 115–38.

Clayton, Jeffrey J. "'Here Is a Land Where Life Is Written in Water': Re-writing Western Water Law in the 21st Century." *University of Denver Water Law Review* 5, no. 2 (spring 2002): 525–44.

Combs, Susan. "Liquid Assets: The State of Texas' Water Resources." Austin: Texas Comptroller of Public Accounts, 2009.

Davis, Jeff J., and McElroy, Scott B. "Revisiting Colorado River Water Conservation District v. United States—There Must be a Better Way." *Arizona State Law Journal* 27 (summer 1995): 597.

De la Teja, Jesús F. "Land and Society in 18th Century San Antonio de Bexar: A Community on New Spain's Northern Frontier." PhD diss., University of Texas, Austin, 1988.

Dean, Lyn E., and Johnson, Russell S. "The Changing Face of Water Rights in Texas 2003." State Bar of Texas, 2003.

"Drifting toward Disaster: The (Second) Rio Grande." *Texas Observer*. December 2022. https://www.texasobserver.org/rio-grande-water-drifting-toward-disaster.

"Drought Emergency Declared for All of Southern California." *Huffpost*. December 15, 2022. https://www.huffpost.com/entry/drought-emergency-california_n_639aad84e4b0804966b3ad22.

Drummond, Dylan O. "Groundwater Ownership in Place: Fact or Fiction?" Paper presented at Texas Water Law Institute, Austin, Texas, December 3–5, 2008.

———. "Texas Groundwater Law in the Twenty-First Century: A Compendium of Historical Approaches, Current Problems, and Future Solutions Focusing on the High Plains Aquifer and the Panhandle." *Texas Tech Administrative Law Journal* 4 (2003): 173–225.

———. "Texas Groundwater Rights and Immunities: From East to Sipriano and Beyond." Paper presented at the 115th Texas State Historical Association Annual Meeting, El Paso, Texas, March 3–5, 2011.

Duhigg, Charles. "As Sewers Fill, Waste Poisons Waterways." *New York Times*. November 22, 2009.

Dumars, Charles T. "Changing Interpretations of New Mexico's Constitutional Provisions Allocating Water Resources: Integrating Private Property Rights and Public Values." *New Mexico Law Review* 26, no. 3 (summer 1996): 367–91.

Dumars, Charles T.; O'Leary, Marilyn; and Utton, Albert E. *Pueblo Indian Water Rights: Struggle for a Precious Resource*. Tucson: University of Arizona Press, 1984.

Duncan, Robert. "Amicus Brief for The Edwards Aquifer Authority and the State of Texas v. Burrell Day and Joel McDaniel, Cause No. 08–0964." (Letter sent to Mr. Blake A. Hawthorne). Texas Senate District 28, June 2010.

Dunlap, Philip. "Border Wars: Analyzing the Dispute over Groundwater between Texas and Mexico." *Law and Business Review of the Americans* 12, no. 2 (spring 2006): 215–42.

Eckstein, Gabriel. "Application of International Water Law to Transboundary Groundwater Resources, and the Slovak-Hungarian Dispute over Gabcikovo-Nagymaros." *International Water Law Project* 19, no. 1 (2010): 67–116.

———. "Precious, Worthless, or Immeasurable: The Value and Ethic of Water." *Texas Tech Law Review* 38, no. 4 (summer 2006): 963–72.

Elder, Robert, Jr. "Water Wars in Texas." *Cox News Service*. August 24, 2003.

Ellis, Gregory M. "Regulatory Takings and Texas Groundwater." Unpublished.

Ellis, Gregory M., and Houston, Jace A. "Overview of Regulatory Methods Available to Groundwater Conservation Districts." May 2004.

Flannery, Tim. *The Eternal Frontier: An Ecological History of North America and Its Peoples*. New York: Atlantic Monthly Press, 2001.

Fox, Nicole. "Should Groundwater Be Owned by the State of Texas?" Charles Porter (August 2011).

"Frequently Asked Questions." California Department of Water Resources Sustainable Groundwater Management Office.

"Frequently Asked Questions: Water Rights in Washington." Department of Ecology, Washington State University. November 2013. https://apps.ecology.wa.gov/publications/documents/961804swr.pdf.

Galant, Carl R., and Johnson, Russell S. "Exempt Uses of Groundwater and Surface Water." Oil, Gas, and Energy Resources Law Section Report. *State Bar of Texas* 33, no. 3 (March 2009).

Galbraith, Kate. "Texas' Water Rights System Gets Tested in Drought." *Texas Tribune* 2012.

"Georgia Water Law." HG.org Legal Resources. https://www.hg.org/legal-articles/georgia-water-law-32945.

Glennon, Robert. *Water Follies: Groundwater Pumping and the Fate of America's Fresh Waters*. Washington, DC: Island Press, 2002.

Gray, Brian E. "The Reasonable Use Doctrine in California Water Law and Policy." In *Sustainable Water: Challenges and Solutions from California*, ed. Allison Lassiter. Berkeley: University of California Press, 2015.

Green, Donald E. *Land of the Underground Rain: Irrigation on the Texas High Plains, 1910–1970*. Austin: University of Texas Press, 1973.

Greenhill, Joe R., and Gee, Thomas Gibbs. "Ownership of Ground Water in Texas; The East Case Reconsidered." *Texas Law Review* 33 (1955): 620.

Gutierrez, Tony. "When the Water Runs Out." *Austin American-Statesman*. August 2011.

Gvirtzman, Haimi. "The Truth behind the Palestinian Water Libels." BESA Center Perspectives Paper No. 238. Ramat Gan: Begin-Sadat Center for Strategic Studies, February 24, 2014. http://besacenter.org/perspectives-papers/truth-behind-palestinian-water-libels.

Hall, Katy. "Dry Fire Hydrants Helping Counter Rural Wildfires." March 1995. http://www.texas-fire.com.

Hardberger, Amy. "What Lies Beneath: Determining the Necessity of International Groundwater Policy along the United States-Mexico Border and a Roadmap to an Agreement." *Texas Tech Law Review* 35 (summer 2004): 1211–57.

Harrison, Sylvia. "The Historical Development of Nevada Water Law." *University of Denver Water Law Review* 5, no. 1 (fall 2001): 148–82.

Hassan, Mohammad Masud. "GAM Run 10–050 MAG Version 2." Texas Water Development Board, February 2011.

Hays Trinity Conservation District. "Hays Trinity Groundwater Conservation District Rules." State of Texas, June 2007.

Horton, Alex W. "Where'd All the (Ground) Water Go? Three Approaches to Balancing Resource Efficiency with Rural Sustainability in Texas." *South Texas Law Review* 691 (spring 2008).

House Research Organization, Texas House of Representatives. "Behind the US-Mexico Water Treaty Dispute." *Interim News* No. 77-7. April 30, 2002.

Howell, Emily. "Is the TCEQ 'Hearing' Impaired? The Impact of City of Marshall v. City of Uncertain on the Availability of Contested-Case Hearings for Water Use Permit Amendments." *Texas Tech Administrative Law Journal* 299 (summer 2007).

Hutchins, Wells A. *The Texas Law of Water Rights*. Austin: Texas Legislature and Texas Board of Water Engineers, 1961.

Janner, Jay. "Rising Bills Tapping Central Texans Dry." *Austin American-Statesman* December 2011.

Johnson, Russell S. "Water Market Transfer and Value Issues." 2002.

Kaiser, Ronald, and Skillern, Frank F. "Deep Trouble: Options for Managing the Hidden Threat of Aquifer Depletion in Texas." *Texas Tech Law Review* 32 (2001): 249–304.

———. "Water Marketing in Texas." Texas A&M University (2001).

Kelton, Elmer. *The Time It Never Rained*. Fort Worth: TCU Press, 1984.

Kunkel, Eric B. "The Spanish Law of Waters in the United States: From Alfonso the Wise to the Present Day." *McGeorge Law Review* 32 (2001): 341.

Lashmet, Tiffany Dowell. "Eminent Domain in Texas (Part 1)—What Is It?" *Texas Agriculture Law Blog*. March 17, 2014. https://agrilife.org/texasaglaw/2014/03/17/eminent-domain-in-texas-part-1-what-is-it.

MacKinnon, Anne. "Historic and Future Challenges in Western Water Law: The Case of Wyoming." *Wyoming Law Review* 6, no. 2 (2006): 291–330.

"Maine Activists Protest Nestle's Potential Sale of Poland Spring Water to Private Equity Firm." *Bangor Daily News*. February 12, 2021.

Marin, Carlos. "Bi-national Border Water Supply Issues from the Perspective of the IBWC." *United States–Mexico Law Journal* 11 (Spring 2003): 35–39.

Mashhood, Farzad. "Legislator Draws Up Water Plan." *Austin American-Statesman*. January 2012.

Mason, Thomas G., and Melvin, Robin A. "New Developments in Texas Water Law, Planning and Management." Presented to the Austin Bar Association Real Estate Section Meeting, March 6, 2012.

McCleskey, Robert A. "Maybe Oil and Water Should Mix—At Least in Texas Law: An Analysis of Current Problems with Texas Ground Water Law and How Established Oil and Gas Law Could Provide Appropriate Solutions." *Texas Wesleyan Law Review* 1, no. 1 (spring 1994): 207–24.

Menger, Johnowene Brackenridge Crutcher. "M. Eleanor Brackenridge, 1837–1924, a Third Generation Advocate of Education." Master's thesis, Trinity University, 1964.

Morgan, Bobbie Whitten. "George W. Brackenridge and His Control of San Antonio's Water Supply, 1869–1905." Master's thesis, Trinity University, 1961.

Motal, Becky. "LCRA Setting Up for Long Drought." *Austin American-Statesman*. January 2012.

National Research Council. *A New Era for Irrigation*. Washington, DC: National Academy Press, 1996.

Neal, Basil Young. "George W. Brackenridge: Citizen and Philanthropist." Master's Thesis, University of Texas, Austin, 1939.

Negro, S., and K. S. Porter. "Water Stress in New York State: The Regional Imperative." *Journal of Water Law* 20 (2009).

Neuman, Janet C. "The Good, the Bad, and the Ugly: The First Ten Years of the Oregon Water Trust." *Nebraska Law Review* 83 (2004): 432.

Partlow, Joshua. "Officials Fear Complete Doomsday Scenarios for Drought-Stricken Colorado River." *Washington Post*. December 1, 2022. https://www.washingtonpost.com/climate-environment/2022/12/01/drought-colorado-river-lake-powell.

Pisani, Donald J. *From the Family Farm to Agribusiness: The Irrigation Crusade in California and the West, 1850–1931*. Berkeley: University of California Press, 1984.

———. *To Reclaim a Divided West: Water, Law and Public Policy, 1848–1902*. Albuquerque: University of New Mexico Press, 1992.

———. *Water, Land and Law in the West: The Limits of Public Policy, 1850–1920*. Lawrence: University Press of Kansas, 1996.

Pleven, Liam. "Betting on a Water Boom." *Wall Street Journal*. Updated December 5, 2011. https://www.wsj.com/articles/SB10001424052970203611404577046510511478718.

Raines, Ben. "Alabama's Rivers Are Crashing Thanks to Water Rules That Favor Industry." AL.com. November 15, 2016. https://www.al.com/news/mobile/2016/11/alabamas_rivers_are_crashing_t.html.

"Record Low Water Levels on the Mississippi River in 2022 Show How Climate Change Is Altering Large Rivers." *The Conversation*. December 14, 2022. https://theconversation.com/record-low-water-levels-on-the-mississippi-river-in-2022-show-how-climate-change-is-altering-large-rivers-193920.

"Regulating Water Withdrawals in New York: The Water Resources Protection Act." Hudson Valley Regional Council. November 2015. https://hudsonvalleyregionalcouncil.org/wp-content/uploads/2015/11/Regulating-Water-Withdrawal-in-NY-s.pdf.

Reich, Peter L. "The 'Hispanic' Roots of Prior Appropriation in Arizona." *Arizona State Law Journal* 27 (summer 1995): 649.

Reis, Ronert I. "Connecticut Water Law: Judicial Allocation of Water Resources" (1967). *Special Reports* 3. Connecticut Institute of Water Resources. https://opencommons.uconn.edu/ctiwr_specreports/3.

Rice, Jenny. *Distant Publics: Rhetoric and the Subject of Development Crisis*. Pittsburgh: University of Pittsburgh Press, 2012.

Rodriguez, Sylvia. *Acequia: Water Sharing, Sanctity, and Place*. Santa Fe: School for Advanced Research Press, 2006.

Sahs, Mary K. "Groundwater Regulation in Texas." State Bar of Texas, 2005.

Sansom, Andrew. *Water in Texas*. Austin: University of Texas Press, 2008.

Sawyers, Gary. "A Primer on California Water Rights." University of California Agricultural Issues Center. https://aic.ucdavis.edu/events/outlook05/Sawyer_primer.pdf.

Schorr, David B. "Appropriation as Agrarianism: Distributive Justice in the Creation of Property Rights." *Ecology Law Quarterly* 32, no. 1 (2005): 3–71.

Skores, Alexandra. "Texas' Worst Drought in a Decade Could Rival 2011 Economic Losses." *Dallas Morning News*. December 16, 2022. https://dallasnews.com/business/economy/2022/12/16/texas-worst-drought-in-a-decade-could-rival-2011s-economic-losses.

Smith, Garland F. "The Valley Water Suit and Its Impact on Texas Water Policy: Some Practical Advice for the Future." *Texas Tech Law Review* 8 (1977): 577–636.

Smith, Tiziana. "Overcoming Challenges in Wastewater Reuse: A Case Study of San Antonio, Texas." Cambridge, MA: Harvard College, March 2011.

"Some of America's Biggest Vegetable Growers Fought for Water. Then the Water Ran Out." *NPR*. December 15, 2022. https://www.npr.org/2022/12/15/1139932893/some-of-americas-biggest-vegetable-growers-fought-for-water-then-the-water-ran-o.

"State Water Board Issues Notice Containing Important Information about the Curtailment Status of Water Rights and Claims of Right within Delta Watershed." *Maven's Notebook*. August 20, 2021. https://mavensnotebook.com/2021/08/20/this-just-in-state-water-boards-initial-order-imposing-curtailments-and-reporting-requirements-in-the-delta-watershed.

Texas Alliance of Groundwater Districts (TAGD). "Legislative Wrap-Up: Groundwater-Related Bills." TAGD. 2011. https://texasgroundwater.org/wp-content/uploads/2020/12/2011legeupdate.pdf.

———. "Position Paper for the 82nd Legislature." TAGD. July 29, 2010.

Texas Farm Bureau. "Joint Position Statement on Groundwater Ownership."

Texas Natural Resource Conservation Commission. "Rights to Surface Water in Texas." 2002.

Texas Water Code. Water Rights, Chapter 11. Texas Natural Resource Conservative Commission, 1977.

Texas Water Development Board. "100 Years of Rule of Capture: From East to Groundwater Management." Report 361. Austin: Texas Water Development Board, June 2004.

———. *The Texas Manual on Rainwater Harvesting*. 3rd ed. Austin: Texas Water Development Board, 2005.

———. "Water for Texas 2007." Austin: Texas Water Development Board, January 2007.

Turlock, A. Dan, and Krueger, Vicki C. "Water Rights: A White Paper Report." National Association of Realtors. September 2015. https://realtorparty.realtor/wp-content/uploads/dlm_uploads/2020/07/State-Local-Issues-Water-Rights-2.pdf.

Underwood, Laura. "Better Late Than Never: States Regain the Right to Regulate Stream Flows under the Clean Water Act: PUD No.1 of Jefferson County v. Washington Department of Ecology." *Texas Tech Law Review* 26 (1995): 187.

United Nations Conference on Trade and Development. "Report on UNCTAD Assistance to the Palestinian People: Developments in the Economy of the Occupied Palestinian Territory." New York: United Nations, 2015.

US Environmental Protection Agency. "Drinking Water from Household Wells." EPA 816-K-02-003. January 2002.

Vataman, Dan. "The Court of Justice of the European Union after the Reform Established by the Lisbon Treaty." *International Journal of Law and Jurisprudence* 5, no. 2 (July–December 2015).

Votteler, Todd H. "The Little Fish That Roared: The Endangered Species Act, State Groundwater Law, and Private Property Rights Collide over the Texas Edwards Aquifer." *Lewis & Clark Law School Environment Law* 845 (winter 1998).

———. *Texas Water Journal*. College Station: Texas Water Resources Institute, September 2010.

Walker, Andrew. "Mexican Law and the Texas Courts." *Baylor Law Review* 55 (winter 2003): 225–63.

Water Resources Action Project. "A Comparative Study of Water Data Across Israel, West Bank and Jordan." 2013.

"Water Rights in Oregon: An Introduction to Oregon's Water Laws." Oregon Water Resources Department. 2018. https://www.oregon.gov/owrd/WRDPublications1/aquabook.pdf.

"What Are Atmospheric Rivers?" NOAA. March 14, 2023. https://cleantechnica.com/2023/03/14/what-are-atmospheric-rivers.

White, A. A., and Wilson, Will. "The Flow and Underflow of Motl v. Boyd: The Problem." *Southwestern Law Journal* 9, no. 1 (winter 1955): 1–26.

"Who Owns the Water: A Summary of Existing Water Rights Laws." Water Systems Council. 2003. https://watersystemscouncil.org/download/wellcare_information_sheets/other_information_sheets/1836033IN_WHO_OWNS.PDF.

Wilcox, Erin. "Water, Property Rights and the Public Trust Doctrine." Pacific Legal Foundation. February 4, 2019. https://pacificlegal.org/water-property-rights-and-the-public-trust-doctrine (first published in the *Daily Journal* on January 30, 2018).

Williams, Michael L. "Can Oil and Water Mix? The Impact of Water Law on Oil, Gas, and Mineral Production." *Texas Bar Journal* 68 (October 2005): 816.

Wolf, Aaron T., and Newton, Joshua T. "Case Study of Transboundary Dispute Resolution: The Indus Water Treaty." Oregon State University. https://transboundarywaters.science.oregonstate.edu/sites/transboundarywaters.science.oregonstate.edu/files/Database/ResearchProjects/casestudies/indus.pdf (accessed March 3, 2016).

Index

www.ingramcontent.com/pod-product-compliance
Ingram Content Group UK Ltd.
Pitfield, Milton Keynes, MK11 3LW, UK
UKHW021026150926
475561UK00004B/183

9 781641 434133